"'Blessed are the peacemakers' (Mt. [...] listening to others. This book unique [...] of peacemaking by its author's willingness to listen to and value those inside and outside the biblical counseling movement—even those with whom he disagrees. What a gift to us all! May it have wide influence among biblical counselors, supporters (like me), and those Christian counselors who themselves have listened too little to biblical counselors."

Eric L. Johnson, Senior Research Professor, Southern Baptist Theological Seminary

"Jeremy Lelek has given a gift to the church and, frankly, a gift to me. As I read *Biblical Counseling Basics,* I found myself saying, 'Oh, now I understand.' I understood why some counseling (mine included) didn't work and why some counseling (mine included) did. It wasn't true or false because it worked or didn't work . . . it worked or didn't work because the basics were either true or false, biblical or pagan, from God or from the dark side. This book is so very important, and every Christian needs to read it. You will not only say, 'Oh, now I understand,' you will rise up and call Jeremy Lelek blessed for having written it."

Steve Brown, Distinguished author, Christian broadcaster, and visiting professor of Practical Theology at Knox Theological Seminary and Westminster Theological Seminary

"Bringing together the historical narrative of the biblical counseling movement and the eternal truths of Scripture that are preeminently relevant to the emotional, mental, and relational struggles of our day, *Biblical Counseling Basics* is a resource that will encourage and equip believers in their ongoing development as biblical counselors. If you desire to learn the foundations of this craft, and how to practically apply Scripture to the maladies of the soul, I highly recommend this book."

Elyse Fitzpatrick, Author of *Counsel from the Cross*

"Here is a clarion call to grasping the rich history of biblical counseling with its solid commitment to the sufficiency of Scripture; healthy interaction with secular thought, using the Scripture as the measure of all knowledge; advocacy of surgical accuracy in the use of Scripture and acute avoidance of proof texting; the centrality of theology proper as the context for counseling; and thoughtful challenge regarding law and ethics."

Howard A. Eyrich, Director of DMin in Biblical Counseling, Birmingham Theological Seminary; Fellow, Association of Certified Biblical Counselors

"Biblical counseling needs more scholars, teachers, leaders, and practitioners like Jeremy Lelek, nuanced in their approach and willing to embrace the complexities of the human psyche. I commend *Biblical Counseling Basics* to anyone desiring a practical primer on how the Scriptures relate to the care of souls."

Greg Wilson, Lead Counselor at Soul Care Associates; care deacon at The Village Church, Flower Mound, TX

"*Biblical Counseling Basics* is an important book in the field of Christian counseling. Lelek provides a much-needed balance to the negative and often uninformed debates that permeate the field. He examines biblical, historical, and contemporary perspectives; identifies the foundational counseling principles; and emphasizes the importance of a transformed heart, not just external behavioral changes. His view is uncompromising in acknowledging the authority and role of Scripture in counseling. In the process, he uncovers the nuanced variety of views in biblical counseling, as he follows the biblical mandate to seek unity in Christ within the fellowship of the saints (1 Cor. 1:10, Eph. 4:3)."

Ian F. Jones, Professor of Psychology & Counseling, Chairman of the Division of Church & Community Ministries, and Baptist Community Ministries' Chair of Pastoral Counseling, New Orleans Baptist Theological Seminary

"If you're a Christian entering the world of counseling, it may seem like you're traveling in a small boat into a vast ocean. The philosophical currents are strong. The history is deep. The possible directions of travel are endless. What are the dangers? How do you navigate the relentless ideological waves? Whose words do you trust? How does God fit, or you fit, or Scripture fit? Where do you begin? *Biblical Counseling Basics* tackles these kinds of questions. Jeremy Lelek gives you a good place to begin. He maps some relevant history, helps you gather bearings in the present debates, and invites you to set a course into ministry that takes God, Scripture, and theology seriously when it comes to the wise care of human souls."

John Henderson, Associate Pastor, Del Ray Baptist Church, Alexandria, VA; author of *Equipped to Counsel*

"*Biblical Counseling Basics* is a thorough, accessible, practical resource that will be at home in the hands of licensed practitioners, pastors, and everyday disciple-makers. If you are called to walk wisely and biblically alongside people as they navigate the precarious terrain of the heart, this Christ-centered work will bless you and help you."

Chris Freeland, Senior Pastor, McKinney Church, Fort Worth, TX

"Lelek's book does what no other biblical counseling book does. It gives you a helpful history, it defines what it really means to counsel biblically, and it offers guidance for the future of soul care. If you have been called to care for people, this book should be in your library."

Paul David Tripp, President of Paul Tripp Ministries; author of *New Morning Mercies*

"This is more than biblical counseling basics. It is a wise telling of the history of biblical counseling, a useable systematic theology for counselors, and a thoughtful welcome to those who don't quite know what to make of it all. Thank you, Jeremy, for moving us ahead."

Ed Welch, Faculty member at CCEF; bestselling author of *Side by Side: Walking with Others in Wisdom and Love*

"When an accident left me a quadriplegic, I collapsed emotionally. I vaguely knew that the Bible probably contained answers, but I had no idea where to look. Thankfully, I was introduced to a biblical counselor who made all the difference. He wasn't a trained professional; he simply loved Jesus and wanted to make him a reality in my life. Friend, you have the same counseling potential. It's why I love *Biblical Counseling Basics*. Want to help wounded people find life-giving hope? This book is for you!"

Joni Eareckson Tada, Joni and Friends International Disability Center

"*Biblical Counseling Basics* is an excellent primer for distinctly Christian counseling, as it clearly explicates the necessity and relevance of Scripture in the care of souls. Written in a narrative style, within the framework of a robust evangelical theology, it challenges readers to love struggling people with the mercy and grace of God in Christ."

Sam R. Williams, Professor of Counseling, Southeastern Baptist Theological Seminary

BIBLICAL COUNSELING BASICS

ROOTS, BELIEFS, AND FUTURE

JEREMY LELEK

New
Growth
Press

www.newgrowthpress.com

New Growth Press, Greensboro, NC 27404
www.newgrowthpress.com
Copyright © 2018 by Jeremy Lelek.

Unless otherwise indicated, Scripture quotations are taken from *The Holy Bible, English Standard Version.* Copyright © 2000; 2001 by Crossway Bibles, a division of Good News Publishers. Used by permission. All rights reserved.
Scripture verses marked NIV are taken from the *Holy Bible, New International Version*. NIV. Copyright © 1973, 1978, 1984 by International Bible Society. Used by permission of Zondervan. All rights reserved.
Scripture verses marked NKJV are taken from the New King James Version®. Copyright © 1982 by Thomas Nelson. Used by permission. All rights reserved.

Cover Design: Faceout Books, faceoutstudio.com

ISBN 978-1-945270-85-7 (Print)
ISBN 978-1-945270-87-1 (eBook)

Library of Congress Cataloging-in-Publication Data

Names: Lelek, Jeremy, 1973- author.
Title: Biblical counseling basics : roots, beliefs, future / Jeremy Lelek.
Description: Greensboro, NC : New Growth Press, 2018.
Identifiers: LCCN 2018003918 | ISBN 9781945270857 (trade paper)
Subjects: LCSH: Counseling--Religious aspects--Christianity.
Classification: LCC BR115.C69 L45 2018 | DDC 253.5--dc23
LC record available at https://lccn.loc.gov/2018003918

Printed in the United States of America

25 24 23 22 21 20 19 18   1 2 3 4 5

To a few amazing scholars in Christian soul care and my cherished brothers and sisters in Christ:

Thank you for your unending work in the body of Christ, and especially for taking time from your inconceivably busy schedules to participate in a long, arduous, time-consuming PhD dissertation. I am forever grateful!

Don Arms, MDiv

Howard Eyrich, DMin

Stephen Greggo, PsyD

Eric Johnson, PhD

Ian Jones, PhD

Robert Kellemen, PhD

Phil Monroe, PsyD

David Powlison, PhD

Eric Scalise, PhD

Timothy Sisemore, PhD

Winston Smith, DMin

Joshua Straub, PhD

Paul Tripp, DMin

Steve Viars, DMin

Ed Welch, PhD[1]

Confidential Contributors[2]

Contents

Acknowledgments

A cknowledging the giants imperative to the completion of this book, I must mention the most significant giant of all. Without the continual encouragement from my wonderful wife, Lynne, neither my dissertation (from which this book is drawn) nor this book would have ever seen completion. Lynne, you have been a model of Christ to me when I was overwhelmed by the stress and fears associated with writing. You have listened patiently as I read sections of this book and not once were you too busy to lend your wisdom. You are one in a million, and I love you very much.

To my amazing children with whom I am totally captivated, Aaron, Caleb, Hannah, and Eden, I am overwhelmed with gratitude that God gave your mother and me such treasured gifts. You make my life brighter, and God uses you daily to give my life glorious purpose!

Dad and Mom, what can I say? You raised me to love the Bible and to love our God. You helped ground me from a young age. From the day I decided to leave our tiny West Texas hometown of Colorado City and move to Lynchburg, Virginia, to attend Liberty University, you have always been my biggest supporters. Were you not there during the early years of my PhD work, faithfully watching my kiddos (especially Aaron and Caleb), there is no way this book would exist. I love you both.

Ronnie McElroy, you are a friend of friends, a brother of brothers. So many times I was challenged with completing my PhD as well as this book, and you were my faithful encourager. I have never met a more sacrificial saint with a passion to honor Jesus through his service. Thank you for being you!

Dr. James Sells, you have been an amazing guide and mentor to me as a professional and as a growing counselor. Thank you!

Jerry Meade (who sadly passed during the publishing process) was seminal in my early development as a biblical counselor, and he shaped my worldview of soul care in ways that continue to influence my work. His impact on me is threaded throughout the pages of this book.

The Board of Directors of the Association of Biblical Counselors have been some of my dearest and most dedicated friends during the past several years. Craig, John, Margaret, Michael, Mike, Ronnie, Scott L., Terri, and Tim, you are the team that has stood by me for many years, and you are the team serving with me now. You are treasured, and I am beyond blessed to serve with you. Our future is bright!

Metroplex Counseling staff (present and former), you are the silent servants in God's kingdom. You serve behind the scenes, impacting lives in ways that are incomprehensible. Tim, Kathy, Tammy, Derrick, Gary, Jonathan, Joel, Kelsey, Lauren, Matt, Rachael Rosser, Rachel Kuchem, Steve Clay, Steve Beatty, Scott Busby, Alley, Wes, and Sharon—you are the salt of the earth. I am honored and humbled to know and serve with you.

My pastor, my friend, Darwin Jordan—you are one of the most brilliant, caring, and creative people I have ever met, and your ability to preach God's Word blesses me every Sunday. You dedicated so many hours to speak into the theological aspects of this book. Without your support and input, this book would have been a failure. Thank you for the example you present to me as a humble leader. I cannot believe the Lord has allowed my family and me to sit under your exceptional teaching and leadership for so many years. We are beyond blessed by your wisdom.

Liberty University changed my life. While I could mention many who were responsible for this experience, I want to acknowledge some very specific people who radically influenced me in shaping my worldview as a counselor—Philip Captain, Marilyn Gadomski, Bev Lowry, and Barbara Sherman. You challenged me in ways that encouraged growth and maturity. You will never completely understand the positive impact you had on my life, and while it has been many years since I sat in your classrooms, your influence is evidenced in this book.

To the amazing elders of my church, *Fort Worth, PCA*: thank you for your constant and ongoing support for my work at ABC. Thank you for trusting others into our care.

Paul Tripp, you have been a friend and mentor. I spent almost a decade getting to know you, and I am beyond privileged to have learned from you. You have taught me what it means to be a leader, and through our work together, you have lived out the message you so faithfully teach throughout the world. Knowing you has changed my life for the glory of God. Thank you!

Ed Welch and Eric Johnson, thank you both for taking valuable time from your busy schedules to review my manuscript. Your input was extremely helpful, not to mention that your profound wisdom (along with that of Powlison and Tripp) is a major influence on every word written in this book!

David Powlison was one of ABC's most ardent supporters in our early years when crisis threatened our very existence. You never faltered in your encouragement and loyalty as a brother in Christ when so many in the BC world were extremely hesitant to give us a chance. Thank you!

I would certainly be remiss if I failed to thank the amazing team at New Growth Press for the outstanding work they put forth in transforming my meager manuscript into this final product. Barbara Juliani, thank you for taking a chance on me! Ruth Castle, Elizabeth Sloan Hart, and Irene Stoops, your editorial wisdom profoundly improved this book. Cheryl White and Gretchen Logterman, your efforts to keep this project moving forward were invaluable. I'm very honored to be a part of the NGP family!

One final and very important person I would like to thank is an old but cherished friend, Daren Martin (author of the books, *Company of Owners* and *Whiteboard: Business Models That Inspire Action*). Daren was the creator behind the brainchild of the Association of Biblical Counselors, and he is also the one who took a skeptic of biblical counseling (me) and transformed me into an ardent proponent of this wonderful craft. Brother, I was privileged to work in your shadow for almost seven years. God used you to model the attributes of a wise counselor, passionate leader, and faithful friend. I miss you, and I miss those days. While life has not been simple nor easy since our time together as counselors, we have both learned the beauty of our Lord's gospel in that his faithfulness to us in this journey is what matters most—and oh, how faithful he has been. In all sincerity, had the Lord not brought you into my life in 1999, I would not be a biblical counselor today. You opened my eyes to a whole new world with a convincing articulation of truth and took me under your wing to train me in the ways of his magnificent Word. For that, my friend, I dedicate this book to you. May the God of our salvation bless you greatly for all you have done in and for his kingdom. Love you, friend!

Author's Note

    This book is a cursory outline of the basic tenets of biblical counseling as well as an attempt to offer case wisdom in applying abstract theological ideas to humanity's tangible here and now struggles. It is drawn from my work during completion of my PhD study at Regent University as well as twenty years of counseling experience in private practice. While current social norms tend to place counseling exclusively under the headings of particular professional disciplines (i.e., psychologist, Licensed Professional Counselor, Licensed Social Worker, et cetera), biblical counseling enters the conversation with assumptions that do not limit the practice of counseling in such a way. Instead, biblical counseling builds upon Scripture's teaching that as believers in Jesus Christ, we are all called to counsel. As such, this book is written for any Christian who seeks a deeper understanding on how the Bible applies to the often complicated mental struggles we unfortunately witness among ourselves, our friends, and our families.

    You may be among the skilled professionals cited above (as am I). While you have expertise in particular areas of mental health, maybe you have never read a book that connects the worlds of theology and psychology. If that is the case, this book is for you. Perhaps you are a pastor seeking to increase your knowledge base in practical theology—the art of applying theology to actual lived experiences. This book will serve that objective well. You may be a student or a lay counselor hoping to frame a counseling approach that squares with the teachings of the Bible. This book is a starting point. Wherever you find yourself on this spectrum, my prayer is that you will be drawn closer to God as you read through each and every page.

Part One

. . . .

Roots:
History and Context

CHAPTER ONE

. . . .

BATTLE LINES:
THE ORIGIN AND DECLINE OF
BIBLICAL CARE

Biblical psychology is no science of yesterday. It is one of the oldest
sciences in the church. —Franz Delitzsch[1]

For psychology is now again the path to the fundamental problems.
—Friedrich Nietzsche[2]

The book you are reading attempts to unpack the single question, What is biblical counseling? The answer is multifaceted.
Biblical counseling is a model of care that brings Scripture to bear
on the multitude of struggles that plague the human soul, while
simultaneously offering scriptural, gospel-saturated insight on how
human beings can flourish. Biblical counseling aims to glorify God,
esteem the Bible, celebrate science, and prioritize Jesus's commands
to love God and neighbor. It offers divine understanding to important life issues while bringing clarity to the believer about the nature
of human psychology (i.e., "the study of the soul").[3] Biblical counseling comprises a theological system that informs basic questions such
as Who are we?, What motivates us?, What actually brings about
genuine transformation?, and How can we maintain lasting change
to the glory of God? Certainly, biblical counseling answers many
more questions, but these are central and worth considering in the
pages that follow.

Biblical counseling also affirms that its source, the Bible, has been revealed by an omniscient God who designed every soul that exists. As such, failing to bring the wisdom of this God to the forefront of the counseling process is considered a failure to provide the deepest counsel available to those in need. While science may be helpful in psychology's ongoing development to treat the maladies of the mind, for people to know themselves most accurately, they must comprehend more than empirical data or theoretical assumption. They need God's perspective on life issues such as sin, suffering, and the ongoing process of human transformation.

To that end, followers of Jesus who want to broaden their understanding of biblical counseling need to do so with a spirit that seeks humility from God. Biblical counselors are continually engaging the Bible for guidance and wisdom. As a result, they daily enter into a divine narrative that provides occasion for rich, personal reflection as it pertains to God's activity in their own lives. Their interaction with God's Word is far from a futile practice of mere data gathering. Knowing the right answers from the Bible is not the be all and end all of providing authentic biblical care. While biblical knowledge is an imperative aspect of this craft, mere knowledge is a doorway to self-centered pride. When people seek counseling, they are seldom searching for facts. They may be searching for answers, but the manner in which such answers are given will drastically shape the counselee's experience. Quoting a Bible verse to a person in the throes of depression falls short of genuine biblical care. In order to offer more, biblical counselors will first need to consider how the piercing truths of God's Word are relevant to their own hearts. Studying biblical counseling should itself change the counselor. When engaging penetrating truth, such ongoing personal transformation is actually essential to becoming an authentic biblical counselor.

How will this book deepen readers' understanding of biblical counseling? Section one will offer a brief history of Christian soul care within the church as well as various circumstances that led many pastors to abandon the role as counselor and instead defer to the secular practitioner when counseling was needed. Thankfully, history does not stop there. Biblical counseling experienced a resurgence where men such as Jay Adams (the father of the modern biblical counseling movement), David Powlison, Ed Welch, and Paul Tripp (second generation pioneers in the movement) began to articulate a model of care that was comprehensive in scope and accessible to anyone belonging to the body of Christ.

Section two will cover the central theological tenets of biblical counseling. These tenets provide a general foundation upon which Christians can build. Section two addresses the use of Scripture in counseling, God's role in the counseling process, a basic biblical understanding of human nature, a general discussion about the process of change, an explanation on the role of the church in biblical counseling, and an overview of basic counseling methods.

The final section will take a look at areas within biblical counseling where the movement is still growing and maturing. Leaders within biblical counseling acknowledge that the movement is still quite young, and some aspects of development are still in process. This section will provide insight as to where biblical counseling can be further developed. Personal recommendations for the movement's future are also offered.

In the Beginning . . .

I want to begin with a very countercultural assertion—counselors are desperate for the divine. This statement might seem a bit confusing, given the current culture where much of counseling's foundation, modern secular psychology, has historically assumed an innate autonomy from faith and spirituality. The present and prevailing trend of mental health care has boldly continued down this path by further enmeshing itself with a myopic materialist philosophy that ascribes to the notion that humans are exclusively biological beings. In such a spiritually emaciated context, people of faith should address the basic question, Where did the practice of counseling others actually originate? Otherwise, the study of counseling becomes constricted by a modernist fallacy, and the assertion that spirituality is a valuable element of a healthy psychological makeup is sadly lost.

Typically, when authors attempt to locate psychology's origin, they will initiate their analysis by highlighting the great Western philosophers such as Plato, Aristotle, and Socrates. Next, they usually move from the archaic hypotheses of the classical philosophers to thinkers such as Descartes who coined the phrase, "I think therefore I am,"[4] to philosophers such as Hume, Comte, and Locke who represent the era of rationalism. Readers are then typically introduced to the pioneering talk therapies driven by staunch modernists—men such as Sigmund Freud, Carl Rogers, Fritz Perls, and Albert Ellis. There are a plethora of such books that have sought to chronicle the history of counseling and psychology, and each of them fails to consider the influence of the sacred.

Operating on the premise that people need the divine in order to offer authentic counsel, this study will initiate the discussion at a point in history that far predates Freud or the renowned philosophers of the West. The survey of counseling that you are about to read begins with a poignant thought by Dr. John Henderson:

> Godly or "biblical" counsel began in the Garden of Eden. God created Adam and then God counseled Adam concerning the blessed course of life and the cursed one, "From any tree of the garden you may eat freely, but from the tree of knowledge of good and evil you shall not eat, for in the day that you eat from it you will surely die." The counsel of God was truthful, His Word for human life and loving. His counsel revealed Himself to Adam and maintained a right relationship with Adam.[5]

If the biblical account of the creation expresses actual, historical data, then the believer's analysis of counseling's origin will be vastly different from secular sources in that it will inevitably begin at the Garden of Eden. The founder of the biblical counseling movement, Jay Adams, emphasized this many years ago, "From the beginning, human change depended upon counseling. Man was created as a being whose very existence is derived from and dependent upon a Creator whom he must acknowledge as such and from whom he must obtain wisdom and knowledge through revelation."[6]

Adams asserts that counseling has been part of the human experience dating back to the very first man and woman, and therefore, this practice has always been intricately connected to God. Can you imagine what it must have been like for Adam and Eve as they were privileged to sit under the infinite wisdom of the One to whom Scripture refers as the Wonderful Counselor (Isaiah 9:6; John 15:26)?

Since the Bible reveals that counseling finds its birthplace in the person and activity of God, it is not a recent, secular novelty. Rather, rightly understood, counseling is an eternal gift graciously transferred to humanity in order that humanity might gain knowledge of the supreme fullness of life, namely God. The wisest of his day, King Solomon, declared that knowledge begins with "the fear of the Lord" (Proverbs 1:7). Within the context of humanity's interpersonal relationship with God, his precious counsel is given in the form of Scripture. Once received through the active work of the Holy Spirit, the Lord's counsel is shared with others in the form of "one another" ministry—counseling. This brand of counseling is particular among all others since it possesses a unique conceptual framework of human psychology. It is a framework that positions the modern human-centered versions of counseling as antithetical to God's original (Mark 12:30–31).

If counseling has always been part of God's interaction with humankind, it should, therefore, be considered a critical aspect of the Christian life today. This rich heritage has been well documented by many thoughtful saints. It is a history that has unfortunately remained unspoken in psychology's modern classroom, at times even among those institutions that bear the name "Christian." As professionals, pastors, parishioners, or students, we are all wise to take up the mantle left before us and recapture the treasures of Scripture that powerfully equip us in our ongoing development as competent counselors—wise physicians of the soul.

Before defining and unpacking the construct of biblical counseling, however, I would like to engender a genuine appreciation for this rich heritage as well as gain perspective on how the church surrendered the turf of soul care to the discipline of psychology by offering a brief overview. I believe that knowing history will shed light on current trends within the field as well as embolden counselors to walk in their divine call to counsel from the Word of God.

The Bible: A Treasure of Case Studies

In the creation story, Adam and Eve ultimately rejected the counsel of God (Genesis 3). Their rebellion brought forth the fall of creation and separated humanity from its Creator. For the first time in the biblical narrative, corrective counsel was required since people now operate from a sinful heart destined to wander from the Lord's wisdom and knowledge (Romans 7:7–25).

One of the most prominent examples of God's counsel is represented in the Ten Commandments. God speaking to Moses through these commands sets a familiar cadence throughout the entire Old Testament (Exodus 20) calling people to obedience. For example, God spoke to Nathan who then confronted David with his sin (2 Samuel 12). God warned Isaiah of the dangers of rebellion (Isaiah 1) and encouraged him with the coming hope of a Redeemer (Isaiah 8—9). He anointed Jeremiah to speak about the certain calamities associated with falling away from God. He called a stubborn Jonah to go to Nineveh where Jonah finally, yet reluctantly, spoke God's words to the people, and God transformed their hearts. Throughout the Psalms and Proverbs, God speaks words of wisdom and comfort to those subject to folly and pain. The Old Testament sets an undeniable precedent where God repeatedly spoke to his people who then spoke God's words to others. The rhythm of Scripture is guided by the continual drumbeat of "God said."

The New Testament continues this familiar rhythm beginning with the Gospels. Matthew, Mark, Luke, and John provide historical accounts of Jesus's life, and his actual words of counsel. Jesus introduces himself as the way, the truth, and the life (John 14:6). As part of his vast counsel in the New Testament, Jesus invites every professing believer to share in the call to counsel. This call is also known as the Great Commission: "And Jesus came and said to them, 'All authority in heaven and on earth has been given to me. Go therefore and make disciples of all nations, baptizing them in the name of the Father and of the Son and of the Holy Spirit, teaching them to observe all that I have commanded you. And behold, I am with you always, to the end of the age'" (Matthew 28:18–20).

While at first glance it may seem odd to refer to counseling as a form of discipleship, this is precisely the function of biblical counseling. It is the art of bringing God's Word to bear on the intricate issues of the soul or the complicated struggles that often arise in relationships. It is a means to help others flourish in their walk with God. Such discipleship (or counseling) typically occurs along a continuum. Biblical counseling may look like one follower of Jesus applying a passage of Scripture to the struggles of another over a cup of coffee. It may look like the more skilled or trained follower of Jesus (i.e., a trained biblical counselor) offering in-depth biblical guidance and utilizing specific methods drawn from a formal biblical counseling model. Both of these scenarios fall within biblical counseling. All Christians dating back to the earliest prophets of Scripture, in varying contexts, have been personally invited to take part in the symphony of voices echoing the counsel of God. We are all called to counsel.

Jesus calls people to follow his lead. He was the most brilliant counselor to ever grace the earth. He brought profound insight into the human experience, and his counsel was iconoclastic to the religious assumptions of his day. Unlike others in his culture, Jesus frequently emphasized that the location of human struggle and the target for human change was not found in religious ritual, but it was centered within the human heart—the seat of human thinking, feeling, desiring, and doing. For example, he taught (i.e., counseled) that adultery was not a mere external act. He said, "You have heard that it was said, 'You shall not commit adultery.' But I say to you that everyone who looks at a woman with lustful intent has already committed adultery with her in his heart" (Matthew 5:27–28).

An initial reading of this verse may not seem to fit with the modern construct of counseling. It lacks much therapeutic fluff. Yet biblical counsel often incorporates direct teaching as a useful methodology. In this case, people widely believed that individuals were only guilty of adultery if they actually participated in the physical act. Jesus, on the other hand, pointed out that adultery is simply an outward expression of an inward problem—lust. He focused people's attention upon the real focal point—where the core issue resided. Biblical counseling aims to do the same. Rather than engage excessively in behavioral modification (although behavior is important), biblical counsel will always take time to consider the heart issues at play.

However, it would not represent Jesus's counsel accurately to claim that he focused exclusively on the internal heart. Jesus also (and often) called people to action. Consider his counsel regarding interpersonal conflict, "Pay attention to yourselves! If your brother sins, rebuke him, and if he repents, forgive him, and if he sins against you seven times in the day, and turns to you seven times, saying, 'I repent,' you must forgive him" (Luke 17:3–4). Jesus counseled his disciples, instructing them on relational upheaval. Whereas many relationships crumble because people avoid conflict and attempt to sweep issues under the rug, Jesus's counsel provided a divine restorative model. Jesus instructed his disciples on practical steps to take when sinned against that would provide the opportunity for reconciliation.[7]

Whether he was teaching the famous Sermon on the Mount, explaining the myriad of parables, summarizing every command in Scripture to only two (love God and love your neighbor) or living his life by loving the Father and caring for others, Jesus unquestionably epitomized the name "Wonderful Counselor" (Isaiah 9:6). Repeatedly within the Gospels, Jesus provided wisdom and instructive care to those around him (especially his disciples).

Jesus's beloved disciples and apostles build upon his pattern throughout the New Testament. Drawing from Jesus's relational wisdom, Paul offers similar and striking counsel. He wrote:

> If possible, so far as it depends on you, live peaceably with all. Beloved never avenge yourselves, but leave it to the wrath of God, for it is written, 'Vengeance is mine, I will repay, says the Lord.' To the contrary, 'if your enemy is hungry, feed him; if he is thirsty, give him something to drink; for by so doing you will heap burning coals on his head.' Do not be overcome by evil, but overcome evil with good. (Romans 12:18–21)

Paul's wisdom was taken from the instruction of God in the Old Testament (Deuteronomy 32:35) and mirrors Jesus's counsel in the New Testament (Luke 6:27–29). Paul serves as a steady guide on how to relate to others when confronted with hurtful, even evil, actions or words. His counsel points people to image how Jesus, when sinned against, did not retaliate, but he entrusted himself to the just judge of the universe (1 Peter 2:23–24).

Jesus's apostles in the New Testament offered an abundance of counsel to people of their day. Peter urged those suffering under unfair leadership to continue to do good (1 Peter 2–3). James tackled the candid question often relevant to marriage and friendships, Why are you fighting? (James 4:1–8). He diagnoses the root of the problem (coveting) and prescribes steps toward change (seek humility, submit to God, resist the devil, and enter into passionate repentance). The writer of Hebrews provides counsel that brings divine context to the purposes of suffering, yet honestly admits this process is often quite painful (Hebrews 12:7–14). While the apostles offered much of this counsel through epistles, it was nonetheless counseling. Their written record (the New Testament) will inform anyone seeking to practice biblical counseling today. In one way, when counselors draw from Scripture it is as though counselees are also receiving the counsel directly from Paul, Peter, James, and the author of Hebrews who all received their wisdom directly from God.

It is undeniable, God spoke to his people, his people spoke what they were given, and lives, hearts, and cultures were transformed. This counsel is still alive today in the form of the Bible, and it is because God has spoken and this revelation has been recorded on the pages of Scripture that biblical counselors are privileged to provide eternal truth relevant to the most complex mental, emotional, or relational struggles of the day.

The Early Church Fathers and Reformers

The early church certainly understood the invitation of Jesus and imitated the authors of Scripture in the call to provide godly counsel. Dr. Eric Johnson offers a chronology of "soul care" rooted in both the Old and New Testaments that ultimately shaped many first-century authors.[8] Johnson notes early Christian scholars, such as Clement of Rome (c. AD 96), and credits them with the ministry of early soul care since their scholarship and work "contributed to a notable reformation of individuals' thinking and behavior that led to a growing sub-community distinguished by a certain way of life shaped by Scripture."[9] Historian Morton Hunt concurs with such life-shaping influence, noting that when Augustine introduced his version of biblical soul-care, his ideas dominated the arena of psychology for eight centuries.[10]

In addition to Augustine, history also points to other early church fathers, such as Thomas Aquinas and John Cassian, designating them as deeply thoughtful men who sought a comprehensive understanding of the human soul. Dr. Rebecca Konyndyk DeYoung notes, "The ancients and medievals sought this sort of self-knowledge as part of the ethical life, as is clear from the inscription at Delphi, 'Know Thyself,' and the mission of Aquinas's Dominican order, namely, 'the care of souls.'"[11]

She quotes Cassian at length, emphasizing the significance he placed on self-knowledge and human well-being, "Looking at [their struggles] as in a mirror and having been taught the causes of and remedies for the vices by which they are troubled, they will also learn about future contests before they occur, and they will be instructed as to how they should watch out for them, meet them, and fight against them."[12] Cassian, here, is describing what people today would call counseling. As sufferers contemplated their own struggles (as though looking in a mirror), it was commonplace for them to receive biblical insight concerning the etiology (or cause) of their issues as well as receive prescriptive and preventative methods to guide them. Continuing with Cassian:

> As is the case with the most skilled physicians, who not only heal present ills but also confront future ones with shrewd expertise and forestall them with prescriptions and salutary potions, so also these true physicians of the souls destroy, with a spiritual conference as with some heavenly medicine, maladies of the heart just as they are about to emerge, not

allowing them to groin in the minds of young men but disclosing to them both the causes of the passions that threaten them and the means of acquiring health.[13]

The people of Cassian's day sought counsel from their spiritual leaders who both diagnosed the causes of their mental, emotional, and spiritual ills as well as prescribed biblical means toward "acquiring health."

Both Aquinas and Cassian model a mindset that was dominant in their day—a mindset shaped by Jesus and the authors of Scripture. Soul care was not splintered away from the church toward a skilled, secular practitioner, but it was a craft embedded in the DNA of the Christian life.

Following in the church fathers' footsteps, men of the Reformation, such as Martin Luther and John Calvin were major contributors to developing philosophies and theologies of human nature, human motivation, and personality development.[14] Calvin's *Institutes of the Christian Religion* and Luther's *The Bondage of the Will* contain some of the most fascinating and comprehensive theologies of human nature ever postulated. These books rival the depth and breadth of any personality theory developed by modern psychology.

Luther's and Calvin's conceptual framework, however, included the impact of sin and depravity on the human estate, the subjection of the will to evil passions and desires (and even the devil), the essential need for grace to awaken and free the one enslaved by sin, and the sovereign power of God actively at work in every aspect of the human experience. Luther, Calvin, and others of their day tackled with a distinctively theological framework the very questions in which psychology would become immersed centuries later.

A Puritan "Psychology"

Continuing in the Reformers' tradition, another group of Christians were deeply invested in understanding human nature from a theological vantage. They were known as the Puritans. While the Puritans were far from a perfect people, it is also unfair to characterize them exclusively as "witch-hunting lunatics." That is a profoundly skewed caricature of saints who brought many grace-filled goods to the suffering souls of their day.

Leaders within this tradition developed highly "sophisticated diagnostic casebooks containing scores and even hundreds of different personal problems and spiritual conditions."[15] These casebooks had as their basis a rich theology derived from the pages of Scripture.[16] Such casebooks were possible because the Puritans, who consisted of some of the most brilliant thinkers, philosophers, and theologians of their time, esteemed the Bible as relevant to the soul issues of their day. They held a genuine belief that God's revelation in Scripture contained the keys to address humankind's mental and emotional maladies.

One such theologian was Jonathan Edwards, a renowned Puritan who briefly served as the president of Princeton University prior to his untimely death. In his treatise on the human will, he (as Luther and Calvin before him) outlined a very elaborate and rigorous theology of motivation. The difference between Edwards and secular theorists, however, is that his ideas were derived from a comprehensive understanding and application of biblical doctrine. Analyzing the nature of volition, Edwards once wrote, "The choice of the mind never departs from that which, at that time, and with respect to the direct and immediate objects of that decision of the mind, appears most agreeable and pleasing, all things considered."[17]

Edwards echoed the sentiments of Peter, Paul, and James in that he placed the crux of human activity in one's longings—the affections (Romans 8:5–8; Ephesians 4:22–24; James 1:13–16). In Edwards's view, it was under the influence of such desires that the human will was constantly subjected and within which the heart was perpetually at war. It was an idea Jesus put forth centuries before Edwards when he taught, "For where your treasure is, there your heart will be also" (Matthew 6:21). Fundamentally, according to Edwards, a biblical view of motivation is centered in the idea that the heart is captured and ruled by what it desires most in a given moment. On this subject, he artfully elaborates:

The Author of the human nature has not only given affections to men, but has made them very much the spring of men's actions. . . . Such is man's nature that he is very inactive, any otherwise than he is influenced by some affection, either love or hatred, desire, hope, fear, or some other. These affections we see to be the springs that set men a-going, in all the affairs of life, and engage them in all their pursuits: these are the things that put men forward, and carry them along, in all their worldly business; and especially are men excited and animated by these in all affairs wherein they are earnestly engaged, and which they pursue with vigour. We see the world of mankind to be exceeding busy and active; and the affections of men are the springs of the motion.[18]

For Edwards, human motivation was not driven by unmet emotional needs but by humanity's inner springs of motion, what he calls the affections. Edwards's conceptual framework of the human will is nothing less than brilliant.

The English Puritan John Owen discussed the imperative nature of God's activity in the process of healing and change:

Now, self-healers or men that speak peace to themselves do commonly make haste; they will not tarry; they do not hearken what God speaks, but on they will go to be healed [Isa. 28:16] . . . Which is worst of all, it amends not the life, it heals not the evil, it cures not the distemper. When God speaks peace, it guides and keeps the soul that it "turn not again to folly" [Ps. 85:8]. When we speak it ourselves, the heart is not taken off the evil; nay, it is the readiest course in the world to bring a soul into a trade of backsliding . . . In God's speaking peace there comes along so much sweetness, and such a discovery of his love, as is a strong obligation on the soul no more to deal perversely [Luke 22:32].[19]

Owen understood the arduous nature of change, and he exposed motives for change that can actually impede the process. As he stated, the "self-healer" has an agenda, and that agenda is typically egocentric. It is not centered in the glory of God nor a genuine desire to reflect Christ—two imperative aims of biblical care. Instead, Owen conceptualized the process of inner healing aimed at acquiring peace and relief for their own sakes as counterproductive to spiritual flourishing. Contrary to such hedonistic methods, in order for genuine transformation to occur in one's psychological and spiritual states, he believed God's activity, through his Spirit, was essential. Owen's views judiciously articulate the tenets of Scripture (Ephesians 2).

Contained within his body of work, Owen continually spoke the language of counseling, though he might not have used modern psychological lingo. Referencing his style, Kelly Kapic notes, "Using classic faculty-psychology categories of the mind, the will, and the affections, Owen consistently attempts to present a holistic perspective of the human person, and this informs his view of sin and sanctification."[20]

Both Owen and Edwards were men of deep faith and conviction. In their attempts to conceptualize humankind, they formulated detailed logical systems of understanding that were shaped by biblical doctrine. Their works within the realm of soul care remain highly regarded among theologians and scholars today as some of the most brilliant in Christendom. In his introduction to Owen's treatise on the Holy Spirit, Sinclair Ferguson reminds us, "The Puritans were pastors and physicians of the soul. But they understood that the basic counseling sessions of every Christian's life should take place in the context of the exposition of the Scripture."[21]

These examples are two of hundreds worth considering from the Puritans. Their work in soul care is quite voluminous, and their expertise striking. J. I. Packer points out "that behind the studied simplicity of the Puritan practical books lies the care and competence of brilliant and deeply learned theologians."[22] Johnson adds, "While our era far outstrips theirs in terms of an understanding of the created mechanics of human development and soul change, ours is dwarfed by theirs with regard to the more important expertise of applying the Bible to the greatest needs of the soul."[23]

Biblical Psychology's Deep Roots in Church History

The rich heritage of soul care within the body of Christ reveals that such practices were not anomalies. They were common ministerial duties for which the people of God felt they were responsible. Throughout history, many published, scholarly contributions have sought to formulate a rich psychology rooted in the Bible's teachings. Many far predate Wundt (recognized as the father of psychology) or Freud. To further illustrate this heritage, consider just a few titles that were published from as early as the mid-1500s through the late nineteenth century (listed in chronological order):[24]

- 1538: Bucer, M. *Von der Waren Seelsorge und Dem Rechten Hirtendienst (Concerning the True Care of Souls and Genuine Pastoral Ministry)*
- 1692: Burnet, G. *A Discourse of the Pastoral Care*
- 1769: Roos, M. F. *Fundamenta Psychologiæ Ex Sacra Scriptura Collecta* (tr. *Outlines of Psychology Drawn from the Holy Scriptures*).
- 1799: Gerard, A. (1799). *The Pastoral Care*
- 1843: Beck, J. T. *Outlines of Biblical Psychology*
- 1853: Rauch, F. A. *Psychology; or, A View of the Human Soul; Including Anthropology*
- 1855: Delitzsch, F. *A System of Biblical Psychology*
- 1871: Gall, J. *Primeval Man Unveiled: Or, the Anthropology of the Bible.*
- 1873: Forster, J. L. *Biblical Psychology: In Four Parts*
- 1874: Sutherland, G. Christian Psychology: A New Exhibition of the Capacities and Faculties of the Human Spirit, Investigated and Illustrated from the Christian Standpoint

These authors illustrate the long and consistent stream of history in which Christians now operate as believers participating in the modern current of biblical soul care. Christians have worked on this turf for a very long time, and we should not shy away from a confident, biblical approach to one-another care even as we may experience the resistance, even ridicule, from the post-Christian culture in which we have been called to serve.[25]

A Changing Tide—The Decline of Biblical Soul Care

People operating as Christian counselors find themselves in a stream of history that flows back to the first two people on earth. From the Bible to at least the time of the Puritans, counseling and soul care held a prominent position within the prescribed functionality of the body of Christ. And while this emphasis remained for centuries, this tradition eventually gave way to the emergence of modernism with its emphasis on logical positivism and empiricism—the idea that facts are valid so long as they can be proven through scientific study. From these two paradigms emerged a scientific age wherein truth was ultimately determined by the rigors of applying scientific methodology. As a result, if a truth claim, construct, process, or phenomenon could not be measured and verified by a very specific research process, the scientific method, it was not considered viable. If a microscope or mathematical formula could not measure it, then one could not assume it was universally true for all people at all times.

Modernism ultimately gave birth to what is known today as the science of psychology.[26] The implication of this change meant that the spiritual became subservient to the scientific and reshaped a profoundly new orthodoxy for understanding the human soul. Gone were the days of interpreting the psychology of humankind through the lens of the Bible. Men like Aquinas, Augustine, Luther, Edwards, and Owen were often redefined from being valued contributors to the understanding of people to neurotic individuals in need of therapeutic analysis by the new practitioners of the day.[27]

Since logical positivism does not acknowledge variables that fail the test of empirical validation, the psychology it produced by and large dismissed the validity of the spiritual; this dimension could not literally be measured. Exceptions to this rule were rare but included occasional theorists such as William James and Carl Jung. Both had an interest in the supernatural, mysticism, and the occult, but denied any form of true Christian orthodoxy.

In America, researchers like G. Stanley Hall went to great lengths to disprove the spiritual as a valid aspect of psychological science.[28] Within this modernist context, individuals such as Sigmund Freud and Carl Rogers began to rise in prominence as the new authoritative voices regarding human nature and the mind.[29] These were men who basically relegated spiritual interests to the category of neurosis, emphasizing instead theoretical ideas that were completely influenced by Darwinian evolution and humanistic philosophy.

Boisen, Rising Empiricism, and a Church Virtually Muted

While Modernism was rising in the West, the overall influence of the church on issues pertaining to psychology radically declined. The conservative wing of the church was distracted from participating in what had become accepted as an exclusively scientific endeavor.[30] John Bettler recalls, "While evangelicals spent the first half of the twentieth century defending the faith and struggling to save their seminaries and churches from liberal takeover, those same liberals were free to define and develop pastoral counseling as they wished without input or opposition from those upholding full biblical authority."[31] Powlison wrote that during this time conservatives "virtually ignored counseling."[32]

The vacuum created by the silence of conservative evangelical thinkers was not left vacuous for long, however. The liberal factions within the church poured themselves into addressing humanity's mental health needs. To a large degree, they were prompted toward greater action by the convicting call of a man named Anton Boisen. Boisen was one of the first to challenge Christian seminaries by admonishing them to offer clinical training for seminary students in the realm of mental health.[33] He had suffered several mental breakdowns and was unable to find help within the church for his ailing soul.[34] In 1936, he scorned the church's disinterest in such affairs:

> It seems truly an astounding situation that a group of sufferers larger than that to be found in all other hospitals put together, a group whose difficulties seem to lie for the most part in the realm of character rather than in that of organic disease, should be so neglected by the church. Notwithstanding the fact that the church has always been interested in the care of the sick and that the Protestant

churches of America have been supporting 380 or more hospitals, they are giving scarcely any attention to the maladies of the mind.[35]

Within the void caused by this scarce attention, Boisen posited a new emphasis within the body of Christ wherein pastors could receive practical training in effectively treating what he referred to as "the maladies of the mind." But, for Boisen, this new emphasis would require a blending of psychology and theology—a synthesis that would demand a "giving up of dogmatism and the beginning of that humility which is a precondition of entrance into the Kingdom of heaven."[36] He ultimately contended, "Even though the conservative attitude might succeed in holding the lines a little longer, it offers no solution."[37] Sadly, his prophetic words proved glaringly true in the years that immediately followed.

Influenced by the call of Boisen, The Council for Clinical Pastoral Training (CCPT) was eventually formed, and a new liberal era was born in the field of Christian ministry.[38] This liberal leaning was not necessarily the intent of Boisen, but much of his work initiated a synthesis of the secular field of psychology with a majority liberal religious consensus—both shifting momentum away from orthodox Christian doctrine. Carter and Narramore observed that

> In reacting to what they thought were negative emphases
> on hell, depravity, personal salvation, and the inerrancy of
> Scripture, the liberal wing of the church began to focus more
> on human potential and social action. Under the influence
> of German liberalism, they rebelled against a "pessimis-
> tic" view of the human being and began to hold out hope
> that through increased human effort workable solutions to
> humanity's dilemma would be found.[39]

Adding to the liberal influences, supervisors responsible for training clergy within the CCPT largely began to adopt the models of Freudian and later Rogerian psychology as their primary guides for conceptualizing people and their problems.[40] This was a significant shift toward a liberal and secular way of thinking, given that Freud believed religion offers nothing more than foolish illusions[41] and Rogers was a devout humanist. Rogers once wrote, "Experience is, for me, the highest authority . . . Neither the Bible nor the prophets—neither Freud nor research—neither the revelations of God nor man—can take precedence over my own direct experience."[42]

These worldviews were primary among practitioners overseeing seminary students in clinical settings. Inevitably, these same students acquired positions within local churches, and secular ideas embraced by Freud, Rogers, and others eventually seeped into the fabric of the church under the banner of pastoral counseling. Before long, many of these pastors reinterpreted sin as sickness.[43]

E. T. Charry noted, "Liberal churches were psychologized with the creation of the field of pastoral counseling, and soon theological education followed by providing clinical, pastoral education."[44] B. Narramore highlighted that during the infancy of pastoral counseling, an "approach that gave much attention to specific biblical teaching seemed somehow suspect and unscientific. In the minds of the intellectual liberals, any strong reliance on scriptural teaching smacked of authoritarianism and the fundamentalist mentality."[45] With such a stigma attached to scriptural teaching in the realm of counseling, from the 1920s to the 1970s, the discipline of pastoral counseling was almost exclusively shaped by secular thought influenced by the likes of Freud's dynamic needs theory and the client-centered therapy of Carl Rogers (himself a former seminary student).[46]

A major shift had taken place in the culture. The psychiatric clinician replaced the church, an entity once considered the very epicenter of soul care. The expertise of psychoanalysis and psychology supplanted the cherished value of theology regarding the human estate. Reflecting on this seismic historical shift, David Powlison soberly concluded, "The church of Christ lost her heartland, the understanding and cure of souls."[47] This was a scarring development indeed. Thankfully, however, as the church was relenting to the intimidation of the establishments of psychology and psychiatry, the Lord was raising up an influential voice to confront this tragic and disturbing trend.

O. Hobart Mowrer, a Surprising Ally and a New Call to Action

Psychology made significant progress in convincing pastors to relinquish their roles as counselors. However, not all pastors were content with doing so. For pastors who maintained the practice of counseling as part of their ministry duties, psychologists had convinced seminaries (where these men were receiving their pastoral training) that the best context for such training would be the psychiatric hospital. While this may have been appealing initially, given how modernism and materialist ideals were surging, this arrangement did not bode well for pastors who wanted to practice counseling from the foundation of orthodox Christian teaching.

A misconception was embraced—that biblical teaching was for the church, for preaching, or for prayer. However, when it came to real mental issues, something far more advanced than the Bible was deemed essential. A false-dichotomy was born wherein psychology was presumed to be the antidote for the soul (psyche) while theology was considered to be food for the spirit—a very different perspective than church history suggests. This created an unnecessary and more importantly, an unbiblical division in which the student of Scripture was made dependent on the secular psychological scholar. Embracing this idea forced pastors into environments where advanced therapeutic skill could only be found in the practitioner of psychology who likely opposed the very God in which these pastors professed faith and allegiance—the very God in whom their call was rooted. A crisis was beginning to develop, and for a while, no real opposition was offered. That is, until a man named O. Hobart Mowrer asserted his voice into the conversation.

Mowrer was one of the first ardent critics of the liberal movement evolving in pastoral counseling. He was deeply concerned about the development of a psychological discipline overrun by what became known as the medical model. In his view, this model was decimating the idea of personal responsibility. As the former president of the American Psychological Association (1954), Mowrer contended that the religious community had made a strategic mistake by embracing exclusively medical explanations of human dysfunction. In 1961, he wrote, "At the very time that psychologists are becoming distrustful of the sickness approach to personality disturbance and are beginning to look with more benign interest and respect toward certain moral and religious precepts, religionists themselves are being caught up in and bedazzled by the same preposterous system of thought as that from which we psychologists are just recovering."[48]

Mowrer further articulated,

> The present situation is, I believe, a very serious one and far from what Dr. Boisen originally intended. During the clinical internship and the propaedeutic seminary courses, students are typically schooled in the view that psychopathology is only indirectly a religious concern. They are deeply indoctrinated with the view that neurosis and psychosis arise from too much "morality," rather than too little, and that the minister must carefully recognize his "limitations" in dealing with such problems. The total impact of this experience has, it seems, not been a good one.[49]

It is from such concern that Mowrer penned his oft-repeated questions, "Has evangelical religion sold its birthright for a mess of psychological pottage? In attempting to rectify their disastrous early neglect of psychopathology, have the churches and seminaries assimilated a viewpoint and value system more destructive and deadly than the evil they were attempting to eliminate?"[50]

For Mowrer, a return to the constructs of sin and responsibility were essential to developing a truly effective therapeutic model. For some who came after him, the construct of sin was critical to psychology if society was expected to maintain a sense of moral obligation.[51] Others cited the inherent dangers of adopting a model of mental care dominated by a medical system that ascribed to a mythical and illogical idea of mental illness.[52] Still, some dismissed psychoanalysis and the medical model altogether, replacing it with ideas that emphasized personal freedom and responsibility.[53]

From the mid to early years of the twentieth century until the 1950s, there was no substantial evidence that the conservative evangelical community as a whole actively engaged in the emerging debates surrounding psychology and Christianity.[54] However, in 1956 the silence among evangelicals was broken. The Christian Association for Psychological Studies (CAPS) was formed, serving as a significant catalyst in the development of what came to be known as Christian psychology.[55] It also marked the beginning of a new practice within psychology that would eventually be known as integration.[56]

Influential contributions to these new approaches to Christian care were found in the works of men like Clyde M. Narramore,[57] John Carter, Bruce Narramore,[58] Gary Collins,[59] and Larry Crabb.[60] Later, Minirth and Meier[61] also contributed extensively to the growing body of literature analyzing what these practitioners believed was a proper interrelation between psychological science and orthodox Christian teaching. With these new Christian professionals, the presuppositions of the secular models would finally be scrutinized. A notable distinction among most of these men and the individuals involved in Boisen's CCPT years earlier was that they tended to approach the topics of psychology and theology from a more conservative orthodoxy within evangelicalism. For most of them, the authority of the Bible within their respective spheres of expertise remained a high priority, at least in theory.

Counseling Considerations

1. Have you ever considered the idea that counseling originated in the Garden of Eden when God spoke to Adam and Eve regarding the Tree of the Knowledge of Good and Evil? What does this reality reveal about God and his relationship to his people?
2. What are some differences that you believe arise between the way the church fathers, the Reformers, and the Puritans viewed humanity and the process of change compared to men such as Sigmund Freud and Abraham Maslow?[62] Is this relevant to you as a biblical counselor? Why?
3. What are your thoughts about the church handing over the work of counseling to the secular professional? Is this still a concern for today? Why?

Resources For Further Reading

- *The Confessions of St. Augustine*
- Edwards, Jonathan. *The Freedom of the Will.* Morgan, PA: Soli Deo Gloria, 1996.
- Luther, Martin. *The Bondage of the Will.* Grand Rapids, MI: Fleming H. Revell, 2003.
- Mowrer, O. Hobart. *The Crisis in Psychiatry and Religion.* New York: Litton Educational Publishing, 1961.

CHAPTER TWO

. . . .

A BIBLICAL PARADIGM EMERGES

It is time that Christian ministers and other counselors asked again,
"Who has bewitched you . . . having begun by the Spirit, are you now
being perfected by the flesh?" —Jay Adams[1]

Soft days for evangelical Christians are past, and only a strong view
of Scripture is sufficient to withstand the pressure of an all-pervasive
culture built upon relativism and relativistic thinking.
—Francis Schaeffer[2]

John Carter and Bruce Narramore, serving as professors of psychology at the Rosemead School of Psychology, were among the first evangelicals to recognize and write about the epistemological tensions between secular psychology and theology.[3] They emphasized that the field of psychology operates from the "assumption that empiricism is the only valid means for aiming at scientific knowledge."[4] On the other hand, the field of theology "embraces revelation that is beyond that of rationalism or empiricism."[5] Psychologist Gary Collins made the same observations. He was an influential leader credited for bringing the American Association of Christian Counselors into prominence (1986), and Collins recommended the development of a new psychology built "on a religious foundation, and specifically on a presuppositional base derived from and in accordance with the teachings of the Bible."[6] Their emphasis on scriptural truth exposed the distinction between the humanistic ideology of psychology and the views of Christian doctrine.

Christian Analysis, Two Levels of Knowing, and the Birth of Integration

Carter and Narramore agreed with this greater emphasis on biblical revelation and confirmed the inevitability of emerging distinctions. They postulated the concept of "levels of explanation," a view that acknowledges how the two disciplines of psychology and theology are frequently addressing the same issues from different levels of knowing (e.g., the empirical and the spiritual). For example, psychology addresses cognitions and so does theology. The goal then was to consider what the two separate disciplines had to offer while appreciating the mutual contribution of each. Carter and Narramore believed this was a position that could protect Christian professionals from "forced or artificial attempts at integration."[7] Similarly, Collins believed that psychology and theology were "two separate but unique fields shedding light on our understanding of similar issues."[8] For Narramore and Carter, where the two disciplines spoke to the same issues, they should "mutually enrich, complement, correct, clarify, and/or corroborate one another."[9]

Larry Crabb, on the other hand, was among the first to introduce the phrase "biblical counseling" into the discussion. He developed a process of synthesis known as integration, a method of "spoiling the Egyptians."[10] Under the banner of "common grace," Crabb's approach asserted that Christian professionals and the church "can profit from secular psychology if we carefully screen our concepts to determine their compatibility with Christian presuppositions."[11] As the others, Crabb believed there was potential value in the vast body of literature that had accumulated in the field of secular psychology. Unlike his colleagues, however, Crabb wanted to go beyond the methods put forth by the "levels of explanation" approach. He wanted to appropriately synthesize the ideas of psychology and theology. Holding firm to this conviction, the task of integrating these ideas into a Christian worldview became an utmost priority for Crabb and others during the 1970s.

While there are significant distinctions Carter's and Narramore's, Collins's, and Crabb's approaches, each of them believed that responsible interaction with secular research literature was a necessary exercise if Christians wanted to develop a competent model of care. Without this process, constructing a valid empirically based model of Christian soul care seemed improbable if not impossible. Here are a few rationales that scholars offered to substantiate this position:[12]

- All truth is God's truth.
- The Bible and psychology are allies.
- Psychology serves to bring understanding to human functioning.
- Greater knowledge of the psychological literature prepares Christians to articulate their potential opposing positions effectively.
- The vast body of research in psychology may lend to a more efficient work in Christian ministry.
- Psychology must come under the authority of Scripture.

As a result of their commitments, a new era was born in evangelical ministry that generated much discussion, development, and debate.[13] Leading thinkers offered meticulous criticism about the wedding of psychology and theology.[14] It was an era within Christendom that introduced the counseling wars.[15] Ultimately, I believe it was a time when genuine believers holding diverse views were each doing their best to formulate models of care that would most benefit the people of God. Even though I personally disagree with many of the conclusions offered by some of these well-intentioned individuals, it was a time when they were desperately seeking to provide Christian answers in an era where secular psychology was taking the culture and the church by storm.

Adams, Nouthetic Counseling, and the Rethinking of Integration

Referring to this time as the "counseling wars" may sound harsh, but during this season, the profound rise of secular thought in psychology forced the church to address some very complex and difficult questions: Does the new psychology have a role in Christian care? What role do pastors play in counseling? Should the new psychology be integrated into a Christian model of care? Is the Bible relevant for issues of the mind? Is the Bible sufficient to develop a rich model of care? These questions and more created a fiery and necessary debate among evangelicals that ultimately divided them into camps that continue to exist today.

Without question, the most vocal dissenter in this growing debate regarding the relationship between modernist psychology and biblical theology was Jay Adams. Adams may be considered the founder of biblical counseling's modern movement. His seminal work has produced what is now known as nouthetic counseling.[16]

Early in Adams's pastoral study, he became disillusioned with pastoral counseling since it mostly embraced a Freudian view of psychology. Adams rejected the compatibility of most psychology with a Christian worldview. Instead of utilizing the methods he was being taught as a seminarian, he began using "hit-or-miss patterns of counsel growing out of on-the-spot applications of scriptural exhortations."[17] Adams found this approach to be quite effective, not to mention far more congruent with his convictions as a pastoral student.

In 1965, as part of his seminary training, Adams began working in two state mental institutions with O. Hobart Mowrer, who vigorously opposed the emerging trends of amorality he was witnessing in psychology.[18] Under the guidance of Mowrer, who demanded his clients take responsibility for their actions, Adams's suspicions of psychology and the medical model were emboldened. In 1970 when *Competent to Counsel* was published, he shared that he became "engrossed in the project of developing biblical counseling."[19] Unlike other evangelical writing on the topic of counseling in the church, Adams's presuppositions did not allow for a synthesis of secular psychological theory with orthodox scriptural teaching when such psychology overstepped its bounds into the realm of theology. Instead, Adams argued,

> And, when compromisers talk about all truth as God's truth, they call it "common grace." They abuse this concept too. They mean by such use that God revealed truth through Rogers, Freud, Skinner, etc. God does, of course, restrain sin, allow people to discover facts about His creation, etc., in

common grace (help given to saved and unsaved alike), but
God never sets up rival systems competitive to the Bible.[20]

Adams dedicated his work to formulating a comprehensive
model of counseling that was built upon a very specific presupposition: the Bible is sufficient to make a believer competent in the
work of counseling. The model assumed the name "nouthetic,"
derived from the word *nouthesis*, which is translated "admonish,"
"warn," and "teach."[21] This approach to counseling strongly emphasized theology, centered itself upon the doctrine of Jesus, and was
dependent upon the Holy Spirit's work.[22] Unlike dominant theories
of the time, Adams's nouthetic approach was considered authoritative and directive since it rested upon biblical precepts. According
to Powlison, "Adams believed that the Bible—understood by literal, grammatico-historical exegesis, and partly systematized in the
creeds of the Reformation" provided three essential components to
reshape the affairs of counseling that had developed in the church.[23]
First, nouthetic counseling formulated "a comprehensive system,
defining truth about people, their problems in living, and the processes of change." Second, it offered "a methodology for the cure of
souls." Third, it assumed "a particular institutional and professional
locus for helping people: the church and the pastoral role."[24] Adams
believed these to be "the answer to eclecticism."[25]

Adams's model reflected all the essentials of a viable counseling
model. Such components, as cited by Robert Roberts, include an
account of basic human nature, a set of personality traits that characterize a fully functioning and mature person, successful development,
and a diagnostic scheme.[26] According to Adams, such categories
were thoroughly informed by one's study of the Bible. To utilize
Roberts's criteria, the nouthetic model conceptualized basic human
nature as sinful and corrupt; it characterized a fully functioning and
mature person as more and more reflective of Jesus Christ; it defined
successful development in terms of the doctrine of justification and
sanctification; and it offered a diagnostic conceptual scheme that was
shaped by the precepts of theological doctrine. Nouthetic counseling
gained significant momentum with the publication of *Competent to*

Counsel in 1970, and it grew to earn a prominent place in shaping the history and work of counseling within the church.

Formal Training in Biblical Counseling

From his initial book to the present day, Adams has been uniquely influential in the realm of nouthetic and biblical counseling. Throughout the past forty years, some have concluded that nouthetic counseling has become one of the most, if not the most, dominant model of biblical counseling.[27] Emerging from Adams's early work, the Christian Counseling Education Foundation (CCEF) was founded and expanded to ensure that individuals could receive practical training and quality higher education in nouthetic counseling. Others, like John Broger, established the Biblical Counseling Foundation (BCF) and emphasized training laity in the work of biblical counseling. Diverging philosophical viewpoints were clear. Adams emphasized the essential role of the nouthetic counselor as being pastoral. Broger's vision was to equip the "Christian in the pew."[28]

Concerned about the quality of training and literature in this emerging movement, Bettler (as cited by Powlison) "proposed that there was a need for a professional organization to ensure the quality control of nouthetic counseling."[29] The result of this proposal was the formation of the National Association of Nouthetic Counselors (NANC) in 1976. NANC became the alternative to state licensure in the Christian counseling movement. It was during this time that the *Journal of Pastoral Practice* was also founded.

A Second Generation Emerges

Many counselors and pastors such as John MacArthur and Wayne Mack[30] followed suit with the nouthetic movement and contributed to its development. As the second generation of leadership in nouthetic counseling evolved, it found among its ranks individuals such as Louis Priolo,[31] David Powlison,[32] Ed Welch,[33] Paul Tripp, Elyse Fitzpatrick,[34] and Richard Ganz.

Among these, Mack, Priolo, and Ganz eventually became more prominent within NANC, which separated from CCEF in 1978. The separation transpired at the urging of Bettler who "concluded that it was irregular for the accrediting organization to be subordinate to the chief educational institution" of CCEF.[35] Eric Johnson writes, "Though there are exceptions, by and large, most of the members of these institutions and organizations adhere very closely to the emphases of Jay Adams."[36]

In the wake of this transition, the faculty of CCEF, consisting primarily of Powlison, Welch, Tripp, and Bettler, continued to refine Adams's nouthetic model. This refining process produced particular nuances within the biblical counseling community. For example, Adams's model tended to focus more on behavior, while the second generation of authors began to place a greater emphasis on the heart.[37] Reminiscent of Augustine, Luther, Calvin, Owen, and Edwards, these emerging authors considered the heart to be the "crucible" of human functioning,[38] the "source of all human motivation,"[39] and the place from which idolatry emerges.[40]

Powlison criticized the nouthetic movement for its strategic failure in focusing on obedience to the exclusion of inward motivation.[41] While Powlison, Welch, and Tripp renewed a theological emphasis on the heart, Powlison's criticism recognized that classic nouthetic counseling still acknowledged the heart's influence upon motivation. When it came to the process of change, the classic nouthetic model strongly embraced the idea that changing habits fosters a change of heart.[42] Adams considered the heart important, but the means of change tended to be more (though not exclusively) behaviorally oriented via repentance and obedience to God. For Powlison and his colleagues, their earlier works emphasized, among other things, the inner workings of the heart.

The second-generation authors also underscored the importance of repentance and obedience as vital aspects of change; yet, there is distinction in these two approaches. These second-generation authors reintroduced elements of the human makeup, such as desires (or affections) and thoughts (or cognitions) as important variables in biblical counseling. Among these authors, behavior was an aspect of the change process, but it was not considered the primary focus.

Despite their existing nuances, there continues to remain a significant commonality among what Johnson refers to as traditional (e.g., Adams, Mack, Ganz) and progressive (e.g., Powlison, Welch, Tripp) biblical counselors.[43] While some have resisted the categories cited by Johnson, my own interaction with each group as well as the interactive research I conducted with them confirms noticeable differences between them. Even so, both the traditional and progressive groups embrace the presuppositions that have undergirded nouthetic counseling from its inception.

One of the most concise illustrations outlining these presuppositions may be found in Powlison's acronym COMPIN, that "there are COMP*rehensive* IN*ternal resources* in the Christian faith enabling us to construct a wisely Christian model of personality, change, and counseling."[44] In other words, the Bible serves as a sufficient lens through which Christians may analyze, evaluate, and understand everything about counseling, and it stands sufficient in formulating a rich, conceptual biblical model of soul care without the aid of outside research.

This perspective stands in contrast to the views upheld by many counselors and psychologists in the broader evangelical community who have historically embraced what Powlison calls VITEX, the "VIT*al* EX*ternal contribution* that secular psychologies must make to the construction of a wisely Christian model of personality, change, and counseling."[45] In other words, if the believer seeks to develop an authentic, rich, comprehensive approach to Christian soul care, the external contribution of secular theory and research are absolutely essential.

If we accept Powlison's categories of VITEX and COMPIN,[46] then the classic and progressive biblical counselors find common ground in that both reflect the position of COMPIN. This distinction serves at least two purposes in wading through the myriad of ideas implicit within the modern Christian counseling culture.

First, the assumptions inherent in the two maintain a distinguishable line between those who find the need for secular psychology essential to developing the core of a Christian counseling model and those who do not. Second, it allows for differences among those in biblical counseling so long as the basic presupposition of scriptural sufficiency is maintained in developing a comprehensive model of care. In this regard of holding to a proper view of Scripture's sufficiency, the tenets of Adams's earliest works continue to thrive in the modern biblical counseling movement.

A New Age of Unity in Biblical Counseling: A Third Generation of Leaders

During 2011, biblical counselors such as Steve Viars, David Powlison, and Garrett Higbee encouraged a new phase in the biblical counseling movement that convened traditional and progressive biblical counselors. This meeting culminated in the development of the Biblical Counseling Coalition (BCC). Various pastors, professors, and individuals from parachurch organizations comprised the council board of the BCC. These founding board members had experience in organizations such as the Christian Counseling and Education Foundation (CCEF), the Association of Certified Biblical Counselors (formerly The National Association of Nouthetic Counselors, NANC),[47] the Association of Biblical Counselors (ABC), and numerous churches and seminaries throughout the United States.[48] The BCC's mission statement called the organization "to foster collaborative relationships and to provide robust, relevant biblical resources that equip the Body of Christ to change lives with Christ's changeless truth."[49] Variations exist among individuals and groups within the BCC, but it seeks to pursue truth in unity while upholding the basic tenets of traditional biblical counseling.

The Spectrum of Christian Soul Care and the Importance of Peer Dialogue

Throughout its history, biblical counseling has endured and survived some arduous seasons. The counseling wars, I would argue, were necessary and fruitful. The early pioneers of biblical counseling, operating at a time when psychiatry and psychoanalysis were soaring in popularity and power, held their ground and did not allow the novel ideas of psychology to smother the Scriptures. Later generations built upon their firm foundation. Debate is healthy for a developing discipline, and in many ways, it forces people into deeper critical thought as well as humble consideration of ideas outside their circle. The pioneers of soul care each helped, in their own way, to refine a model of care that is distinctively biblical.

Today, biblical counseling is on the other side of the old counseling wars. Philosophies and models have been solidified to a large degree (though development and maturity continue). Those within the formal biblical counseling movement have grown to allow more nuances so long as foundational presuppositions are shared. This is reflected in the development of the BCC. Gone are the days where those in the movement operate in silos.[50] Today, unity in diversity is being celebrated.

I also believe that throughout this growing process others who may not necessarily identify with Powlison's historic COMPIN or VITEX[51] acronyms have also emerged as important contributors in the broader biblical soul care movement. It is my firm opinion that this issue has currently developed into something far more sophisticated than what some in biblical counseling have recently portrayed.[52] For example, scholars such as Eric Johnson, Ian Jones, and Phil Monroe have emerged as men fervently committed to genuine biblical care. Each holds a deep conviction that Scripture is imperative to such work. Within the literature they have produced and the classes they teach, they clearly emphasize building a firm theological base if a person hopes to navigate the plethora of secular research effectively. A key distinction, however, between men such as Johnson, Jones, and Monroe and those embracing Powlison's early concept of COMPIN is that Johnson and his colleagues are functionally more open to utilizing specific findings from research within the counseling process so long as these findings are properly translated through the grid of orthodox, biblical theology. They are asking important questions within their respective spheres of influence, and they are shaping their specific fields in important ways. Their leadership outside of the formal biblical counseling community serves a crucial role within the body of Christ in drawing students and practitioners toward Scripture as their functional authority within the counseling process.[53]

Discussing and critiquing one another's approach to soul care is important and quite fruitful when done so as loving brothers and sisters in Christ. Pushback on particular aspects of one's counseling approach is healthy because it fosters personal growth in one's own understanding. It also serves as a wonderful context to grow in the attributes of Jesus. This type of interaction allows for wise Christian thinkers to develop important relationships. Working alongside brothers and sisters who may not completely agree but who hold deep convictions that the Scriptures must take center stage in counseling will no doubt be a sharpening exercise. Even more important, it will offer a Christ-centered, grace-empowered model to those seeking to develop as Christian counselors and psychologists. Two men who have modeled this well, in my opinion, are David Powlison and Eric Johnson.

I hope soul care's future will see more peer dialogue and a deeper unity in the broader battle.[54] In the end, the adversary is not other counselors, but an enemy unseen promoting a message that is intended to supplant the riches of the gospel as applied to the human soul. It is a version of psychology (i.e., study of the soul) that is antithetical to Scripture, and it is a version of psychology that Christians must ardently resist to the glory and honor of God.

Counseling Considerations

1. Why is Jay Adams's contribution to biblical counseling so important for biblical counselors today?
2. What do you think of the rationales endorsing the idea that engaging secular research is necessary in order to offer genuine biblical care? Do you agree this is necessary to practice as a biblical counselor? Why or why not?
3. Read the Biblical Counseling Coalition's mission statement referenced in the endnotes of this chapter. What stands out to you most as beneficial to the biblical counseling movement? What about for you as a biblical counselor?

4. The final section of this chapter encourages more peer dialogue from biblical counselors with those outside the formal movement. What are your thoughts on this recommendation?

Resources for Further Reading

- ~ Adams, Jay. *Competent to Counsel*. Wheaton, IL: Crossway, 1970.
- ~ Lambert, Heath. *The Biblical Counseling Movement After Adams*. Wheaton, IL: Crossway, 2012.
- ~ MacDonald, James, Bob Kellemen, and Steve Viars, eds., *Christ-Centered Biblical Counseling*. Eugene, OR: Harvest House, 2013.[55]
- ~ Powlison, David. *The Biblical Counseling Movement: History and Context*. Greensboro, NC: New Growth Press, 2010.

Part Two
Beliefs (and Practices)

CHAPTER THREE

. . . .

Biblical Counseling: Theory or Theology?

It is a God-given duty that we should take the content of Scripture and bring it together into a systematic whole. It is plain that we are required to know the revelation that God has given us. —Cornelius Van Til[1]

The work of counseling biblically overlaps a great deal with the work of systematic and practical theology. This reality hit home for me in 2003 when I attended a forty-hour course at the University of North Texas (UNT) to acquire necessary credentials for becoming a Licensed Professional Counselor-Supervisor. I registered for this course to fulfill required qualifications in Texas, but the course deepened my conviction that biblical counseling is a profoundly viable alternative to the myriad of secular models.

UNT is typically rated among the top ten schools in the nation for its counseling program. As far as training secular counselors goes, it ranks among the best. One reason for its excellent ratings is that each incoming student is required to adopt a specific theory of counseling. There are hundreds of such theories from which students may choose, and most select from more prominent models such as client-centered therapy, family systems theory, or Adlerian psychology. This form of training equips students by helping them become experts in a single theoretical model. As future counselors, these students then have a cohesive lens through which to evaluate their clients. Students assimilate the details of their chosen theory into their conceptual framework as they design research papers, evaluate case studies, and participate in counseling internships.

While I do not ascribe to a particular secular theory, I do think this approach to training counselors is extremely effective. As a counseling practitioner, if I am going to provide a helpful service then it is imperative I possess a firm conceptual understanding of human nature, human motivation, and human change. Guiding students to adopt a single overriding theory serves that end while also providing a firm ground from which the student may operate when confronted by the oft-tumultuous moments that arise during a counseling session.

The UNT professor who taught our supervision class explained the school's rationale for their approach. She explained that when people move from book learning in theory to the actual practice of counseling, they can become overwhelmed by the information and issues brought forth in a counseling meeting. When students feel lost and unsure about what to do next in a counseling session, the professors of UNT teach them to ask one simple question, What does my theory say? Since students are emerging experts in a chosen theory, this question will serve them well and inform their process regarding what interventions to implement.[2]

Counseling can be a very unpredictable process. Given UNT's objectives, the professors are doing their students a great service by grounding them in a particular theoretical model. This allows the theory to provide students with a grid through which to understand people, relational struggles, mental maladies, and the methods best suited to address and treat each.

When the professor shared her rationale for having students embrace a single theory, I was struck with how biblical counseling is similar. It brings particular assumptions to the counseling process. These assumptions inform the counselor's understanding of human nature, the etiology (cause) of neurosis and their symptoms, a conceptual view of wellness, methods to foster change, and guidelines to shape ethical norms. The critical difference, however, is the source from which counselors draw their ultimate understanding for diagnosis, treatment, and practice. This difference is in the realm of something known as epistemology—a term that may be defined as how people know what they know.[3]

Epistemology is the ultimate ground or final basis of knowledge. In the world of psychology, epistemological assumptions are derived from research, and often this research shapes theory. Therefore, science's epistemological base is the ground from which theory (the guiding lens of all things counseling) emerges.

A parallel may be drawn for biblical counseling. Unlike science, however, biblical counseling's epistemological assumptions are drawn from the Bible. Viewing the Bible as the ultimate authority of truth, biblical counselors develop a theology from the content of Scripture that serves the same purpose as theory does within the secular arena. Or, as we stated regarding science, the Christian's epistemological base—the Bible—is the ground from which theology (the guiding lens of all things biblical counseling) emerges.

The epistemological differences are clear. While secular models are rooted in theory, biblical counseling is rooted in theology. Echoing the sentiments of the UNT professor, I would submit that one of the most prominent goals to which biblical counselors must aspire is to set their hearts on becoming experts in systematic and practical theology. If biblical counselors are going to counsel others biblically, then right theology will be viewed as an absolute priority. This is true not only at the academic level, but at the applied level as well. Scholars in biblical counseling have always stressed good theology.[4]

Similar to UNT's training approach, when sessions become complicated, or when moving pieces need to be put together, or when ethical decisions must be made, biblical counselors will rely on sound theology to serve as their ground of understanding. Just as UNT students are taught to ask, What does my theory say? the counselor operating from a biblical footing will learn to ask, What does my theology say? This book, I pray, will equip readers in rightly answering this question to the glory and praise of God.

What Is Theology's Relationship to Counseling?

Ron Hawkins and Tim Clinton have affirmed the imperative nature of the Bible in the counselor's care for others. They assert, "We believe the future of effective caregiving belongs to those who dare to press in closer to the heart of God and to apply treatment strategies that are firmly anchored in Scripture and divine revelation."[5]

I concur with Clinton and Hawkins, and I want to add that in order to apply Scripture adequately, Christians will need to engage in the diligent work of developing a sound theological framework from which to operate. Without such a framework, a counselor's capacity to apply the riches of God's Word accurately becomes extremely limited. Without a sound theology, counselors become vulnerable to misapplying Scripture or, even worse, offering counsel that is heretical or antithetical to biblical doctrine.

Discussing theology may trigger a mental lockdown for some. Many people assume that theology is nothing more than a dry, emotionless, intellectual pursuit of biblical knowledge. There are many who may mistakenly view the purpose of studying theology as simply acquiring facts from within the Bible for their own sakes. For individuals passionate about helping others on a relational level, such a perspective of theological development will certainly come off as mind numbing, boring, and sterile. Thankfully, however, theology is not simply learning data for the sake of learning data. Theology informs people's worldview, shapes their counseling practices, and presses them deeper into one-another care.

John Frame helps biblical counselors connect theological acumen with their soul care work. He writes, "the work of theology is not to reproduce the emphasis of Scripture (to do that precisely would require the theologian merely to quote the Bible from Genesis to Revelation), but to apply Scripture to the needs of people."[6] According to Frame, theology's purpose is interpersonal.

First, Christian theology presupposes the self-existence of God[7] who has spoken wisdom through his Word in order that those saved by his grace may know and live for him. Therefore, studying Scripture brings glory to a person as people relate to his divine revelation. When people immerse themselves in God's Word, they are privileged to glean from eternal wisdom originating from him, and from that wisdom, they learn of their place and purpose in the universe. People are given understanding pertaining to their origin, design, struggles, suffering, hope, and purpose. People's capacity to rightly understand this wisdom is also interpersonal; it is the Holy

Spirit who empowers them with eyes to see, ears to hear, and hearts eager to pursue God.

Secondly, theology also informs people on how they may best serve the needs of others. Studying theology is preparation for becoming a wise and skilled counselor. Theology's aim is not simply to gather data from the Bible's pages; rather, it is to consider how people may effectively love and serve both believers and unbelievers with the treasures they glean from sacred truth.[8]

If theological study is an interpersonal endeavor, some may ask, who is qualified to study theology? Contrary to what many may assume, studying theology is not a practice exclusive to pastoral training. All Christians are free and encouraged to participate in theological study and debate. Wayne Grudem writes:

> I am convinced that there is an urgent need in the church today for much greater understanding of Christian doctrine, or systematic theology. Not only pastors and teachers need to understand theology in greater depth—the WHOLE CHURCH does as well. One day by God's grace we may have churches full of Christians who can discuss, apply and LIVE the doctrinal teachings of the Bible as readily as they can discuss the details of their own jobs or hobbies—or the fortunes of their favorite sports team or television program.[9]

Theology is about life lived before God within a community of fellow believers. Virginia Holeman writes,

> Christian theology has a particular content (God and the God-centered life) that is derived from particular source materials (the Bible, church history and Christian traditions) for particular purposes (so that God may be glorified through the way that Christ's followers live). In the broadest sense, *theology shapes who we are and how we live* by helping us to better understand who God is and how we can live together as members of God's family in this world that God created and loves.[10]

Theology is not mere information, it is divine truth intended to shape the hearts and lives of people as they are introduced to the Lord of creation.

Dr. Jay Adams emphasized how counseling and theology are inseparable. He argued that the two disciplines are "organic" and that "counseling cannot be done apart from theological commitments."[11] He offered exceptional wisdom on this matter at a time when little attention was being given to Scripture within the discipline of psychology. He warned,

> Every act, word (or lack of these) implies theological commitments. On the other hand, theological study leads to counseling implications. The attempt to separate the two must not be made; they cannot be separated without doing violence to both. The separation is as unnatural (and perilous) as the separation of the spirit from the body. Paraphrasing James, we may say that counseling without theology is dead.[12]

Christians would do well to meticulously apply these words in their ongoing development. It is this deep conviction that has motivated men and women in recent decades to create and continually refine a rich theology of soul care.

The Bible, Theology, and Counseling: A Shared Purpose

Biblical counseling is drawn from eternal, unchanging revelation. The book of Isaiah declares of this revelation: "The grass withers, the flower fades, but the word of our God will stand forever" (Isaiah 40:8). While biblical counseling is a discipline in process, it is anchored in immutable truth. What the biblical authors penned thousands of years ago still holds true today. Biblical counseling did not emerge *ex nihilo* (from nothing) nor did it develop from a scientific paradigm. Instead, it has always been anchored in the eternal wisdom of God.

This idea is captured well in the statements of one panelist who participated in my doctoral study. He noted, "The Bible is about what counseling is about."[13] At a very basic level, this comment points to the fact that the Bible references counseling as an aspect of the human experience. For example, the Scriptures warn against submitting to bad counsel (Psalm 1:1) while encouraging believers to engage in the arts of learning, teaching, and speaking practical wisdom for life (Colossians 3:16). From the very beginning, God has engaged in such practices with his people. Therefore, when Christians consider speaking wise counsel into the lives of others, they find a model of care from none other than the God of Scripture. He has faithfully offered his counsel to humanity, dating back to the first person on earth. He has persisted in exercising this practice throughout the Old and New Testaments, and he continues to do so today through his inspired revelation to humankind—the Bible.

Yet, even though the Bible is replete with examples of God's counsel to mankind as well as admonitions for people to counsel and instruct each other, the panelist's statement goes much deeper. The panelist's comments imply a presenting ethos within Scripture that encapsulates all of counseling. This ethos includes the assertion that Scripture itself is God's divine counsel to mankind. His revelatory counsel offers humanity knowledge about himself and is infused with divine power that grants to believers "all things" pertaining to "life and godliness" (2 Peter 1:3). Some components of this revelation include mankind's origin and purpose (Genesis 1; Revelation 4:11); the historic rebellion initiating human need for corrective counsel (Genesis 3); the relentless variables that contribute to people's ongoing neurosis and rebellion (Romans 3:9–18; Galatians 5:16–17; James 1:13–15); the infinite and exclusive cure for the human soul/psyche (Romans 1:16–17; Hebrew 7:22–24); the supreme purpose of change (Romans 8:28–29; 1 Corinthians 10:31); the means and hope of transformation (Ephesians 2:1–10; Titus 2:11–14); the divine model of cure (Hebrew 1:3), and the existential significance that alone brings meaning to the entire process (Psalms 148:9–13; Revelation 21:1–5). These themes and more saturate the pages of the Bible, confirming the panelist's assertion that it is indeed a book about counseling.

A Proposed Definition of Biblical Counseling

If counseling originated with God, and if the Bible is indeed about counseling, then what is biblical counseling? Scholars have made many seminal contributions to address this question. David Powlison has provided foundational affirmations and denials that continue to shape and guide the ongoing development of biblical counseling.[14] Ed Welch has conceptualized it as a "hybrid of discipleship and biblical friendship."[15] Paul Tripp has reminded us of the present redemptive glories that unfold as we engage relationally and biblically with others.[16] Even influential pastors have weighed in on this question providing a rich framework that guides genuine biblical soul care.[17] The Association of Biblical Counselors utilizes an excellent definition by Dr. John Henderson as a means to help Christians conceive of biblical counseling as something to which all believers have been called.[18] Drawing from these examples, it is obvious that there have been many contributions by leading thinkers that have answered the question, *What is biblical counseling?*

When I posed this basic question to dozens of leading scholars interested in contributing to biblical care of souls, the following definition ultimately garnered the strongest consensus among them:

> Biblical counseling endeavors to build a relationship with another person in which God's work of change can thrive. It is therefore dependent on the Word of God, the work of the Holy Spirit and the grace of Jesus Christ. It seeks to build a contextualized understanding of the counselee (past and present) and will view that data through the lens of Scripture. The Biblical counselor rests in the knowledge that he is not the change agent, but a tool in the hands of the One who is. The biblical counselor does not ignore physical issues or emotional data, but seeks to integrate them into a holistic understanding of the person and where change needs to take place. The biblical counselor is not adversarial in his relationship to the psychologies of his culture, but examines research and insights through the lens of Scripture. In his work with the counselee the biblical counselor always recognizes the

sovereignty of God, the transformative grace of Christ, and the insight-giving and conviction-producing ministry of the Holy Spirit. In all of this the biblical counselor sees himself not as an isolated instrument of change, but one whose work is intimately connected to God's primary tool of change: the church, with all of its God-ordained duties, structures and means of grace.[19]

I do not presume that this definition is the final authority on defining biblical counseling, but it is a valuable contribution to the conversation because experts spanning the spectrum of Christian soul care (i.e., Christian psychology, Christian counseling, biblical counseling, and nouthetic counseling) chose it as representing a genuine definition of biblical counseling. My hope is that it will serve individuals in each of these fields to hone their skills in using the Word of God in their work. This definition will shape the flow of the chapters that follow.

Counseling Considerations

1. Why is learning theology so critical to Christian counseling?
2. The Bible ultimately answers the same fundamental questions that have been posed by psychology (and philosophy prior to psychology) for centuries: *Who are we? Why do we do the things we do? How do humans change?* What does Scripture provide in answering each of these questions in a robust way?
3. How skilled are you in the art of applying a rich theology to the counseling process?
4. What does the Bible reveal about the process of change?
5. How does the gospel apply to the process of change?

RESOURCES FOR FURTHER READING

- Frame, John. *Systematic Theology*. Phillipsburg, NJ: P&R Publishing, 2013.
- Henderson, John. *Equipped to Counsel*. Mustang, OK: DareToDream Publishers, 2008.
- Johnson, Eric. *God and Soul Care*. Downers Grove, IL: IVP, 2017.
- Kellemen, Robert. *Gospel-Centered Counseling: Equipping Biblical Counselors Series*. Grand Rapids, MI: Zondervan, 2014.
- Lambert, Heath. *A Theology of Biblical Counseling: The Doctrinal Foundations of Counseling Ministry*. Grand Rapids, MI: Zondervan, 2016.
- Tripp, Paul David. *Instruments in the Redeemer's Hands: People In Need of Change Helping People in Need of Change*. Phillipsburg, NJ: P&R Publishing, 2002.

CHAPTER FOUR

. . . .

THE BIBLE AND COUNSELING

The authority of Scripture means that all the words in Scripture are
God's words in such a way that to disbelieve or disobey any word of
Scripture is to disbelieve or disobey God. —Wayne Grudem[1]

Recently David entered his first semester at a prominent university where he is pursuing his master's degree in counseling.
His course load included *Theories of Personality, Ethical Standards
in Counseling,* and *Human Sexuality.* While David was extremely
excited about his new foray into the world of psychology, midway
through his semester he found himself wondering if he may have
gotten himself into a predicament. David is learning some fascinating theories developed by renowned men like Sigmund Freud and
Carl Rogers, but he also wonders whether as a Christian he will be
able to utilize such knowledge in his counseling practice.

Freud's incessant push that all neurosis originates from sexuality
and an overly consumed moralistic super ego seems to glamorize the
erotic while antagonizing the spiritual. Then there is Carl Rogers who
holds to the idea that people are innately good and if the therapist
simply provides a safe context, the client's inner potential for actu-
alization will emerge. All the answers needed for human flourishing
are assumed to be located within the individual. David is having a
difficult time reconciling Rogers' claims with his own beliefs about
sin and people's need for God's power to change. Further, his ethics
professor asserts that counselors must always operate from a place of
value neutrality.[2]

David's head is swirling with confusion. Scripture outlines important values by which to live one's life—values that David believes could be helpful to the hurting and broken—but the profession he is pursuing urges him to put these values on a shelf and allow the client's inner, subjective values to shape the morality of the therapeutic process. David is connecting the dots and realizing that this could be very troubling for him as a practitioner.

David's most stunning experience unfolded, however, in his human sexuality class. He was floored as he read through the first chapter of his textbook. The authors wrote about various cultural specific norms held by people around the world and stated that such norms should shape acceptable sexual practices among the diverse populations of the continent. One example they cited was a culture in Africa where it is customary for men to choose young boys as sexual partners as a means of introducing them to sexual practices—a deed that would land a man in prison within the United States. David could not believe that the authors seemed to validate this practice since it was culturally driven.

The Ultimate Source

Whether David consults Sigmund Freud and his psychoanalysis, B. F. Skinner and his behaviorism, Carl Rogers and his person-centered approach, or the most advanced researchers in modern neuroscience,[3] each are ultimately seeking answers to the exact same psychological questions: Who are we? Why do we do the things we do? What motivates people? What are the causes of our psychological ills? How do we change? How do we heal? What is the goal of change? These are the inquiries with which psychology has engrossed itself, spanning back to the philosophies of Socrates, Plato, and Aristotle. David is recognizing that they are also the inquiries into which the Holy Scriptures have faithfully spoken throughout the ages.

The literature recording humankind's efforts for deeper psychological understanding is vast. My concern does not lie in the fact that people have vigorously sought such understanding, but that by and large the discipline of psychology has done so while excluding any thought of God that would positively inform the process. This is especially true when we consider the age of modernism in which psychology proper has gained exceptional momentum. As I stated early on, modernism tends to reject any information that cannot be verified through the scientific method, therefore, assigning as the ultimate source of knowing (i.e., epistemology) the discipline of empirical science.

David is experiencing the obvious consequences of this mindset. If data or ideas cannot be measured by some empirical method, then such data becomes irrelevant as far as science is concerned. The inevitable consequence of this approach is that it diminishes the validity of spiritual realities since the spiritual cannot be quantified through statistical means. This is why David is witnessing within his classes a discipline in which God is frequently denigrated, outright denied, and even stigmatized as a symptom of pathology. It is here at the intersection of science and spirituality that biblical counseling could prove helpful to David since it diverges significantly from much that has been purported by historic psychology with its humanistic bent.

Unlike secular psychologists, biblical counselors view the consideration of God as critical in developing a proper view of human nature, and they recognize that the source from which to draw an understanding of God is made possible primarily through the sacred Scriptures. The Bible, therefore, is the ultimate source of knowing (not science, as is the case in secular psychology). Succinctly stated, the Bible is the epistemological basis from which biblical counselors develop their presuppositions regarding all that is counseling.

The Bible Is Not a Footnote or a Filter

As a student of psychology and a devout Christian, David is quickly coming to grips with the fact that he cannot afford to belittle Scripture by making it a mere footnote beneath the insights he is learning from secular psychology. Scripture is not a secondary source to fill in the gaps found within the myriad books he is reading. Likewise, David does not want to make the mistake of examining leading research in psychology as a starting point in order to understand the mind and then filter it through the Bible to see which parts he can accept and which parts he must reject.

To begin anywhere other than the Bible in the pursuit of understanding the fundamentals of human nature undermines, though often inadvertently, people's efforts toward becoming competent counselors who appropriately utilize the Word in their work. It creates a sacred-secular divide that does not exist. Van Til strongly pushed against such dualism.

> We cannot do without God any more when we wish to know about physics or psychology than when we wish to know about our soul's salvation. Not one single fact in this universe can be known truly by man without the existence of God. . . . Now if every fact in this universe is created by God, and if the mind of man and whatever the mind of man knows are created by God, it goes without saying that the whole fabric of human knowledge would dash to pieces if God did not exist and if all finite existence were not revelational of God.[4]

Scripture provides God's perspective on all of reality.[5] Therefore, the Bible is essential "if we are to interpret natural revelation rightly"[6] since there are no such things as " neutral facts, for facts are God's facts."[7] John Frame explains, "Our world is a world that is exhaustively meaningful, because it is the expression of God's wisdom. Among human beings, interpretation is not the work of trying to assess for the first time the significance of uninterpreted facts. Rather, ours is a work of secondary interpretation, interpreting God's interpretation."[8]

If biblical counselors hope to rightly understand anything about human psychology, they must be good stewards of God's Word, making certain that the Bible—more accurately, the God of the Bible—takes center stage. As Christians, if our conceptual lens is not thoroughly shaped by the Bible, then no matter how well trained we may become in brain research, psychological theory, or counseling methodology, we will inevitably miss the mark in developing a psychology that properly reflects a biblical understanding of God's creation.

Given the great need for biblical care in our world and the fact that Scripture speaks overwhelmingly to the issues addressed by secular psychology, one does not necessarily need to be trained in these other disciplines in order to counsel well. If people become ardent students of Scripture, submit to a wise and experienced counseling mentor, and depend upon the work of the Holy Spirit, they will become well equipped to perform a divine duty to which every believer on earth has been called—the duty to make disciples—the duty to offer biblical counsel (Matthew 28:18–20; 2 Timothy 3:16–17).

The Bible Is the Trustworthy Authority

David is beginning to see the importance of understanding Scripture so that he may wisely navigate the content he is learning within the counseling classroom. He is embracing the Bible as authoritative above all other sources.

Consider the following wise words of Kevin DeYoung:

> All religion rests on authority. In fact, every academic discipline and every sphere of human inquiry rests on authority. Whether we realize it or not, we all give someone or something the last word—our parents, our culture, our community, our feelings, the government, peer-reviewed journals, opinion polls, impressions, or a holy book. We all have someone or something that we turn to as the final arbiter of truth claims. For Christians, this authority is the Scriptures of the Old and New Testaments.[9]

If DeYoung's assertion is true, on what basis is he able to make such an absolute claim? How do people know the Bible is authoritative over all other competing voices? Answering this question adequately will require consulting biblical counseling's epistemological base—the Bible.

When writing Timothy, the apostle Paul makes a bold claim about the nature of the Scriptures. He wrote, "All Scripture is breathed out by God and is profitable for teaching, for reproof, for correction, and for training in righteousness, that the man of God may be competent, equipped for every good work" (2 Timothy 3:16–17). This particular verse is rich with implications pertaining to counseling, but for now, simply consider the issue of authority. Paul encourages Timothy to remember that every word found within the Scriptures has a transcendent, supernatural origin–God. He uses a graphic metaphor of God breathing the Scripture to demonstrate that God himself is the author of the words. Here, the inspiration of Scripture is described as the expiration ("breathe out") of Scripture—it comes straight from the person and mouth of God.

If this idea is true—God is there and he has spoken in propositional form through the authors of the Bible[10]—then esteeming the authority of these words over and above any truth claim offered in psychology not only seems plausible, but necessary. Consider further the words of Peter on this issue.

> And we have something more sure, the prophetic word, to which you will do well to pay attention as to a lamp shining in a dark place, until the day dawns and the morning star rises in your hearts, knowing this first of all, that no prophecy of Scripture comes from someone's own interpretation. For no prophecy was ever produced by the will of man, but men spoke from God as they were carried along by the Holy Spirit. (2 Peter 1:19–21)

While men speak prophecies, the words uttered are guided by the inspiration of the Holy Spirit. These words are as a lamp shining in a dark place. Peter's claim certainly applies to the contents of the Bible. There is no question that men actually penned the words upon its pages. However, these men were mere instruments in the hands of another. They wrote what was revealed to them by God. Jay Adams summarizes this idea well.

> The Christian counselor has a Book that is the very Word of the living God, written in the styles of the individual writers,

who (through the superintendence of the Holy Spirit) were kept free from all errors that otherwise would have crept into their writings, and who, by His providential direction, produced literature that expressed not only what they themselves wanted to say, but what God wanted to say through them, so that (at once) these writings could be said to be Jeremiah's or the Holy Spirit's. This is a God breathed book.[11]

To make the claim the Bible is a "God breathed book" is to say it is inspired or directly given by God through his Spirit. That is why all truth claims must be subject to its scrutiny. Since the Bible comes from God, it is perfect and true.

The Bible is also inerrant. The inerrancy of Scripture means the Bible in its original form does not contain mistakes. This does not mean the use of Scripture by fallen man is infallible, but inerrancy points to its actual written content. Consider just a few passages concerning the trustworthiness of God's words (emphases added).

God is not man, that he should lie, or a son of man, that he should change his mind. Has he said, and will he not do it? Or has he spoken, and will he not fulfill it? (Numbers 23:19)

Every word of God proves true; he is a shield to those who take refuge in him. Do not add to his words, lest he rebuke you and you be found a liar. (Proverbs 30:5–6)

Now we have received not the spirit of the world, but the Spirit who is from God, that we might understand the things freely given us by God. And we impart this in words not taught by human wisdom but taught by the Spirit, interpreting spiritual truths to those who are spiritual. (1 Corinthians 2:12–13)

And we also thank God constantly for this, that when you received the word of God, which you heard from us, *you accepted it not as the word of men but as what it really is, the word of God,* which is at work in you believers. (1 Thessalonians 2:13)

So when God desired to show more convincingly to the heirs of the promise the unchangeable character of his purpose, *he guaranteed it with an oath,* so that by two unchangeable things, in which *it is impossible for God to lie,* we who have fled for refuge might have strong encouragement to hold fast to the hope set before us. (Hebrews 6:17–18)

The Bible itself claims divine inspiration and the words given by such means have been affirmed as true and inerrant again and again within its pages. According to these verses, the words of Scripture are trustworthy because an immutable, truthful God has spoken them. Therefore, when people approach the Bible as God's divine revelation, they are given opportunity to trust its wise, loving, perfect, and truthful author.

While it is a stretch to claim that the Bible is a psychology textbook, psychology has often crept onto the Bible's terrain when it comes to devising a proper understanding of the human soul. That is why it is so important that counselors first consult God's divine revelation when approaching the big questions of psychology. Has God weighed in on issues such as human nature, human dysfunction, psychological healing, mankind's purpose, and the nature of change? If so, what has he revealed? The answers to these questions and the significance people ascribe to them will powerfully shape their model of care. If counselors seek to serve others with rich biblical insight, then such answers from the Bible will wield the proper authority due their sacred origin.

Authority in Action

As a counseling student, David has started to understand that embracing the authority of Scripture is paramount in his development as a counselor. However, he is now wrestling with how to exercise such authority on a practical level. If he were to ask me how to do this, I might point him to Albert Ellis's Rational Emotive Behavioral Therapy (REBT) as an example.

According to REBT, it is irrational for people to rate themselves as either being "good" or "bad." In his own words Ellis maintains,

Moreover, both statements—"I am good" and "I am bad"— are overgeneralizations because, as noted above, all people do both "good" and "bad" deeds, and cannot really be categorized under a single, global heading—as being "good" or as being "bad." So the pragmatic solution to the problem of human "worth" is not a very good one, and had better be replaced by the REBT more elegant solution: "I am neither good or bad; I am simply a person who sometimes acts 'well' and sometimes acts 'badly.' So I'd better rate or evaluate what I do and not what I am."[12]

In other words, to view one's essence or one's being as either "good" or "bad" would violate Ellis's basic philosophical assumptions. Such beliefs about self would lend to a propensity for individuals to disturb themselves via emotional guilt, anxiety, or depression. Therefore, rating self is a big no-no in the REBT model. Only one's actions deserve the ratings of good or bad.

How do these assertions square with the Scriptures? Does the Bible differ with Dr. Ellis's conclusions? The answer is an easy one. The Scriptures actually do place individuals within the categories of "good" and "bad" for it teaches that people, by nature, are evil. This may seem wildly negative and exaggerated, but from the Bible's perspective, not trusting God, not showing constant gratitude to God, not honoring and enjoying God, and not loving God's Word and following it faithfully are clear marks of the fundamental evil of man's heart. By nature, people do not have a passion for the true God. Scripture also teaches that people innately live for themselves instead of living for God or for others (2 Corinthians 5:15), and this fundamental evil shows itself in countless ways in each person's life. Thus, Scripture can and does say that humankind has fundamental flaws in their attitude toward God and others. Further, Scripture says this constitutes people's nature as evil.

In contrast, the Scriptures consider believers to be righteous, not because they always feel and think and say and do the right things, but because Christ's righteousness has been imparted to them (2 Corinthians 5:21). As a result of this redemptive work, believers have begun to love, trust, enjoy, and submit to God. Believers have begun to reckon with their own self-promotion and self-pity, while embarking on a new path of humility and sacrificial love to others, a love that more and more reflects the very love of God that he has shown in sacrificing himself for human beings.

This change has come about because Christians have encountered the grace and love of God that is shown in Christ. They have come to know and believe the love God has for them in Christ. In experiencing that love, believers begin to walk in love (1 John 4:16, 19). Thus, trusting in the full favor and acceptance won by Christ's suffering and resurrection, Christians discover the root of change in spiritual and moral behavior. So the "righteous" are paradoxically the humble and broken who have seen their vital need of Christ's work on their behalf and have begun to trust him as their rescuer from the guilt and practice of sin.

Think how differently unbelievers and believers view God, others, and themselves. Unlike Ellis, Scripture does label people as evil or righteous, and though these are not absolute terms—meaning that the former does no good or the latter does no wrong—they are descriptions of fundamental tendencies that manifest themselves over the course of people's lives. Bringing a biblical view of humans to counseling is astonishingly different from bringing Ellis's view of humans. Both views claim authority to provide a comprehensive structure by which to interpret people and their behavior, and it will be no small matter as to which one a counselor ultimately chooses.

David and I clearly see that Ellis's assumptions about the core of human nature ultimately exemplify disbelief in God's words. They create an unbiblical construct of cognitions and the human belief system. As such, I would encourage David to defer to the Bible in orchestrating a richer conceptual framework of thoughts and beliefs. In doing so, David will have rigorously exercised the authority of Scripture in the development of his counseling assumptions and methodologies.

Is the Bible a Topical Encyclopedia?

To facilitate an honorable use of Scripture when counseling others, David will also need a right perspective of the Bible as a whole. Within the biblical counseling community, it is frequently stated that the Bible is not an encyclopedia but a lens.[13] Counselors who utilize the Bible should avoid approaching human struggles on a merely topical basis. In other words, Scripture is not a disconnected book that forces counselors into the horrible practice of careless proof-texting. A "Bible-as-encyclopedia" approach occurs when counselors exclusively rely on passages that correlate with the presented counseling issue(s).

As I converse with David further on this matter, I might offer the following example. Imagine that Sue has come to me for help because she is experiencing some very intense symptoms. Throughout the day, almost every day, seemingly out of nowhere, her heart begins to race at an extremely concerning rate. Her breathing becomes choppy, and she typically experiences light-headedness and a sense that she is going to faint. Sue's mind spins out of control with terrifying thoughts that she is experiencing a heart attack. Her anxiety has gotten so bad that she is only sleeping three to four hours a night. Almost every night, Sue wakes up from her sleep with her heart pounding, palms sweating, and her mind running out of control. Sue has been to the emergency room several times, and results from various tests indicate that she has a healthy heart and is not experiencing a heart attack during these episodes. To exacerbate things, Sue has also developed a fairly intense fear of people. She frequently abandons relationships, believing that others are out to get her. She is resentful about perceived offenses against her that never transpired. She is haunted by a long series of inner conspiracy theories wherein plots intended for her demise are continually at play. Sue is desperate for help.

If I defer to the "Bible-as-encyclopedia" method while counseling Sue, I would simply go to the concordance, and find an applicable passage on anxiety to share in session. I may start with Paul's words, "Let your reasonableness be known to everyone. The Lord is at hand; do not be anxious about anything, but in everything by prayer and supplication with thanksgiving let your requests be made known to

God" (Philippians 4:5–6). From these verses I may offer the following basic insight and counsel:

- The Lord is present, so there is no need to give in to anxiety.
- When you feel anxious, try prayers of thanksgiving.
- God wants to know your requests because he cares for you.
- Maybe you should memorize these verses as a means to relax
  when anxiety strikes.

Indeed, the Bible mentions anxiety, and what it says does have
implications for Sue. There is no question that the points above are
certainly true and potentially useful. However, for someone who suffers the paralyzing impact of severe anxiety, my proof-text counsel
will likely be anything but helpful. Such handling of the Bible as
it applies to Sue's gut-wrenching fears may feel more like salt to a
wound than balm to the soul. If I am not careful, I may sound like
Job's counselors, of whom he agonized, "'I have heard many such
things; miserable comforters are you all'" (Job 16:2). Offering platitudes is never the way of authentic biblical counsel.

This anemic application of Scripture poses other problems as
well. My ability to help Sue becomes limited to passages that mention the word *anxiety*. If my counsel is limited to simply referencing
anxiety passages ripped out of context, my counsel suffers, and even
worse, Sue suffers. For instance, this approach is not going to foster
a deeper knowledge of God. It will not encourage Sue to engage in
a deeper examination of her heart. It will not help her situate her
struggles within the context of Christ's redemptive narrative. It will
not consider the implications of God's sovereignty. Instead, it will
simply point Sue to Bible verses in an attempt to do nothing more
than promote relaxation or terminate her anxious experience. In
my opinion, such an application falls far short of exposing the deep
riches of God's Word as they apply to intense feelings of anxiety.

Further, this approach would either require the Bible to be completely exhaustive on all modern psychological maladies or render it
profoundly insufficient for tending to the human soul. What happens when a person enters my office diagnosed with trichotillomania
(an anxious pattern of behavior characterized by obsessively pulling

out one's hair)? Obviously, the Bible's concordance is not going to have that issue listed. If all I have at my disposal is the "Bible-as-Encyclopedia" model, I will be left in a very unfavorable predicament.

This approach also creates the illusion that the Bible does not speak into the issues that contribute to trichotillomania (or other labels offered by psychiatry). Such misunderstanding leads to the flawed inference that the Bible is irrelevant to maladies not specifically cited within its pages. This apparent deficiency reduces the Bible to being a disjointed book that covers a limited number of human ailments—most of those being very minor. It misleads counselors to think that when it comes to *real* psychological struggles (as labeled in modern terms) the Bible appears to be mostly silent. In other words, psychiatric labels—constructs developed from the modern, secular paradigm of psychiatry—such as obsessive-compulsive disorder, bipolar disorder, major depressive disorder, attention deficit-hyperactivity disorder or severe addictions seem to be beyond the scope of the Bible's purview. This perspective dilutes Scripture and forces it into a subservient position to secular psychology in its capacity to comprehend the deeper struggles plaguing the human psyche. This is an ironic travesty, given the fact that the author of Scripture is also the architect of the human soul. As such, he has offered deeper counsel than the "read two verses and call me in the morning" prescription that has often characterized Christian soul care.

Finally, locating verses topically inevitably abuses the actual meaning of the passage being used. Christians can easily fall prey to twisting the passage to fit their own counseling purposes. Thus, the issue of hermeneutics naturally arises—the proper interpretation of the Bible. If biblical counselors do not consider particular verses in proper context, their hermeneutic will always suffer, and when their interpretation suffers, they run the risk of misleading others in harmful and sinful ways.

If Christians hope to devise a rich biblical counseling model, they will have to have more than simplistic tendencies of quoting a few verses. I believe the Bible offers exceedingly enough wisdom to meet this challenge.

The Bible as Interpretive Lens

Instead of utilizing the Bible as a topical encyclopedia, I would want to help David develop a comprehensive biblical approach to counseling. A robust theology will need to guide his efforts. The Bible is not so much a topical guide as it is a divine narrative written by a sovereign, amazing, and brilliant author.[14] This narrative is the guiding prism that reveals vast shades of color to every detail of life. It alone brings true clarity and meaning to everything people see, do, and experience. Biblical counselors will seek to operate in the illuminating declaration of the psalmist, "Your word is a lamp to my feet and a light to my path" (Psalm 119:105).

Rather than constrict the sacred Scriptures to the "Bible-as-encyclopedia" method, wise counselors will draw from John Calvin's "Bible-as-spectacles" analogy in which he calls for a robust theological system that serves to interpret and shape every aspect of life. Calvin's teaching on this matter as it applies to counseling has been well outlined by Welch and Powlison, "The Bible gives the redemptive lens through which we see everything: politics, art, relationships, war, economics, engineering and psychology. We come to understand ourselves, our problems, and the means by which grace changes us. This lens pervasively alters our vision; the redemptive word of the true God affects all seeing."[15]

A biblical lens comprises of rich, sound theology—of God, of man, and of change. Rather than feverishly locating a quaint verse on anxiety as though it were a panacea for the ailing soul, examining struggles through Scripture as the sacred lens will move biblical counselors to ask significant theological questions. Biblical counselors might ask Sue:

- Who is God in this situation as far as Sue is concerned?
- What attributes of his nature apply to this situation?
- Who is Sue, fundamentally?
- What promises apply to Sue while she is enduring this grueling battle with anxiety?
- What is Sue's goal in counseling and change?
- Who is the agent of change?

- What redemptive themes apply in this situation?
- How is grace being poured upon Sue in her moments of doubt and fear?
- Is sin at play? If so, how?
- What captures and functionally rules Sue's heart?[16]
- How might God be seeking to conform Sue to the image of Jesus through this experience?
- What or who is Sue's ground of trust? God or something else? How does she know?

To answer these questions well, biblical counselors must do at least two things—diligently study the Word of God and lovingly get to know Sue. They will consult wise authors and theologians who have spent their lives asking these same things.

David may ask, "OK, but what if Sue has a serious psychiatric issue like Paranoid Personality Disorder (PPD)? Some of her symptoms seem to infer this as a possibility. The Bible says nothing about PPD." David's question is insightful. Since the Bible is the lens through which we are viewing this situation, David and I are not left empty-handed. While we cannot find that term in our Bibles, Scripture is still relevant to Sue's deepest issues. David and I will need a systematic theology that informs us on the diagnosis that our culture refers to as PPD. As we confer with Scripture regarding Sue's diagnosis, David and I will then unpack this (or any) diagnosis in biblical categories. We will follow the wisdom of David Powlison:

> Let us be ruthless to root out theoretical structures that view people as psychological or socio-psychological abstractions: the phenomena observed are not "ego defense mechanisms" but are pride's offensive, defensive, and deceptive strategies. And let us also forswear the therapeutic assumptions that are consequent to the theory: they are poor and deceptive substitutes for the Gospel of Jesus Christ. If—and it is a large IF—biblical categories control, we can revel in the descriptive acuity and case-study riches of psychologists. With biblical categories, we ourselves will mature as psychologists in the best sense of the word: acute observers of human life,

experienced in cases and case studies, consistently wise in our counseling methods. We will know people deeply enough to know exactly how they need Jesus Christ. We will remember that Christianity is a third way. The alternative to moralism is not psychologism; the alternative is Christianity.[17]

What does it look like to heed Powlison's admonition? For starters, Jesus's words that people's hearts are captured by what they treasure will inform our understanding of PPD or any psychiatric label (Matthew 6:21). How does such divine wisdom inform David's conceptualization of Sue as she is entrenched in obsessive worries? What treasures may influence her anxious patterns and paranoia—safety, security, acceptance, power, or control? Biblical counselors will search the wisdom of God's Word for greater clarity on this matter. How might Sue's inner treasures influence paranoia and fear? Certainly psychiatry has done much to describe the construct of PPD, but what is it, really? Does the Bible weigh in on this matter at all?

The words of the prophet Jeremiah will also frame David's understanding. He warned, "Thus says the LORD: 'Cursed is the man who trusts in man and makes flesh his strength, whose heart turns away from the LORD. He is like a shrub in the desert, and shall not see any good come. He shall dwell in the parched places of the wilderness, in an uninhabited salt land'" (Jeremiah 17:5–6).

What may be producing this dying shrub of thorns and thistles (i.e., paranoia and fear) in Sue's life? This verse clearly points to her object of trust. In whom is Sue placing her trust? This question may lend itself to explaining many symptoms we witness in those struggling with anxiety in its various manifestations (i.e., trichotillomania, OCD, panic attacks, et cetera). If so, the implications of the Bible regarding such struggles are far from absent; they are refreshingly illuminating. To visualize Sue's struggle through a biblical lens, consider the following diagram: [18]

Jeremiah 17:5–6

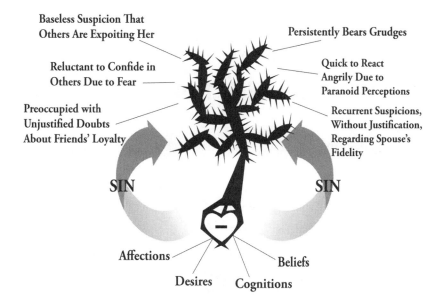

Baseless Suspicion That
Others Are Expoiting Her

Persistently Bears Grudges

Reluctant to Confide in
Others Due to Fear

Quick to React
Angrily Due to
Paranoid Perceptions

Preoccupied with
Unjustified Doubts
About Friends' Loyalty

Recurrent Suspicions,
Without Justification,
Regarding Spouse's
Fidelity

SIN

SIN

Affections

Beliefs

Desires   Cognitions

Object of Trust (Self)

Approaching Sue's struggle in this way will require David to consider the nature of worship to which Jesus and Jeremiah were both pointing. A significant element in Sue's struggle resides in where she places her ultimate faith and trust. The theme of worship will inform the model and means of care while helping David realize how reductionist it would be to ask Sue to memorize passages on anxiety in hopes of teaching her to relax. God's Word dives headlong into the depths of these and many other struggles—confronting them with supreme relevance and precision while also offering divine solutions for people like Sue. As Jeremiah continues, he points Sue to the source of her hope and healing. "'Blessed is the man who trusts in the LORD, whose trust is the LORD. He is like a tree planted by water, that sends out its roots by the stream, and does not fear when heat comes, for its leaves remain green, and is not anxious in the year of drought, for it does not cease to bear fruit'" (Jeremiah 17:7–8).

While Sue's persistent battle with paranoia and fear may prove stubborn to relent, faithful biblical counsel will creatively and consistently work with her to reorient her object of trust toward a loving, kind, trustworthy God who is faithful to produce fruit in her that brings him glory. The image below is a snapshot of our hope for Sue.

Jeremiah 17:7–8

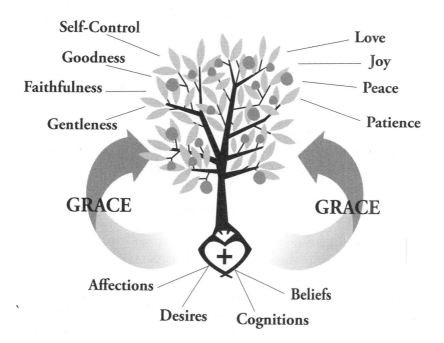

Object of Trust (God)

Wise counselors will also utilize the Bible as their lens when consulting general revelation. Biblical counselors are not "Bible-only" practitioners. In part, this is because biblical counselors understand that humankind bears the image of God (redeemed and unredeemed); therefore, all people possess an amazing capacity for discovery, wisdom, brilliance, and creativity. As a result, biblical counselors will seek to glean from the treasures of gifted scholars who have spent countless hours studying and observing human patterns of thinking, perceiving, relating, and behaving associated with PDD.

Yet biblical counselors must be discerning. Psychological data does not exist in a vacuum, but it always bears the weight of presuppositions and assumptions that must continually be considered and analyzed from a biblical frame of reference. Such consideration often requires a complete reinterpretation of that which the secular establishment deems as truth.

This certainly holds true for the various diagnoses of psychiatry (i.e., trichotillomania, obsessive-compulsive disorder, paranoid personality disorder, et cetera) in that biblical counselors will need to labor to develop the skills to transpose them into biblical categories. The importance of our transposing any diagnosis presented by the American Psychiatric Association (APA) arises because such diagnoses are conceptualized from a purely amoral, medical point of reference. In other words, the underlying assumption of psychiatry (which is the prominent discipline shaping today's views of mental struggles) is that symptoms are mere manifestations of physiological pathology or a diseased brain, and as such, they are not necessarily morally laden or related to God in any way. Human activity is not understood as transpiring in a context where the heart (even the sick one) is operating before the Lord. Existentially, this view is a complete distortion, and for the follower of Jesus, it may even contribute to a sense of despair for the counselee. This model infers that mental illness is separate from and unrelated to one's faith. God becomes irrelevant. Christians are left to suffer with mental maladies in a universe where it is presumed that God is silent on these matters or that Scripture is irrelevant to them.

To push against this distortion David and I consider the following chart that illustrates two perspectives of Sue's issues—the left column represents the lens of psychiatry, the right column, the lens of Scripture.

Psychiatric Explanation of Paranoid Personality Disorder

Pervasive distrust and suspiciousness of others such that their motives are interpreted as malevolent, beginning by early adulthood and present in a variety of contexts, as indicated by four (or more) of the following:

- Suspects, without sufficient basis, that others are exploiting, harming, or deceiving him/her
- Is preoccupied with unjustified doubts about the loyalty or trustworthiness of friends/associates
- Is reluctant to confide in others because of unwarranted fear that the information will be used maliciously against him/her
- Persistently bears grudges, i.e., is unforgiving of insults, injuries, remarks, or events
- Perceives attacks on his/her character or reputation that are not apparent to others and is quick to react angrily or to counterattack
- Has recurrent suspicions, without justification, regarding fidelity of spouse or sexual partner

Biblical Explanation of the APA's Diagnosis Paranoid Personality Disorder

The Bible is very clear in stating: "The fear of man lays a snare, but whoever trusts in the Lord is safe" (Proverbs 29:25). Additionally, Paul attributes evil suspicion and strife to those who do not "consent to wholesome words, even the words of our LORD Jesus Christ, and to the doctrine which accords with godliness" (1 Timothy 6:3 NKJV). With no fear of the Lord in their hearts, these individuals may engage in (Romans 3:18):

- Devising wicked schemes in their hearts (Proverbs 6:18)
- Having feet quick to rush in to evil (Proverbs 6:14)
- Bearing false witness (Proverbs 6:19)
- Pouring out filthy lies (Proverbs 6:19)
- Stirring up dissension (Proverbs 6:19)
- Grumbling against others (James 5:9)
- Having mouths full of cursing and bitterness (Romans 3:14)
- Slanderous accusations (Proverbs 10:18)
- Allowing a "root of bitterness" to spring forth which defiles many (Hebrews 12:15)
- Bearing grudges (Leviticus 19:18)

As we can see by these two lists, while the Bible does not mention the term Paranoid Personality Disorder, it does offer wisdom pertaining to the same symptoms, even going further by providing a cursory etiological explanation for these behaviors in that individuals suffering in the realm of paranoia are likely not giving "consent to wholesome words, even the words of our Lord Jesus Christ, and to the doctrine which accords with godliness" (1 Timothy 6:3–5). This idea is brilliantly captured when the psalmist declares, "Who is the man who fears the LORD? Him will he instruct in the way that he should choose. His soul shall abide in well-being, and his offspring shall inherit the land" (Psalm 25:12–13).

In other words, the one who fears the Lord and follows his instruction will possess a soul (i.e., a psyche) that abides in well-being.

Unlike psychiatry's Bible (the Diagnostic and Statistical Manual of Mental Disorders), the Scriptures help biblical counselors shape their counseling lens to see in Sue's struggles themes of worship, idolatry, love, sin, dependence, conformity to Christ, faith, trust, and divine empowerment. These constructs possess meaning if God truly exists.

So are biblical counselors forced to completely discard the descriptions offered by psychiatry? No. These descriptors will likely prove helpful. However, they only articulate symptoms; they do not offer a cure. This is where the Bible brilliantly displays its superiority—it boldly offers rich understanding on symptoms, cause, and cure.

Even for the more severe mental struggles, these variables are always at play. This approach brings biblical meaning, purpose, and understanding to the counseling process and to Sue's agony. As such, operating from a biblical perspective, counselors will be prompted to pose further probing questions—questions that are theological in nature—questions that address Sue as a beloved person created in the image of God. For example,

- What is going on?
- How is it impacting you?
- What life experiences may be contributing factors?
- Who is God in this moment? What do you think he is up to?
- Do you feel you are being punished?
- What do you want most in this situation?
- What do you want most from counseling?
- Why do you want the outcome you have mentioned?
- What does healing and change look like to you?
- How are you functionally relating to God in the midst of this trial?
- Does God love you? How do you know?
- How does the gospel apply in the midst of this struggle?

- Are you doing this alone or are you letting others in to help?
- Are you harboring shameful sin? If so, why do you think you need to do that?
- How does the finished work of Jesus Christ apply to the sin you hide?

Anxiety may be the primary problem that Sue is presenting in counseling, but the above questions begin to press in to the deeper issues at play—issues centered in her belief about God, the gospel, people, her life history, and grace as well as the functional reality of sin and its role in human motivation and perceptions. Biblical counselors do not simply want to address the symptom (i.e., anxiety in its various forms). They want to address the root of the problem. These questions get to the heart where God's truths can transform.

My hope for David is that as he continues his journey into the world of counseling, he will become fascinated by and engrossed in the robust nature of the Bible. It deeply touches the diverse, often severe, maladies he will eventually encounter in the counseling room.

Counseling Considerations

1. Do you possess a rich theology of human motivation derived from the Bible?
2. Do you possess a rich theology of human change derived from the Bible?
3. Do you possess a rich theology of human nature derived from the Bible? If you answered no to any of the first three questions, what steps can you take to begin to develop in these areas? How might you develop in these areas?
4. If there were no extra-biblical data offered by psychology or self-help (theory and research) regarding relational, emotional, and mental problems, have you developed a system of theology that would effectively address these issues? Would you be able to offer more than a verse and a prayer?
5. When seeking to become a better counselor, which of these excites you most: growing in your wisdom of Scripture as it

applies to the practical struggles of life or reading the latest self-help book?

RESOURCES FOR FURTHER READING

- Calvin, John. *Calvin: Institutes of the Christian Religion.* Ed. J. T. McNeil, trans. F. L. Battles. Louisville, KY: Westminster John Knox Press, 1960.
- Frame, John. *Systematic Theology: An Introduction to Christian Belief.* Phillipsburg, NJ: P&R Publishing, 2013.
- MacDonald, James, Bob Kellemen, and Steve Viars, eds. *Christ-Centered Biblical Counseling.* Eugene, OR: Harvest House, 2013.

CHAPTER FIVE

COUNSELING AND THE USE OF SCRIPTURE

Incline my heart to your testimonies, and not to selfish gain!
—Psalm 119:36

Religion is just mind control. —George Carlin[1]

The Bible is a very powerful book. The writer of Hebrews described it as "living and active, sharper than any two-edged sword, piercing to the division of soul and of spirit, of joints and of marrow, and discerning the thoughts and intentions of the heart" (Hebrews 4:12). According to Powlison, when Christians utter the words "The Bible says," it "ought to engender hard thought, close observation and careful discussion—not freeze our minds, end the conversation and close our eyes to life as it is lived."[2] For this reason, it is imperative that the one drawing from Scripture exercise humility and unyielding discernment.

Horror stories abound where people have twisted the meaning and intent of specific biblical passages in order to manipulate and brainwash the naïve, trusting, and unsuspecting. Who can forget the massacre in Jonestown; the evil, twisted justifications of the Ku Klux Klan in their case for white supremacy; the abuse of Scripture in mistreating homosexuals or blowing up abortion clinics? While these are obvious travesties, in truth the extremists are not the only ones capable of mishandling the Bible. Well-intended believers can fall into this trap as well (and often do). Biblical counselors must take very seriously the fact that when they utilize the Bible inappropriately, they open others up to devastating consequences. Even worse, they fail to glorify God.

Depending upon the Bible for counsel is a high call that warrants a reverent fear of the one whose words are translated to others. The apostle John explains, "I warn everyone who hears the words of the prophecy of this book: if anyone adds to them, God will add to him the plagues described in this book, and if anyone takes away from the words of the book of this prophecy, God will take away his share in the tree of life and in the holy city, which are described in this book" (Revelation 22:18–19). John is referring specifically to the book of Revelation, but his terrifying and sobering words are applicable for the whole of Scripture generally. Tampering with God's words is a dangerous endeavor. Counselors' hearts should tremble at the possibility of misapplying his wisdom.

All books in the Bible are as equally sacred as Revelation; therefore, the spirit of John's stern warning merits our attention and is affirmed elsewhere in the Old and New Testaments. Consider the following, with emphases added:

Every word of God proves true; he is a shield to those who take refuge in him. *Do not add to his words, lest he rebuke you and you be found a liar.* (Proverbs 30:5–6)

Do your best to present yourself to God as one approved, a worker who has no need to be ashamed, *rightly handling the word of truth.* (2 Timothy 2:15)

Not many of you should become teachers, my brothers, for you know that *we who teach will be judged with greater strictness.* (James 3:1)

These authors incite a relational imperative when mentioning the use of Scripture. The writer of Proverbs points to a person committed to rebuking those who mishandle his words. Likewise, Paul is encouraging Timothy to handle the Word of Truth wisely for the purpose of presenting himself approved by God. James warns of a higher standard by which teachers of the Word will be judged by

God. Concerning this relational imperative Tim Keller reminds, "To understand the Scripture is not to simply get information about God. If attended to with trust and faith, the Bible is the way to actually hear God speaking and also to meet God himself."[3] How beautiful it is to consider that the biblical counselor's work is a means to introduce their counselees to the very God of the universe. It should actually be their primary aim.

The way counselors choose to represent, utilize, and interact with the Bible horizontally (while counseling others) has enormous implications vertically (in our relationship to the Lord). No wonder D. A. Carson warns, "Make a mistake in the interpretation of Shakespeare's plays, falsely scan a piece of Spenserian verse, and there is unlikely to be an entailment of eternal consequence; but we cannot lightly accept a similar laxity in the interpretation of Scripture. We are dealing with God's thoughts: we are obligated to take the greatest pains to understand them truly and explain them clearly."[4]

Counselors must never forget this transcendent reality: As they divide the Word of Truth with others, they are perpetually and simultaneously relating to God either as his faithful ambassador or his despised enemy (James 4:4–6).

Hermeneutics: The Use (or Misuse) of Scripture in Modern Soul Care

Since people are fallen, those with the best intentions have failed to represent God's truth well. Counselors must always operate with a keen awareness of this possibility, remembering that they are susceptible to exercising poor hermeneutics—a poor practice of biblical interpretation. Surveying the use of Scripture by those trained in psychology, Stanton Jones and Richard Butman, both psychologists, offer this assessment:

> We will admit that some Christian psychologists doing integration have not been above sloppy biblical interpretation and farfetched theological speculation. The critics of integration do not have to look far to find examples of

unsubstantiated clinical speculation, sloppy logic, careless biblical interpretation, theological naiveté or fideism, and unbridled self-promotion.[5]

Maier and Monroe admit, "Christian therapists sometimes pay lip service to the importance of biblical hermeneutics, but little is done to promote its study in the field of Christian psychology."[6] As parishioners, professionals, or pastors, biblical counselors must be passionate in their aim to undo this concerning trend by challenging themselves to become careful stewards of Scripture.

Sadly, biblical and nouthetic counselors have also been guilty of poor biblical interpretation. Ed Welch and David Powlison have acknowledged, "Within our tradition there have certainly been forays into proof-texting, examples of shoddy exegesis, and times when we have been too dependent on a concordance. But the goal is to understand Scripture in context in order to apply it to people in context."[7]

Powlison soberly reminds and graciously exhorts anyone offering counseling shaped by Scripture that all people are influenced by sin. Therefore, people are "clumsy thinkers, clumsy practitioners, clumsy theologians, clumsy exegetes, clumsy cultural analysts. We all get pigheaded, shortsighted and stuck in those forms of error that contain partial truths. All error has a perverse logic, but we may hold to errors and semi-truths without being wholly perverted people. May God make us more skillful—together."[8]

As Christians hone the art of biblical counseling, they must continually remember that when they fail to rightly divide God's Word, lives are harmed and God is offended. John Bettler reminds, "All teaching and counseling must be based on a careful and accurate understanding of the Scriptures. To avoid the error of proof-texting by which the Bible is simply added to pre-existing ideas, biblical counselors must know how to handle the Bible."[9]

This is a potent reminder to those who hold the Bible in high esteem. Poor conceptualization of biblical ideas, including those such as the sufficiency of Scripture, may actually impede appropriate understanding of particular texts.[10] A weak definition of this concept wrongly applied can conveniently lead to the fallacies of "pat answer, legalism, pietism, or triumphal separatism."[11] Christian counselors are wise to admit that no one is exempt from the ongoing responsibility to interpret Scripture carefully while resisting the tendency of proof-texting in order to support their pre-existing views.

Exegesis: "Exe-What?"

Whether you are a self-studied lover of the Bible, a student completing a seminary degree, a counselor pursuing licensure, a pastor seeking to learn the practical application of the Bible, or a seasoned Christian psychologist, rightly interpreting Scripture must remain a paramount priority. One means by which to maintain high standards in this interpretive task is through careful exegetical methodology. Exegesis is the critical interpretation of a specific text, verse, or verses in the Bible. When Christians exegete a passage well, they will interpret the passage in a manner that most closely reflects the original meaning the author intended. But people often misconstrue the meaning of a text in order to force it into a particular agenda, paradigm, or preexisting idea. When this happens, very poor exegesis occurs, and the interpretation of the passage ultimately gets twisted or has little to do with what the author originally intended.

Wise counselors who depend upon Scripture must take significant measures to sharpen their exegetical skills. Too often, Christians are so concerned with giving pat answers or fitting a verse into their own ideas that they fail to search the depths of a particular passage as it applies in the context of the broader themes of Scripture. Failure in this regard often leads to the fallacy of eisegesis, wherein the interpreter forces a foreign meaning onto the passage that ultimately changes it entirely.

Love God and Neighbor . . . and Self?

Robertson McQuilkin, former president of Columbia Bible College and Seminary (now Columbia International University) once noted:

"But if the hermeneutics of Scripture, the basis of interpreting Scripture, is from the perspective of cultural anthropology or naturalistic psychology . . . Scripture is no longer the final authority. Cultural relativism, environmental determinism and other anti-Biblical concepts seep in and gradually take control."[12]

If Christians interpret Scripture through the lens of what psychology tells them about humans, the ramifications are disastrous. Interpretation of the Bible will invariably become skewed. During the late 90s, when I was completing my Master's degree in counseling, I witnessed this phenomenon on a fairly regular basis. A particular passage that consistently seemed to have its original meaning hijacked by the theoretical assumptions of psychology is when Jesus commands, "The most important is this, 'Hear O Israel: The Lord our God, the Lord is one. And you shall love the Lord your God with all your heart and with all your soul and with all your mind and with all your strength.' The second is this: 'You shall love your neighbor as yourself.' There is no other commandment greater than these" (Mark 12:29–31).

Good exegesis of this passage, in part, will conclude that there are only two commands here—love God and love neighbor. This emphasis keeps the primary focus on God and the secondary focus on others. During the proliferation of self-help guides during the late 70s and early 80s, some in Christian psychology came along, and based on popular psychological theory of the day added a third command—love yourself.[13] Some went so far as to say that a prerequisite to loving God and others resided in a healthy self-love, "Only when I have accepted my *self* can I let go of it, can I become selfless."[14]

The reasoning they offered went something like this: "How can you love anyone else if you don't first love yourself. You can't give something you don't already possess." By forcing a foreign theoretical idea of psychology onto the Bible, proponents distorted the actual meaning of the passage and completely reoriented the emphasis of Jesus's words from loving God and neighbor to loving self. Regarding this form of self-love, Anthony Hoekema writes, "The term *self-love* may imply that we are to love what we ourselves are by nature, apart from God's grace. Love of this kind is next door to pride; a Christian ought therefore not to indulge in it."[15]

According to this "self-love" translation, Jesus's words moved from being theocentric to being egocentric. Dr. Ian Jones further elaborates, "The secular understanding of high self-esteem is closely related to the biblical meaning of pride and what the King James Version quaintly refers to as 'a haughty spirit' (Proverbs 16:18). Such people are filled with overconfidence, arrogance, pride, conceit, and an unrealistic self-importance, and their behavior may cause harm to others and ultimately to themselves."[16]

The adoption of this self-esteem language suffocated the transcendent beauty of the great commandments in the dingy confines of an already self-consumed soul. Commenting on the issue of self-love, theologian, Jochem Douma, remarks, "The words 'as yourself' do not contain a duty of self-love, but rather rest on observable fact. We do in fact love ourselves, and the intensity of that self-love can serve as a measurement for our love towards our neighbor."[17]

Yet the misinterpretation by many within Christian mental health placed the human ego at the center of fulfilling the most foundational commands found in the Bible and swept the Christian community by storm. People began to flood Christian therapists' offices to learn how to love themselves and boost their self-esteem. Some experts assured them that these were the new prerequisites to being able to love God. This idea countered the promise that God's grace gives Christians everything they need for life and godliness (2 Peter 1:3). Since followers of Christ trusted the experts who were, with good intention, dispensing misinformation, many unsuspecting Christians bought into a gross misinterpretation of the Bible. They began to follow a false doctrine that was the antithesis of the Christian ethic.[18] Consider the vivid contrast from the following verses (emphases added):

> And calling the crowd to him [Jesus] with his disciples, he said to them, 'If anyone would come after me, *let him deny himself* and take up his cross and follow me. For whoever would save his life will lose it, but whoever loses his life for my sake and the gospel's will save it. (Mark 8:34–35)

And he [Jesus] said to all, "If anyone would come after me, *let him deny himself and take up his cross daily* and follow me." (Luke 9:23)

I protest, brothers, by my pride in you, which I have in Christ Jesus our Lord, *I die every day!* (1 Corinthians 15:31)

Have this mind among yourselves, which is yours in Christ Jesus, who, though he was in the form of God, did not count equality with God a thing to be grasped, but *made himself nothing, taking the form of a servant*, being born in the likeness of men. And being found in human form, *he humbled himself* by becoming obedient to the point of death, even death on a cross. (Philippians 2:5–8)

Interpreting Mark 12:29–31 or Matthew 22:37–40 in light of these passages on the self, it is impossible to assume Jesus was teaching a self-love doctrine. Nonetheless, the self-help books encouraged Christians to love self, raise self-esteem, and improve self-confidence, in contrast to God's eternal words. The sad reality of the practice of "loving self" in such an egocentric way actually reduces one's concept of a proper, biblical self-image—a healthy and rich view of self that is captured by the realization that people were made by God and for God.[19] Human beings are given dignity in Christ, and their confidence lies in what God has done and will do for them.

Exegesis: Basic Methodology

Proper hermeneutics and proper exegesis are important practices for any counselor. Here are a few pointers to begin wise hermeneutical and exegetical practices:[20]

1. Select and identify the passage.
    *   Start by browsing the whole book to see the whole picture.

2. Explore the general meaning of the passage.
    *   What does it say?
    *   What is it?
    *   Who is the author?

- What is the intent of the passage?
- What is the major theme?
- What is the story line?

3. Explore the specific meaning of the passage.
   - How is the passage arranged?
   - What is the sequence of thought?
   - What are the contexts and/or background?
   - What is the grammatical structure, such as nouns, verbs, et cetera. Examine the significance of individual words and phrases. Look at other translations.
   - What are the intentions and propositions? What are the problems and solutions?
   - Are there any theological terms that need to be researched?

4. Explore the context.
   - Who is the author and what does he bring to the passage? When and where was the book written? To whom was the book written?
   - What is the historical setting? What was going on in that time of history?
   - What are the cultural considerations?
   - What is the literary setting?
   - What precedes and follows the text?
   - What are the relationships to other passages?
   - What are the facts? How do they compare to your opinions?

5. Explore the contents.
   - What are the different topics involved and how do they relate?
   - Are there phrases or words repeated? Why?
   - What are the ethical teachings?
   - What are the precepts?
   - What do you recognize and what do you need to research?

6. Put it all together.
   - Be sure that teaching rather than experience dictate your interpretation/teaching.

- Adhere to the proper interpretation of Scripture by not twisting verses to justify your opinions.
- Avoid dogmatic statements that are not justified biblically, such as method of dress, movie attendance, et cetera.

Other Useful Counseling Tips

Ask questions:
- What is the theme of this passage? What is it really about?
- What is the context of the verse(s) I am studying?
- What do all the particular words (notice every word by emphasizing them) and phrases mean?
- What do I learn from the connections between phrases?
- What is the flow of thought?

Use other tools:[21]
- Use the cross-references in your study Bible. Always compare Scripture with Scripture. Again and again, other passages that talk about similar subjects will help you understand the passage you are studying. *This is one of the most important things you will do.*
- Closely related to the cross-references, look up important words from your passage in the concordance in the back of your study Bible where you will find other passages that use the same word.
- Read the notes in your study Bible (the ESV has excellent articles on Bible doctrine and Bible ethics that will provide help on many subjects). Eventually buy good commentaries recommended by your leaders that can give you further help in particular books of the Bible you want to study.
- Look up difficult words in a dictionary, or use the articles in the back of your study Bible.
- Write down what you do understand about the passage as you make observations.

- Write down questions about what you don't understand. Ask your spouse, your parent, your pastor, or leader or Sunday school teacher about things you simply cannot understand.

The Bible's authority is a cornerstone within biblical counseling, but biblical counselors also need to be aware of how the Scriptures can be abused. To abuse God's Word means others are abused, and this practice unfortunately runs rampant. Throughout history, people have used the authority of the Bible to support evil delusions, some even leading to mass suicide and abuse. However, one does not have to be an extremist egomaniac to fall prey to poor interpretation of God's Word. Many within the evangelical community have flourished in their ministries by offering views of Scripture that are far more shaped by personal agendas and psychological theory than careful study. All are susceptible. Honoring God in the counseling room means making proper exegetical practice an ethical and a moral obligation. Accurate, thorough exegesis and a continued dependence upon the Holy Spirit for Christlike love, humility, discernment, and guidance must guide biblical counselors.

Counseling Considerations

1. If you have never taken a class in biblical hermeneutics, consider doing so.
2. Work to develop your skills in biblical interpretation by engaging your pastor or someone with more advanced skills than you. Share your interpretation of passages and how you arrived at your conclusions. Be open to learn. Be willing to consider new ways of seeing.[22]
3. Be at ease with admitting error. It is a part of the process of growing and developing as a student of Scripture.
4. Find solid biblical commentaries and consult them often.
5. As you grow in your ability to rightly divide the Word of Truth, pray for and pursue continual humility and guidance from the Holy Spirit.

Resources for Further Study

- MacArthur, John. *The MacArthur New Testament Commentary.* Chicago, IL: Moody Press, 1985.
- Monroe, Philip. "Guidelines for Effective Use of the Bible in Counseling." *Edification: Journal of the Society for Christian Psychology* 2, no. 2 (2008): 53–61.
- Moo, Douglas. "The Epistle to the Romans," in *The New International Commentary on the New Testament.* Grand Rapids, MI: Wm. B. Eerdmans Publishing, 1996.
- VanGemeren, Willem A. "Psalms," in *The Expositor's Bible Commentary Revised Edition.* Vol. 5, eds. Tremper Longman III and David Garland. Grand Rapids, MI: Zondervan, 2008.
- Wilkin, Jen. *Women of the Word: How to Study the Bible with Both Our Hearts and Our Minds.* Wheaton, IL: Crossway, 2014.

CHAPTER SIX

. . . .

COUNSELING WITH GOD IN MIND

> Praise God from whom all blessings flow;
> praise him, all creatures here below;
> praise him above, ye heav'nly host:
> praise Father, Son, and Holy Ghost. Amen.[1]

John and Sara are in desperate need of marriage counseling. They have been married for only six years, and their relationship became strained when John began to pull away from Sara. He started to join his coworkers for happy hour, and now he frequently arrives home late. While hanging out at the pub one evening, John shared with one of his female colleagues that he has a troubled marriage. He complained that Sara is far too demanding, and she offers little affirmation or encouragement to him. Feeling unappreciated, he has decided to do his own thing, to show Sara how bad things are when he is not around. "Maybe she'll get the point that I'm important and change her tune," he surmised. However, his vengeful tactics to gain attention are devastating the marriage. In the meantime, John has enjoyed his visits with his female coworker, and feels extremely understood by her. He is definitely attracted to her willingness to show such interest in him.

Sara is utterly confused by John's recent actions. As a stay-at-home mom, she works hard throughout the day raising their two sons. Before John attended happy hour, he would come home, barely acknowledge Sara, and plant himself in front of the television. Any request from Sara for help with the boys was met with a harsh response. John's body language let Sara know that she had another thing coming if she expected him to help out around the house following a long, exhausting day at work. After years of such treatment, Sara withdrew from John. Her heart was broken because John did not love her enough to partner with her in the household duties. Sara admits to resenting her husband, and she does not see how the marriage is going to survive.

John and Sara are both confessing believers, but they admit that they have not been diligent in recent years to read Scripture or attend church. They are both making serious demands as conditions to continue in the relationship. Their primary hope for counseling is that it will help the other person make significant changes that will facilitate a deeper compatibility.

Counseling Is about God

John and Sara are experiencing major relational and existential disorientation. The mutual and chronic pain experienced by each within the marriage has suffocated their awareness of God. They have lost sight of the final purpose of their lives and the very reason God initially brought them together as husband and wife. Counselors will need to reorient them toward their ultimate purpose as creatures of God. Their motives for change will need to be anchored in something far more secure than a patched up relationship or deeper compatibility. Sara and John need to learn what it means to anchor themselves in God, while praying he will cultivate a passion in them to relate to one another primarily for his glory.

The Glory of God

God's plan from all eternity is that his name would be glorified. This is even true for John and Sara as they find themselves in a desperate place. God created human beings with the amazing capacity to perceive and delight in his glory and beauty. Glorifying God means that within their own hearts, people seek him to cultivate a growing awe and joy over all he has done in creation, providence, and redemption. People will seek to be more and more gripped and stunned and amazed at who God is and what he has accomplished for them. People will live a life of expanding gratitude, increasingly recognizing all that God provides for them materially, culturally, physically, relationally, and spiritually. People will seek to live out Christ's gracious, kind, humble, patient love. People will honor his authority by a growing joyful obedience. People will worship him faithfully and passionately among other believers in corporate worship. People will have, as the goal of all they do, to enhance his reputation and admiration by their faithfulness, diligence, mercy, and forgiveness. *Glorifying God is biblical counseling's primary goal.*

God deserving glory in all things is an idea thoroughly expressed in Scripture. The prophet Isaiah offers a fascinating glimpse of what living for God's glory means.

> You have never heard, you have never known, from of old your ear has not been opened. For I knew that you would surely deal treacherously, and that from before birth you were called a rebel. For my name's sake I defer my anger, for the sake of my praise I restrain it for you, that I may not cut you off. Behold, I have refined you, but not as silver; I have tried you in the furnace of affliction. For my own sake, for my own sake, I do it, for how should my name be profaned? My glory I will not give to another. (Isaiah 48:8–11)

God's agenda is clear. His plans and purposes for dealing with Israel in the manner he chooses centers upon his "name's sake," his "praise," his "own sake," and his "glory." The motives behind God's interactions with humanity are driven by an untainted zeal to be glorified on the earth. This theme resonates throughout the pages of the entire Old Testament. The authors honored the God of Moses, Abraham, and Isaac as worthy of all honor, glory, and praise.

> Declare his glory among the nations, his marvelous works among all the peoples! For great is the LORD, and greatly to be praised, and he is to be held in awe above all gods. (1 Chronicles 16:24–25)

Declare the glory among the nations, his marvelous works among all the peoples! For great is the LORD, and greatly to be praised; he is to be feared above all gods. (Psalm 96:3–4)

Though the fig tree should not blossom, nor fruit be on the vines, the produce of the olive fail and the fields yield not food, the flock be cut off from the fold and there be no herd in the stalls, yet I will rejoice in the LORD; I will take joy in the God of my salvation. (Habakkuk 3:17–18)

The Son of God, Jesus Christ, most eminently personified God's glory. Consider, in his own words, the driving passion of Christ's heart:

Father the hour has come; glorify your Son that the Son may glorify you. (John 17:1b)

I have glorified you on earth, having accomplished the work that you gave me to do. (John 17:4)

My food is to do the will of him who sent me and to accomplish his work. (John 4:34b)

Glorifying the Father nourished the redeemer's life and heart. Therefore, it is no surprise that Christ's disciples and apostles reflect his passion throughout the New Testament.

For from him and through him and to him are all things. To him be glory forever. Amen. (Romans 11:36)

So, whether you eat or drink, or whatever you do, do all to the glory of God. (1 Corinthians 10:31)

As each has received a gift, use it to serve one another, as good stewards of God's varied grace: whoever speaks, as one who speaks oracles of God; whoever serves, as one who serves by the strength that God supplies—in order that in every-thing God may be glorified through Jesus Christ. (1 Peter 4:10–11)

God has created a universe in which all creation is designed for his glory (Psalm 19:1). The practice of counseling must reflect this cosmic orientation, even when working with a couple like John and Sara. Counselors are wise to ask themselves whether glorifying God is their primary aim within the counseling context. Is it their ultimate concern when choosing the methods they employ with couples like John and Sara? If not, it is important they reconsider their starting point. Hearts enamored by God's glory must drive counseling practices.

Unfortunately, John and Sara have lost their awe of God and the privilege they have been given to live for his glory. Their pain, suffering, anger, frustration, loneliness, resentment, and entitlement have caused them to collapse upon themselves. The result of this implosion is now a seemingly justified selfishness within their marriage. In order to escape this lethal trap, both of their hearts must once again become captured by God's glory.

Knowing God: A Prerequisite to Self-Knowledge

If creation is about God's glory, then it follows that people, as part of that creation, are fundamentally creatures of worship designed to glory in God (Romans 1; 1 Corinthians 10:31). The universal variable that all secular theorists miss is the failure to consider God's glory in their constructs of wellness or health. In order to practice in the spirit of true Christianity, biblical counselors must factor in God's glory. This is precisely where biblical counseling offers something unique, setting it apart from every other theoretical model. It is an idea that has deep roots within the Church. One prominent Reformer has famously written, "Again, it is certain that man never achieves a clear knowledge of himself unless he has first looked upon God's face, and then descends from contemplating him to scrutinize himself."[2]

John Calvin believed that knowing God is a prerequisite to authentic self-knowledge. People cannot ultimately know themselves unless they know the Creator. Biblical counseling affirms with the psalmist that God has made and fashioned people and that they were created for his purposes (Psalm 119:73). Therefore, as biblical counselors help people like John and Sara conceptualize the core of their personhood—spiritual beings made to worship—the entire process becomes oriented around their chief purpose as human beings—the glory of God.

Biblical counseling, like no other form of soul care, recognizes that if people fail to consider God first, then it becomes impossible to understand themselves psychologically (human nature and motivation), ontologically (the nature of being and becoming), and existentially (the purpose and meaning of existence). Accurate self-knowledge becomes illusory when the purpose of counseling—the glory of the Creator—becomes entangled with the man-centered ideology of self-comfort.

Although relief from suffering and difficulty is an important aspect of biblical counseling, it is not the primary concern of biblical counseling. A biblical worldview embraces the idea that suffering is an aspect of the human experience. God uses hardship to mature believers so that they lack nothing (James 1:2–4). As such, biblical counseling concerns itself with a transformation that finds satisfaction in God—a change made possible only through the Spirit's supernatural work in people's hearts (2 Corinthians 3:18). Change progressively moves the counselee towards authentic inner peace (Philippians 4:4–7). Better marriages and balanced emotions are worthy pursuits, but these goals alone are far too small. The human soul is designed for satisfaction in the Lord of glory.

This aim means counseling is situated within the context of a larger drama. The stories of individual lives are transpiring within the gospel narrative—creation, fall, and redemption. This is the grand drama of the universe written by the author of all creation in which God progressively reveals himself within his own story through the Old and New Testaments. God's glorious narrative continues to be written by his sovereign hand today, and part of this story is that God faithfully rescues, transforms, and heals people in and through all things (Romans 8:28–29). Biblical counselors will need to assist counselees as they rediscover the meta-narrative of the Bible in which their story is being experienced. Biblical counsel will attempt to help them recognize that their personal stories are sentences in a much larger story.

To love John and Sara well, biblical counselors will need to help them reconnect with the divine narrative of the gospel. The Bible affirms that it is God's ultimate will to change them (1 Thessalonians 4:3). Therefore, John's and Sara's life story is primarily about a personal Lord, loving and saving them while rewiring their hearts according to his purposes, timing, and will. Through biblical counseling, God can change human hearts on a deeply psychological level so that they want what they were created to want, find complete satisfaction in that for which they were designed, and long for something far bigger than personal peace. Counseling is about falling in love with the Creator and Sustainer of the universe. So now let us consider, who exactly is this God worthy of such glory who is meticulously involved in his own narrative of redemption?

The Attributes of God

The hope of Christian counselors should be that John and Sara develop a deeper knowledge of God through the counseling process. Such an aim should lead counselors to ask, "Who is God, and how am I to communicate about him effectively to my counselees?" In order to adequately answer this question, biblical counselors must be able to articulate God's character in a way that resonates with the counselees' needs. God's attributes are deeply relevant to John's and Sara's marital breakdown. The Bible provides adequate knowledge of God that can change counselees' understanding of their most difficult mental, emotional, and relational struggles.

God's unchangeable attributes reveal his eternal, immutable, holy, merciful, beautiful, and trustworthy motives within the process of psychological and relational healing. There are many wonderful and highly recommended resources that thoroughly unpack the attributes of God.[3] The following list of God's attributes, in particular, may be incorporated into a responsible model of biblical care.

Attributes Belonging to God Alone and Counseling Implications

Omnipresence—God is everywhere at all times.

John and Sara are feeling alone in their marriage. Each longs for deeper intimacy and closer relationship, but in their deepest heartache they are not alone. The omnipresent God abides with them and is committed to their final good. Counseling will need to bring this realization back onto their radar. It might be helpful to have them read Psalm 139 or Lamentations 3 and journal about and mediate on God's presence, even during terrible circumstances.

Omniscience—God has complete and perfect knowledge of all things, including the past, present, future, and everything actual or potential.

God is not only present with John and Sara, but he is also perfectly aware of everything going on in their marriage. He knows about their pain, their sin, and their sorrow. He cares. God intimately knows their circumstances, their marriage, and their hearts. It might be useful for them to read and journal through Genesis 2—3 and consider both God's goodness and love for the first couple in history. God knew Adam's longings, and in kindness, designed a perfect mate for him. Additionally, it might be helpful for John and Sara to consider the catastrophe that unfolded when Adam and Eve resisted the wisdom of their Creator. What does this story reveal to them regarding operating in pride and selfishness while ignoring God's all-knowing counsel?

Omnipotence—God is all-powerful and able to do all that he wills.

God wields the power to execute his will in John and Sara's current situation. What is God's ultimate will for them? If they are Christians, then Scripture is clear that his will is their sanctification (1 Thessalonians 4:3). Their marriage struggles are a context in which God's power to execute his will in transforming them will ultimately be realized.

Immutability—God does not change in his essence, character, purpose, or knowledge but does respond to people and their prayers.

John and Sara may feel that so much has changed between them that they are beyond repair. Nothing in their relationship is currently stable. They are searching for hope, peace, and stability in places that are only disrupting their lives. A loving reminder of God's immutable nature in the midst of the chaos could prove helpful to them. Though they have both sinned terribly against God, his forgiveness awaits them (1 John 1:9). Though they have acted selfishly in their pain, God's love continues to flourish for them (Romans 8:37–39). Even in their current tumultuous storm, the Lord remains steadfast in his commitment to transform them into creatures of glory (Titus 2:11–14).

Eternality—God has no beginning or end and is not bound by time, although he is conscious of time and does work in time.

God is eternal, therefore, the problems John and Sara are experiencing are not catching him by surprise. God knew John and Sara before the foundations of the world were formed. If John and Sara are indeed regenerate believers, then from God's eternal nature, he has designed for them a very specific purpose—to share himself with them and to work in their hearts throughout their lives, during both the ups and downs, that they would more and more reflect him (Ephesians 1:3–4). Their lives are not random. An eternal God is working out all things according to the perfect counsel of his eternal will (Ephesians 1:11).

Sovereignty—God is supreme in rule and authority over all things although he does allow human freedom.

In their sin and their pain both John and Sara are being taken by the illusion of their own self-sovereignty. They are making absolute demands of how things must be in order for them to exercise love within the marriage. They both want to control the conditions for their obedience to God. Rather than demand control over the other's behavior, they will need to submit to God's sovereignty and begin to ask how their own hearts need to change according to his divine purposes, while diligently seeking the power of the Holy Spirit to bring about their own transformation. A counselor could ask them to consider Jesus in this matter by reflecting on Matthew 7:3–5.

God's unshared attributes offer Christians a glimpse into aspects of his character. These aspects of God's personality bring hope and trust to people, for they remind them that self-reliance is not the viable option when seeking change, healing, and transformation. God is a person who is present and empowers his people toward change that will shape them for their ultimate good—to live for the glory of God.

God's Attributes Bestowed upon Humanity and Counseling Implications

Holiness—God is separate from evil. God's redemption is to share his beauty by fashioning his people to reflect his holiness.

The Lord has predestined that John and Sara would grow in holiness throughout their lives (Ephesians 1:3–4; 1 Thessalonians 4:3). Their marriage is a rich context in which this eternal work may be realized. Maybe they need to make an assessment of their own behavior, words, and thoughts and consider whether or not these reflect holiness. What behaviors, words, or thoughts might they need to "put on" that would more properly reflect the holiness of God?

Love—God ever moves out from himself to give of himself. God satisfies others with his goodness.

The Lord is committed to shaping the hearts of John and Sara that their love for one another would reflect his love for them, "Greater love has no one than this, that someone lay down his life for his friends" (John 15:13). If love for one another is no longer the motive driving their interaction, then they will both need to consider what desires have become more important—affection, appreciation, pleasure, comfort, et cetera. Asking them to read and discuss James 4:1–8 may foster a deeper understanding regarding what transpires when individuals desire things to the point of sin. Coveting blinds people to their most fundamental call to love God and others.

Truth—God is the source of all truth. He is the embodiment of truth.

John and Sara will need to consider what truths are currently guiding their lives. For example, John believes that in order for him to be a loving husband, Sara will first need to affirm and appreciate him. John will need to consider how this belief squares with 2 Peter 1:3–11. John also believes that his escapades during happy hour have been caused by his wife's lack of affection. He will need to measure this assumption with God's eternal truth as found in James 1:12–15. Sara holds to her own versions of truth as well. In her pain she has allowed herself to covet attention and affirmation. Such idolatry has allowed her to give herself permission to neglect her husband. She will need to confront these issues biblically in order to gain sound understanding and insight. Reading, journaling, and meditating on the relevance of Romans 12, Philippians 2:1–8, or 1 Peter 2–3 to her current situation might serve as an eye opening exercise for her.

Righteousness—God always deals in perfect fairness and justice, always doing the right thing for every being in every circumstance.

God's agenda for John and Sara is that they would reflect his righteousness in how they relate to one another. Are they fair, just, and good in their responses toward each other's sins? Do their thoughts, affections, decisions, and behaviors reflect God and his treatment of his children in the face of sin?

Mercy—God shows kindness, patience, grace, and favor toward people who are helplessly broken and evil.

Ephesians 2 is extremely applicable for John and Sara in regards to them growing in mercy as husband and wife. Extending mercy to one another is to live lovingly with each other in spite of the other person's sins and selfishness. It is to give what may not have been deserved or earned.

Beauty—God's holiness, love, mercy, and goodness combined to form his beauty. God's holiness exposes the loveliness of his sheer and pure goodness.

God's beauty is reflected upon this earth as John and Sara begin to image him more and more in their relationship. They become more beautiful as they escape "the corruption that is in the world because of sinful desire" (2 Peter 1:3–4) and instead reflect God in his holiness, love, truth, righteousness, and mercy. Their relationship holds potential to become a dim shadow of the eternal beauty that resides within the Trinitarian relationship of the Father, Son, and the Spirit.

God's shared attributes tell people something of himself and themselves. People cannot know themselves unless their understanding is grounded in the character of God. Counseling is left with an arbitrary understanding of health and growth if the model is not securely anchored in God and his supreme, unchanging nature.

The Trinitarian God

While understanding God's attributes is important for biblical counselors, so is their understanding of the Trinity and each person's role in the process of change. Knowing God is one thing, but recognizing his personal activity in people's lives is another. Theologian Wayne Grudem provides a succinct summation of the biblical teaching concerning the Trinity by offering the following three statements:[4]

1. God is three persons.
2. Each person is fully God.
3. There is one God.

These statements illumine the rich complexity of God. It is quite difficult for people to wrap their limited minds around how God is three distinct persons yet only one God. To some, such a proposition may even appear contradictory. Why would Christians assume the statements are true? There is only one acceptable answer: each statement is taught and affirmed in the Bible.

For example, Jesus mentions all three persons of the Trinity when giving the Great Commission to the saints, "Go therefore and make disciples of all nations, baptizing them in the name of the Father and of the Son and of the Holy Spirit, teaching them to observe all that I have commanded you. And behold, I am with you always, to the end of the age" (Matthew 28:19–20).

The apostle Paul also cites the three persons of the Trinity, "The grace of the Lord Jesus Christ and the love of God and the fellowship of the Holy Spirit be with you all" (2 Corinthians 13:14). Additionally, Paul offers amazing insight into the Trinitarian nature of God in the book of Romans in which he mentions the Holy Spirit's role in interceding for the saints, the Father's sovereign plan for the saints, and Jesus's work of redemption and inseparable love for the saints (Romans 8:26–39). The process of transformative change is utterly dependent on the active work of the Trinitarian God. The Father has created a plan of transformation for every believing counselee; Jesus has executed this plan through his completed work; and the Holy Spirit fully applies this plan in the lives of his people.[5] As a counselor, this is the greatest point of comfort I possess: God in all three persons is actively at work in the process of ongoing change and healing.[6]

The Economic Trinity: God's Role in Soul Care

God is actively at work in the universe he has created. The Bible says, "in him all things hold together" (Colossians 1:17). Jesus is actively maintaining the form and function of everything people see and experience in the cosmos, right now. This includes the particulars of individual lives. I love Spurgeon's take on Colossians 1:17:

> Only think of it; those innumerable worlds of light that make unbounded space to look as though it were sprinkled over with golden dust, would all die out, like so many expiring sparks, and cease to be, if the Christ who died on Calvary did not will that they should continue to exist. Surely, if Christ upholds all things He can uphold me. If the word of His power upholds earth and heaven, surely, that same word can uphold you, poor trembling heart, if you will trust him.[7]

God is not only intimately involved in the continued radiance of a star, but he is also intimately involved in the hearts of his people. Therefore, the Trinitarian God is intimately involved in the counseling endeavor. This conceptual understanding of God is known as the "economic Trinity" or "the Trinity in its relation to creation, including the specific roles played by the Trinitarian persons throughout the history of creation, providence, and redemption."[8] We may further draw from Peter on this idea, "Peter, an apostle of Jesus Christ, To those who are elect of the dispersion in Pontus, Galatia, Cappadocia, Asia, and Bithynia, according to the foreknowledge of God the Father, in the sanctification of the Spirit, for obedience to Jesus Christ and for sprinkling with His blood" (1 Peter 1:1–2).

John Frame notes, "This is a useful generalization about the distinctive roles of the divine persons: the Father plans, the Son executes, and the Spirit applies."[9] Yet, within this generalization, Frame reminds, "Peter is not here describing a precise division of labor. He knows that all of these events require the concurrence of all three persons."[10] The general roles highlighted by Peter simultaneously involve all three divine persons. Therefore, the work of the Father does not exclude or is not executed apart from the Son or the Spirit. The same goes for the particular roles of the Spirit and the Son.

Instead, Peter speaks of the concurrent work of the Trinity in that people are elected according to the foreknowledge of God the Father, in the sanctification of the Spirit, for obedience to Jesus Christ and for sprinkling with his blood. Peter reveals the Father's purpose, the Son's accomplishment (sprinkling) and the Holy Spirit's application (sanctification and obedience).[11]

Paul gives further insight as to the Trinitarian interplay and division of labor, "But when the fullness of time had come, God sent forth his Son, born of a woman, born under the law, to redeem those who were under the law, so that we might receive adoption as sons. And because you are sons, God has sent the Spirit of his Son into your hearts, crying, 'Abba! Father!' So you are no longer a slave, but a son, and if a son, then an heir through God" (Galatians 4:4–7).

The harmony expressed by this divine work is stunning. Reeves articulates a beautiful summation of this eternal dance.

> It is by the Spirit that the Father has eternally loved his Son. And so, by sharing their Spirit with us, the Father and the Son share with us their own life, love and fellowship. By the Spirit uniting me to Christ, the Father knows and loves me as his son; by the Spirit I begin to know and love him as my Father. By the Spirit I begin to love aright—unbending me from my self-love, he wins me to share the Father's pleasure in the Son and the Son's in the Father. By the Spirit I (slowly!) begin to love as God loves, with his own generous, overflowing, self-giving love for others.[12]

Reeves has captured the very essence of biblical counseling and change. Psychological transformation—heart transformation—begins with an eternal love that has always resided within the Trinity.

By sharing this love through the Spirit, people are placed upon the path of healing, being empowered by God to fulfill their design as image bearers as their longing for God and his glory intensify. God rescues people from the depraved inertia of self-love and, as Reeves puts it, rewires us to "love aright." A mind that "loves aright"— a mind that is consumed with an ever-increasing passion to love God and others—is a mind moving toward authentic, grace-driven mental health.[13]

The existence of God is the great presupposition of biblical counseling. Embracing this view orients the counseling process around a person. That person is not the counselee or the counselor but the God of the Bible who deserves glory. The practice of biblical counseling, therefore, is primarily inclined toward the glory of God. It conceptualizes individuals, their circumstances, the process and aim of counseling with a mindfulness of God's character. God's unshared and shared attributes as well as his Trinitarian work within the believer's life brings hope. The Father has created a plan of transformation for every believing counselee, Jesus has executed this plan through his completed work, and the Holy Spirit fully applies this plan in the lives of his people.[14]

COUNSELING CONSIDERATIONS

1. If counseling is situated within the Lord's redemptive narrative, and the Trinity is eternally and continually involved in the redemptive process, how does this shape your understanding of the counseling process?

2. Read Romans 8:18–39. Journal on how this Scripture is relevant to you as a counselor as well as its implications for counselees. What is the point of life (even suffering)? What is the hope that Paul mentions? How is this relevant to counselees who are struggling? How is the Trinity involved moment by moment in the life of the Christian?

3. Review the shared and unshared attributes of God. Write out the relevance and implications of each as it pertains to counseling. How might each of them apply in a counseling context?

4.   Meditate on God's mercy, love, and faithfulness as you consider God's involvement in the change process (redemption) throughout the believer's life span.

5.   Journal a prayer of thanksgiving to God because he has lovingly revealed himself and his activities.

Resources for Further Study

~   Hambrick, Brad. *God's Attributes: Rest for Life's Struggles.* Phillipsburg, NJ: P&R Publishing, 2012.

~   Johnson, Eric, *God and Soul Care: The Therapeutic Resources of the Christian Faith.* Downers Grove, IL: Zondervan, 2017.

~   Owen, John. *The Holy Spirit: His Gifts and Power.* Scotland: Christian Focus Publications, 2004.

~   Packer, J. I. *Knowing God.* Great Britain: Hodder & Stoughton, 1973.

~   Pink, A. W. *The Attributes of God.* Radford, VA: Wilder Publications, 2009.

~   Reeves, Michael. *Delighting in the Trinity: An Introduction to the Christian Faith.* Downers Grove, IL: IVP, 2012.

~   Thorn, Joe. *Experiencing the Trinity: The Grace of God for the People of God.* Wheaton, IL: Crossway, 2015.

CHAPTER SEVEN

. . . .

WHAT IS GOD UP TO IN COUNSELING? (PART 1)
COUNSELING WITHIN THE FATHER'S PLAN

I know that you can do all things, and that no purpose of yours can be
thwarted. —Job 42:2

And we know that for those who love God all things work together
for good, for those who are called according to his purpose. For those
whom he foreknew he also predestined to be conformed to the image of
his son, in order that he might be the firstborn among many brothers.
—Romans 8:28–29

Jessica's story is riddled with trauma. Her father abandoned her
and her mother when Jessica was eight years old. He was addicted
to hydrocodone and extremely volatile. Jessica witnessed him beat-
ing her mother on many occasions and even called 9-1-1 following
one of his rage-filled episodes. He would physically abuse Jessica
when hyped up on his drugs. Jessica's internal world was one of endless contradictions. On the one hand, she hated her father and was
relieved she did not have to deal with him throughout her childhood. On the other hand, at age twenty-two, she often experiences
profound bouts of emptiness and worthlessness because she never
had the opportunity to experience her father's love. She cannot help
but struggle with the idea that she is completely disposable since her
own father did not care for and nurture her. Since the age of fifteen,
Jessica has battled severe depression.

To escape the emotional torture, she has developed several
coping mechanisms. If she pulls up the sleeve on her left arm, there

is a mountain of scar tissue that has accumulated from years of self-harm. A razor to the skin seemed to provide a sense of control over her pain while also distracting her from the internal pain that often consumed her. She also tells of her efforts to gain a sense of worth through many sexual experiences with different guys. The intimacy she hoped to capture only resulted in further shame and worthlessness. Jessica has recently turned to the bottle as a means of solace. Numbing out seems to be her only option for relief. Jessica is wrestling with thoughts of suicide but says she has absolutely no intent to act upon them. She feels very distant from God, even though she attends church on a regular basis.

*****

Counselors often have to think along several tracks at once. Jessica's story contains many complex details to explore. As I sit and listen to her, I am going to have to consider various things at once:

- How is God relevant to Jessica's story?
- Arguably, no question will be more significant in my time with Jessica. In order to offer wise counsel, it will be important for me to have a strong working knowledge of God and his here-and-now purposes within the context of human struggle. What is God up to?
- Am I genuinely listening to Jessica's struggle or am I distracted with forming an answer for her?
- What are the most significant presenting issues that could be exacerbating her struggle?
- Does she seem open to counsel or is there resistance?
- What is her body language expressing to me as she recounts her tragic history?
- What is God up to in Jessica's life?

God the Father: The Sovereign Lord

God is indeed up to something, and part of the counseling endeavor is to help counselees consider his plans, purposes, and intentions.

Christians possess a construct to shape their model of care that is completely absent within psychological literature. God's sovereignty is a theological concept that brings form and order and purpose to everything that exists. It guides every aspect of human transformation. The apostle Paul explains this in Ephesians.

> Blessed be the God and Father of our Lord Jesus Christ, who has blessed us in Christ with every spiritual blessing in the heavenly places, even as he chose us in him before the foundation of the world, that we should be holy and blameless before him. . . . In him we have obtained an inheritance, having been predestined according to the purpose of him who works all things according to the counsel of his will. (1:3–4, 11)

The greatest security for any Christian counselee who is struggling is God's sovereignty. Whether the issue is addiction, obsessive-compulsive disorder, major depression, or homosexuality, these verses possess the everlasting bottom line of human change— God is sovereign over all things, and he is working out a particular plan in human lives "according to the counsel of his will."

Paul is exalting the name of the Father for giving his Son and the wealth of spiritual gifts that accompany relationship with him. Paul explains that this new life in Christ was planned "before the foundation of the world." Counselors and counselees must consciously place the counseling process in its true context, properly situating life experiences within a plan birthed from the infinite mind of God.

The issues counselees experience are not the ultimate focal point, rather they are a smaller piece of a larger narrative.[1] The horizontal experiences of life are always connected to the vertical realities of transcendent purposes. Consider Paul's second letter to the Corinthians where he shares the various hardships he had faced (the temporal/horizontal) by placing their final purpose in the divine plans of God (the eternal/vertical). "For we do not want you to be ignorant, brothers, of the affliction we experienced in Asia. For we were so utterly burdened beyond our strength that we despaired of life itself. Indeed, we felt that we had received the sentence of death. But that was to make us rely not on ourselves but on God who raises the dead" (2 Corinthians 1:8–9).

As Paul recounts the stressors he and his companions endured, he points to the unseen hand of God and his final purposes within the struggle. Paul recognized that though his trials were arduous, they were not meaningless. God's sovereign purposes in redemption were transpiring. God was increasing and transforming Paul's faith.

The same goes for counseling. Jessica's struggle is part of a redemptive plan to conform her into Jesus's likeness. Her life is part of God's divine plan to bring her to final glory. By God's plan, Jessica's trajectory of change is "that she should be holy and blameless before him" (Ephesians 1:4). In the end, nothing Jessica has experienced is surprising to God. A. W. Tozer beautifully captured this concept when he wrote, "Whatever new thing anyone discovers is already old, for it is the present expression of a previous thought of God."[2] One of my roles in counseling Jessica is to recognize that I am a participant in God's divine plan to rescue, transform, and finally perfect her as his beloved daughter.[3]

Paul offers an overview of this process of transformation and sanctification. Consider the following:

> And we know that for those who love God all things work together for good, for those who are called according to his purpose. For those whom he foreknew he also predestined to be conformed to the image of his Son, in order that he might be the firstborn among many brothers. And those whom he predestined he also called, and those whom he called he also justified, and those whom he justified he also glorified. (Romans 8:28–30)

God is working out a divine and glorious good in every detail of people's lives. Everything in people's lives (both joys and sufferings, both sin struggles and holy worship) serves the purpose of perfectly conforming them to the image of Jesus Christ. It is my hope for Jessica that by God's grace, she would recognize the supreme purpose

of all her struggles—in all things God is working to transform her—
so that she experiences the fullness of human life as she increasingly
thinks, wants, and lives like Jesus.

Utter transformation will find completion at Christ's second
coming—when Christians will be glorified with him (Colossians
3:4). Therefore, as I help Jessica pursue present and increasing change,
I will also accentuate the fact that her sure hope of finally being perfectly conformed to Christ's image is when Christ returns and her
body is conformed to the glory of his body (Philippians 3:20–21).

This transformative process, according to Paul, is also predestined. Therefore, before the world ever existed, God planned to
initiate and complete people's ultimate healing (physically, psychologically, emotionally, et cetera). Again, this healing will not be
complete until Christians are glorified in immortal bodies in the
new creation (Romans 8:18–20; 1 Corinthians 15:50ff), but they
are now, by the power of the Spirit, in process toward that final end.

Notice also Romans 8:30 is written in past tense (predestined,
called, justified, glorified). How does this apply to Jessica? It reveals
that her complete redemption is as good as done. Nothing will frus-
trate God's eternal plan of complete and utter restoration. For Jessica
(assuming she is a believer), no moment of compulsion (self-harm),
no addictive impulse (drinking alcohol excessively), no sexual sin,
nothing at all will slow down or stifle God's healing plans. With
God, there is no plan A, plan B, or plan C; there is simply the plan
that is unfolding according to the perfect counsel of his almighty
will. Concerning God's purposes, Job reflects, "I know that you can
do all things, and that no purpose of yours can be thwarted" (Job
42:2). John Frame similarly reflects:

> The logic is inevitable. Anyone whom God savingly fore-
> knows, he predestines to be conformed to the likeness of
> Christ. (That is, he writes the Word on his heart.) And
> anyone so predestined receives an effectual call from God
> sometime in his life, a summons into fellowship with Christ,
> an order that he cannot decline. Those whom God calls he
> justifies: he declares them righteous for Jesus' sake. And
> those he justifies, he glorifies. No one who is foreknown,

predestined, called, and justified can escape glorification. Final salvation is certain.[4]

Frame emphasizes that if people have professed faith in Jesus, they have reason to hope in God's faithfulness to complete his eternal plan in them, despite what may feel like setbacks in their spiritual journey. While Jessica's life has been profoundly difficult, and while her current issues seem to be overpowering her, the God of Scripture will achieve his perfect plan of redemption in her life. If God is for her (and he is) then nothing has the power to thwart his eternal, predestined plan to transform her into the likeness of his glory.

The hope for current and future change—psychological, emotional, spiritual, and relational growth—rests in the faithfulness of God who, by his mercy, has already initiated a process of change that is designed and destined for a sure outcome.[5] God began the work of redemption in counselees who profess Jesus as Lord, and he is faithful to complete his work. Paul affirms, "And I am sure of this, that he who began a good work in you will bring it to completion at the day of the Lord Jesus Christ" (Philippians 1:6). God alone initiated the work, and God is committed to completing his work.

As counselors anticipate this completion, they will seek to foster in counselees a faith in God's timing (Titus 2:11–14; 2 Peter 1:3–4) and a conviction that transformation is sure even if not yet evidenced (Hebrews 11:1). Counselors teach counselees to live in the promise of the apostle John, "For everyone who has been born of God overcomes the world. And this is the victory that overcomes the world—our faith. Who is it that overcomes the world except the one who believes that Jesus is the Son of God?" (1 John 5:4–5).

John's words resound with unmitigated certainty. Everyone who is born of God will overcome, and those who overcome are the ones who have believed that Jesus is the Son of God. Faith is central to ongoing psychological transformation.

Pride's Resistance to a Sovereign God

Humbly accepting God's sovereignty holds the potential to pierce the human conscience like nothing else. Yet Christians face a formidable challenge—pride. Though pride has found its origin in the human heart since Adam and Eve, it has gained a fresh cultural traction in recent decades. Dr. Paul Vitz contends that modern psychology has played a role in reinforcing the heart's pride by its cultural assumptions about self. Vitz concludes that "humanistic selfism" has become a "popular secular substitute religion, which has nourished and spread today's widespread cult of self-worship."[6] Such self-worship has nurtured cultural patterns that Theodore Dalrymple calls "admirable evasion"—socially constructed acceptance of irresponsible behaviors based on doctrines of psychology and psychiatry.[7]

This pride has radically infected the body of Christ too. Church culture has been influenced by the self-centered gospel of psychology—the idea that humanity is the center of all things and that the final aim of the good life is personal comfort and pleasure. Christians have fostered what Dr. Kendra Creasy-Dean and her colleagues cite as Moralistic Therapeutic Deism (MTD)—an unspoken moral code that shapes the modern Western church. Dr. Creasy-Dean describes MTD as follows:

> Moralistic Therapeutic Deism makes no pretense at changing lives; it is a low commitment, compartmentalized set of attitudes aimed at "meeting my needs" and "making me happy" rather than bending my life into a pattern of love and obedience to God. Like the Spiderman symbiote, Moralistic Therapeutic Deism cannot exist on its own. It requires a host, and American Christianity has proven to be an exceptionally gracious one.[8]

She concludes, "We have forgotten that we are not here for ourselves, which has allowed self-focused spiritualties to put down roots in our soil."[9]

These roots have grown very deep indeed. A generation ago, A. W. Tozer artfully described the predicament.

Christianity today is man-centered, not God-centered. God is made to wait patiently, even respectfully, on the whims of men. The image of God currently popular is that of a distracted Father, struggling in heartbroken desperation to get people to accept a Saviour of whom they feel no need and in whom they have very little interest. To persuade these self-sufficient **souls** to respond to His generous offers God will do almost anything, even using salesmanship methods and talking down to them in the chummiest way imaginable. This view of things is, of course, a kind of religious romanticism which, while it often uses flattering and sometimes embarrassing terms in praise of God, manages nevertheless to make man the star of the show.[10]

Tozer's words are decades old, but they apply today more than ever. His concerns are centered in a battle Christians have fought throughout the history of the church. People refusing to glorify God while deifying themselves is part of their fractured spiritual DNA (Romans 3:10–11).

So what is the biblical answer to culture's tendency toward self-centeredness? In 1928, another gifted pastor and author, A. W. Pink, articulated a sobering alternative.

We readily acknowledge that it is very humbling to the proud heart of the creature to behold all mankind in the hand of God as the clay is in the potter's hand, yet this is precisely how the Scriptures of Truth represent the case. In this day of human boasting, intellectual pride, and deification of man, it needs to be insisted upon that the potter forms his vessels for himself. Let man strive with his Maker as he will, the fact remains that he is nothing more than clay in the Heavenly Potter's hands, and while we know that God will deal justly with His creatures, that the Judge of all the earth will do right, nevertheless, He shapes His vessels for His own purpose and according to His own pleasure. God claims the indisputable right to do as He wills with His own.[11]

Pink's words strike at the heart of human pride and popular thought in the West, but they thoroughly reflect the tenets of
Scripture (1 Chronicles 29:11–13; Isaiah 46:9–10; Daniel 4:34–35).
He was urging for what has been called a "big God" theology, an
essential theology for genuine mental health that is centered in God.
It is to embrace God's immutable sovereignty over all things and his
right to do with his creation as he wills. Failure to honor the lordship
of God over all things has resulted in a theology and a psychology
centered more on positive outcomes and pleasant experiences (i.e.,
health and wealth, fixing a problem, or eradicating distress) than on
God's glory in exercising his perfect sovereignty. The pursuit of God
in the midst of what ails human beings is often lost to their pursuit
of constructing an existence in which the ego may reside in an endless man-made euphoria.

God's Purposes in Suffering

Modern culture's failure to acknowledge God's purposes in suffering
has contributed to a false assumption that suffering is not of God
and possesses no innate meaning. Yet, since God is sovereign, nothing stands outside of his ultimate control—not even suffering. God
is not stunned when emotional darkness overtakes someone like
Jessica. He is not baffled when Christian marriages become fractured
by adultery. He is not taken aback when a Christian teenage girl
becomes pregnant. He is not even threatened when a believer's mood
resembles that of psychosis. God's sovereign purposes are working
themselves out in every intimate detail of life, even the difficult ones.
John Piper reminds us,

> Tragedies and calamities and horrific suffering and sinful
> atrocities should not take Christians off guard. "Beloved, do
> not be surprised at the fiery trial when it comes upon you
> to test you, as though something strange were happening to
> you" (1 Pet. 4:12). They are foreseen by God, and he foretold
> them for us to know. God sees them coming and does not

intend to stop them. Therefore, it appears that they some-how fit into his purposes.[12]

God enriches people's faith by revealing the interaction of his providential handiwork in and through their life experiences—both the pleasurable and the painful.

> The heart of man plans his way, but the LORD establishes his steps. (Proverbs 16:9)
>
> Every way of a man is right in his own eyes, but the LORD weighs the heart. (Proverbs 21:2)
>
> The LORD is good to those who wait for him, to the soul who seeks him. It is good that one should wait quietly for the salvation of the LORD. It is good for a man that he bear the yoke in his youth. Let him sit alone in silence when it is laid on him; let him put his mouth in the dust—there may yet be hope; let him give his cheek to the one who strikes, and let him be filled with insults. For the LORD will not cast off forever, but though he cause grief, he will have compassion according to the abundance of his steadfast love; for he does not willingly afflict or grieve the children of men. (Lamentations 3:25–33)

These biblical authors understood that God was sovereignly governing their lives. Comfort is found by resting in his power and his purposes, not in resisting them for one's own egotistic pursuits. Counselors' hearts will break (and sometimes severely) when they witness the evils of sin and the devil ravaging the lives of fellow brothers and sisters, but Christians will sorrow rightly only in the comfort of the Father's omnipotent hand. Christians must adopt Joseph's words as an anthem, "As for you, you meant evil against me, but God meant it for good, to bring it about that many people should be kept alive, as they are today" (Genesis 50:20).

God's sovereign intentions are always good, and even when the evil intentions of man appear to prevail, the good treasures of God's grace in difficult circumstances are unquestionably present.

Emotional difficulties like depression are not diminished to the psychiatric fallacy that such things are exclusively disorders in need of cure. Instead, they are conceptualized as divine taps on the shoulder through which the Holy Spirit calls people to find rest in God alone. Emotional suffering, like everything people experience, can serve as a potent means to draw them closer to the Prince of Peace, the Healer of souls. Randomness and meaninglessness in suffering are myths when considered in God's universe.

If counselors are going to help the mentally, emotionally, and relationally broken, they will be forced to confront their finitude as compared to God's infinite goodness. They may often experience the words of the prophet Isaiah, "For my thoughts are not your thoughts, neither are your ways my ways, declares the LORD. For as the heavens are higher than the earth, so are my ways higher than your ways and my thoughts than your thoughts" (55:8–9).

God's ways are infinitely more wise and good than people's. Sometimes, counselors will not fully understand why people go through particular difficulties. Part of the task as counselors is to relentlessly work against a flawed cognitive dissonance wherein a crisis of faith develops as counselees encounter horrible suffering within the context of God's sovereignty. Counselors must maintain faith in God's Word and continuously work to help discover the infinite faithfulness, kindness, goodness, love, and compassion always present in God's sovereign activities—even those that are quite painful.[13]

God the Father: The Lover of Souls in Joy and Suffering

For some, the idea of God's absolute sovereignty coupled with the reality of suffering might feel constricting, even frightening. If God has so much control, how do people know he really wants their good? This is a thoughtful and fair question that should never be minimized in counseling. Counselors should always emphasize God's love when helping others navigate this inquiry.

Philip Ryken and Michael LeFebvre encourage, "The First Person is commonly called 'Father' because he is the initiator and source of heaven's love."[14] Joe Thorn reminds, "The love of God is his effusive benevolence toward you in Jesus Christ. It accompanies you as you walk through your afflictions, teaching you that God has not left you, nor does he intend to hurt you."[15]

The apostle John ascribes the essence of love to God's very being:

> Beloved, let us love one another, for love is from God, and whoever loves has been born of God and knows God. Anyone who does not love does not know God, because God is love. In this the love of God was made manifest among us, that God sent his only Son into the world, so that we might live through him. In this is love, not that we have loved God but that he loved us and sent his Son to be the propitiation for our sins. Beloved, if God so loved us, we also ought to love one another. (1 John 4:7–11)

Notice that love is not only from God, but that God's *nature* is love. In other words, love is because God is—no God, no love.

The full and ultimate expression of God's love is realized in his willingness to send Christ into the world to redeem his people. While it may not always seem this way, God cannot do anything other than operate in perfect love toward those he has saved. God even extends a profound portion of this love to those who reject him. It is theologically certain, therefore, to conclude that no matter what is going on in the life of a Christian counselee, God's love is present. It can be no other way.

Why is a doctrine of God's love so important to the one suffering? Christians suffering from debilitating mental, emotional, or relational issues often falsely assume that God is angry toward them. I have repeatedly witnessed this during my years as a professional counselor. Unfortunately, when suffering, people often adopt misguided beliefs about God's justice, viewing him as an overbearing tyrant who strikes at any lack of perfection. They conclude, *If suffering is present, God must be angry.*

I believe this dilemma may be addressed adequately not by focusing on God's love exclusively but by reflecting on the intersection of both God's sovereignty and his love. Ephesians illustrates this.

And you were dead in the trespasses and sins in which you
once walked, following the course of this world, following
the prince of the power of the air, the spirit that is now at
work in the sons of disobedience—among whom we all once
lived in the passions of our flesh, carrying out the desires
of the body and the mind, and were by nature children of
wrath, like the rest of mankind. But God, being rich in
mercy, because of the great love with which he loved us, even
when we were dead in our trespasses, made us alive together
with Christ—by grace you have been saved—and raised us
up with him and seated us with him in the heavenly places
in Christ Jesus, so that in the coming ages he might show
the immeasurable riches of his grace in kindness towards us
in Christ Jesus. (2:1–7)

People's relationship with God completely rests in his mercy
toward them. The only reason people know God is because, in love,
he sovereignly extended his grace to them while they were still his
enemies (Romans 5:10). "We love because he first loved us" (1 John
4:19). The commentators of the *Gospel Transformation Bible* express,
"We were dead, but God made us alive in Christ. We were not strug-
glers in need of a helping hand or sinking swimmers in need of a
raft; we were stone-cold dead—spiritually lifeless, without a religious
pulse, without anything to please God. But he loves the loveless, gives
life to the lifeless, and is merciful to those deserving no mercy."[16]

God's willingness to sovereignly extend his mercy brings life to a
lifeless soul. By his regenerating power alone humankind is given the
ability to know and believe in God (Ephesians 2:8–10). God made
certain that people would know and embrace his mercy—that they
would be transformed by his mercy and permanently live in his mercy.
Paul emphatically states that God saves people because of his great love!

Consider just one implication of such divine love: Knowing people's sin far more deeply than they could ever know it themselves,
God loved, sought, and won them. God showed the immeasurable
riches of his grace in kindness toward them in Christ Jesus (including in the midst of sin and suffering).

Why then would any aspect of people's journey between now and eternity be driven by his anger and wrath? Such assumptions completely counter the gospel message as presented in the Bible where God's wrath was supremely satisfied in Christ upon the cross (1 John 2:2).

On the contrary, the author of Hebrews points out that experiencing hardship is evidence of God's parental love (12:7), and it is designed for healing (12:12–14). James encourages believers to take joy in trials because through them God is making saints perfect and complete so that they lack nothing (1:2–4). King David understood the loving God of discipline when in contrition he cried, "Let the bones that you have broken rejoice" (Psalm 51:8). Even in "breaking our bones," God's love is flourishing. While it may be challenging to believe, when caught in the grip of tribulation, biblical counselors must wisely and patiently encourage counselees to cling to these immutable truths. Biblical counselors anchor their hopes in a loving and sovereign Father who created and secured the plan of their redemption (Genesis 3:15).

CHAPTER EIGHT

. . . .

WHAT IS GOD UP TO IN COUNSELING? (PART 2)

THE DISTINCT ROLES OF THE SON AND THE SPIRIT

They that are in Christ Jesus, are one spirit; and therefore, if God loves Christ Jesus, he must of necessity accept of those that are in him and are of him. —Jonathan Edwards[1]

Take away the Spirit from the gospel, and you render it a "dead letter"... There is not any thing done by us that is holy and acceptable to God, but is an effect of the Spirit's operation. —John Owen[2]

God the Son: The Great Redeemer

If Scripture reveals that God the Father is the one who created the plan of redemption, the Bible portrays Jesus as the one who fully accomplished the plan. In Christ, it is revealed what God has done for his people and what he will do for his people. Change is oriented around Christ. Jesus "is the radiance of the glory of God and the exact imprint of his nature, and he upholds the universe by the word of his power." (Hebrew 1:3). In Christ, perfect psychological functioning is exhibited, and it is through his finished work that the Holy Spirit is progressively conforming believers into his perfect image. It is incumbent upon biblical counselors, therefore, to consider how they may present Jesus and his accomplished work to those tormented by the horrors of mental, emotional, and relational anguish.

In his birth and life, Jesus was "made like his brothers in every respect, so that he might become a merciful and faithful high priest in the service of God, to make propitiation for the sins of the people. For because he himself has suffered when tempted, he is able to help those who are being tempted" (Hebrews 2:17–18). Jesus understands mental anguish. He vividly grasps the brutal realities of suffering. He comprehends the nagging torment of temptation. Since Jesus experienced these things in his own life, and since he perfectly responded to each, he is now the believer's holy, merciful, and sympathetic high priest (Hebrews 4:14–16).

Jesus not only became like people in his life, he took their sin in his death. Jesus bore the wrath of the Father for his people's sins (1 Peter 2:24). Jesus did all this because he loves his Father and his children. Humanity's value is derived from being an object of this precious love.[3] Jesus's love for his people is expressed in his willingness to extended mercy by becoming the sacrificial lamb that would take away the sins of the world (John 1:29).

It was through this merciful act that Jesus made it possible for people to relate to the Father in a revolutionary way. Through Christ's priestly work, people became free to connect with and worship God personally and confidently. The author of Hebrews describes what this marvelous work offers to the believer.

> Therefore, brothers, since we have confidence to enter the holy places by the blood of Jesus, by the new and living way that he opened for us through the curtain, that is, through his flesh, and since we have a great priest over the house of God, let us draw near with a true heart in full assurance of faith, with our hearts sprinkled clean from an evil conscience and our bodies washed with pure water. Let us hold fast the confession of our hope without wavering, for he who promised is faithful. (Hebrews 10:19–23)

People are welcomed into a confident relationship with God by the blood of Jesus. Believers may now draw near to God with confidence and faith in what Christ's blood and work has accomplished for their sakes. Remember Jessica from the last chapter? Jesus's finished work is where she will find ultimate hope and rest. It will not be found in her accomplishments in the counseling process, but in what Christ has already accomplished on her behalf.

Furthermore, Jesus himself is presently interceding for Jessica at the Father's right hand, the throne of mercy and grace. Jesus is there now, continuing to serve Jessica and all of his people diligently and faithfully as he intercedes for them. Paul writes, "Who is to condemn? Christ Jesus is the one who died—more than that, who was raised—who is at the right hand of God, who indeed is interceding for us" (Romans 8:34).

The author of Hebrews writes that Jesus literally lives, in this moment, to intercede for his people (Hebrews 7:25). He is passionate to intercede for believers in the midst of their epic failures—their darkest sins. In part, the nature of this intercession may be captured in the beautiful hymn written by Charles Wesley.

Five bleeding wounds he bears, received on Calvary;

They pour effectual prayers, they strongly plead for me.
"Forgive him, O forgive," they cry, "forgive him, O forgive,"
they cry, "nor let the ransomed sinner die!"[4]

What comforting words! The Great High Priest, Jesus Christ, intercedes for the saints, and in return, he beckons them to draw near to his throne of grace that they may receive and experience the full expression of his intercession and love.

I cherish the image portrayed in Isaiah 55 that captures this inviting love.

Come, everyone who thirsts, come to the waters; and he who has no money, come, buy and eat! Come, buy wine and milk without money and without price. Why do you spend your money for that which is not bread, and your labor for that which does not satisfy? Listen diligently to me, and eat what is good, and delight yourselves in rich food. Incline your ear, and come to me; hear, that your soul may live; and I will make with you an everlasting covenant, my steadfast, sure love for David. (55:1–3)

The throne of grace exists by God's mercy for his people to enjoy. Jesus's intercession makes this throne possible. As believers commune at his royal table and feast upon the bread of life (John 6:35), as they quench their parched souls by consuming the life-giving water of God (John 4:14), it is important to consider the delights it possesses so that their minds may be genuinely nourished by its bountiful goods. Counselors must also invite others to feast at this same table so that their broken souls may be effectively nourished.

Jesus Is Our Propitiation

The word *propitiation* might be a word with which you are unfamiliar. Propitiation is the act whereby Jesus willingly received the Father's wrath for all the sins of his people while hanging mercilessly upon the cross. It is a critical part of Jesus's finished work and, therefore, a critical aspect of counseling. First John 2 begins this way, "My little children, I am writing these things to you so that you may not sin. But if anyone does sin, we have an advocate with the Father, Jesus Christ the righteous. He is the propitiation for our sins, and not for ours only but also for the sins of the whole world" (2:1–2).

How might this apply to Jessica who cannot escape her struggle with sinful patterns? She is desperate for an answer since her ongoing struggle with sin, as a result of her suffering, is culminating in extreme shame and self-condemnation.

When John says that Jesus Christ is the propitiation for sins, he means that Jesus bears away sin. This is great news for Jessica. The penalty for the sinful struggles in her life have been received and paid for by Jesus upon the cross. Jesus has taken Jessica's punishment completely away from her and onto himself forever. This is Jessica's final hope. Christian counselors hold a significant responsibility to help counselees effectively deal with sin within the context of the gospel freedom that propitiation brings. Counselors must cradle counselees in Paul's proclamation, "There is therefore now no condemnation for those who are in Christ Jesus" (Romans 8:1).

First John also warns against sin. Counselors should emphasize this with counselees as well. Sin is a terrible enemy and an abject offense against God. Yet John reminds his readers that in the event they engage in sinful activity (both inward sin and outward expressions of sin), they have an Advocate pleading their case before the Father. Even the darkest sins point to the Redeemer (1 Peter 2:24).

Propitiation is exceedingly relevant to Jessica's current struggles. Her hatred toward her father, her futile attempts of control and escape, her sexual escapades, and her alcohol abuse were all placed upon Jesus as though he himself committed such atrocities against the Father (2 Corinthians 5:21). Jessica's true freedom radiates from the finished work of Jesus. My former pastor would say, "Becoming a Christian doesn't free me from struggle but frees me *to* struggle."[5] Jessica does not have to fight her sins as a means to be accepted by God because God accepts her based upon the work of Christ. She is now free to fight sin for his glory.

Helping Jessica meditate upon Jesus's loving kindness may move her toward genuine repentance. It may serve to crush the cycle of sin perpetuated by her dominating sense of shame. Jessica's current mindset exacerbates her sense of worthlessness as she thinks, *I'm tainted; I'm beyond repair; God could never accept me after all I've done.* But propitiation reorients her mind away from herself. Rather than obsessively fixate on her failures to perform for God's favor (itself a form of pride), counseling will encourage Jessica to humble herself and learn to cherish what Jesus has already done on her behalf. She can pray, *God, while my sins are many and dark, I thank you for receiving my just punishment. Only an infinite, loving God could be so good.*

Because Jesus is the propitiation for sin, believers have space wherein they battle against sin without fearing God's condemnation (Romans 8:1–2). Propitiation exposes them to an everlasting love that should foster within their hearts a godly disdain for the horrendous sins (especially their own) that required Jesus to suffer so terribly.

Jesus Is Our Righteousness

Jesus identifies himself with his people's sin and bears their judgment. In this same union, believers are identified with Jesus in his perfect righteousness before the Father. Therefore, they receive the Father's full favor and love. In union with Christ, believers have Jesus's standing before the Father and acceptance with the Father. In union with Christ, the Father delights to do believers good all their days. The words the Father spoke to Jesus—"This is my beloved Son, with whom I am well pleased" (Matthew 3:17)—reveal the Father's anthem toward all believers.

Though certainly the case, it is hard to imagine that the following words are true, "For by a single offering he has perfected for all time those who are being sanctified" (Hebrews 10:14). The atoning work of Jesus has already perfected believers. Christians can literally say that in Christ, they are already deemed perfect. Regardless of believers' mental or emotional state, they have the Father's full embrace and favor in Christ. While it may seem inconceivable that such grace has been granted, it is imperative that Christians root their identity in this truth in order to flourish in the midst of hardship (Jeremiah 17:7–8).

Consider Paul's take on the issue. Referencing the faith of Abraham, he writes the following:

> That is why his faith was "counted to him as righteousness." But the words "it was counted to him" were not written for his sake alone, but for ours also. It will be counted to us who believe in him who raised from the dead Jesus our Lord, who was delivered up for our trespasses and raised for our justification. Therefore, since we have been justified by faith, we have peace with God through our Lord Jesus Christ. (Romans 4:22—5:1)

Additionally Paul teaches, "For our sake he made him to be sin who knew no sin, so that in him we might become the righteousness of God" (2 Corinthians 5:21).

Christ's righteousness applies to every aspect of the Christian's being—including the realm of one's psychological makeup. Chronic anxiety, depression, addiction, or marital problems provide occasion where people's faith may stumble. Since they have been radically influenced by a therapeutic fix-it society, when people are unable to fix it, they may begin to doubt—God, the Bible, and possibly whether or not they are genuine Christians. However, the inability to fix problems in one's own human strength and by human methods is actually an opportunity pregnant with glory, not a reason for doubt.

When the mind is consumed by fear to the point of experiencing a panic attack, it is an occasion to glory in union with Christ. Relapse is occasion to glory in Christ's perfection. These moments give pause to consider Paul's reminder, "For freedom Christ has set us free; stand firm therefore, and do not submit again to a yoke of slavery" (Galatians 5:1).

People often think that because they are struggling, God must be distant or separated. I once had a person lament to me in session, "Dr. Lelek, I know God sees me through Jesus, but my problem is that there is distance between Jesus and me. Until I get my act together and get closer to Jesus, God will look down on me because of my sins." To this, I reached for my Bible and read the following: "If then you have been raised with Christ, seek the things that are above, where Christ is, seated at the right hand of God. Set your minds on things that are above, not on things that are on earth. For you have died, and your *life is hidden with Christ* in God" (Colossians 3:1–3, emphasis added).

No matter the nature of a counselee's struggle, genuine believers exist in "an abiding reality determinative for the whole of the Christian life, to which appeal can be made at all times, in all sorts of connections"[6] that they are objectively united with, clothed with (Galatians 3:27), created in (Ephesians 2:10), and hidden in Christ. Believers do not need to work their way back to Jesus since they were never separated in the first place (Romans 8:38–39).

How would this apply to Jessica? As you may recall, her story includes some very difficult experiences to which her responses have been less than righteous. Rather than place pressure on Jessica to do better, she first needs to understand that all of her failures are hidden with Christ in God. She is not judged on her record, but she has Jesus's righteousness. He experienced every traumatic experience just as she, but did so without sin (Hebrews 2:17–18; 4:15–16). Counseling could begin with Jessica meditating and journaling on how germane Jesus's suffering is to her own life experiences. Jessica can learn how to praise Jesus in his strength as she wrestles in her weakness. Her meditations could include the following examples:

- Jesus exhibited flawless faith in the Father when under extreme mental and emotional duress (Matthew 26:42).
- Jesus remained perfectly faithful in loving the Father when verbally and physically abused in the most horrific manner imaginable (Matthew 27:31).
- Jesus remained perfectly obedient to the Father when he was rejected by his own people and was chosen for crucifixion over a murderous thug, Barabbas (John 18:33–40).
- Jesus refused intoxication that would have alleviated the torturous pain inherent to fulfilling his mission on the cross (Mark 15:23).[7]
- Jesus extended love to the very people who were killing him (Luke 23:34).
- As God's wrath for every single sin of every single believer was being poured out upon him, Jesus did not doubt the Father (Matthew 27:46; Luke 23:46).

Jesus, who willingly and passionately died for Jessica, beckons her, "Take my yoke upon you, and learn from me, for I am gentle and lowly in heart, and you will find rest for your souls. For my yoke is easy, and my burden is light" (Matthew 11:29–30).

The Gospel of Christ reorients counseling away from mere behavior modification or modifying a family system or improving an emotional state. It orients counseling around worship—worship centered in the Christ of the gospel. Within this context, the notion of self-help becomes an absurdity. Without Christ, there is no help and certainly no hope. Genuine biblical counseling, therefore, will aim to encourage counselees to rest within the echo of Jesus's stunning declaration, "It is finished" (John 19:30).

Jesus Is the Resurrected and Ascended Savior

If counselors fail to consider the resurrection of Jesus, then they miss the grandeur of his completed work (John 19:30). Paul was clear on this issue.

> Now if Christ is proclaimed as raised from the dead, how can some of you say that there is no resurrection of the dead? But if there is no resurrection of the dead, then not even Christ has been raised. And if Christ has not been raised, then our preaching is in vain and your faith is in vain. We are even found misrepresenting God, because we testified about God that he raised Christ, whom he did not raise if it is true that the dead are not raised. For if the dead are not raised, not even Christ has been raised. And if Christ has not been raised, your faith is futile and you are still in your sins. Then those also who have fallen asleep in Christ have perished. If in Christ we have hope in this life only, we are of all people most to be pitied. (1 Corinthians 15:12–19)

If Jesus has not been raised from the dead, then people have no hope. If Jesus has not risen, then Christians are pitiful creatures waiting for the dreadful perishing of their souls. But Jesus was indeed resurrected, and believers have hope both in this life and the life to come (John 20:17).

The resurrection assures believers that Jesus's work will continue in their lives. It assures Jessica that God will remain faithful to her in her times of weakness. It is evidence that the Lord, once dead, now has a new life and new body and guarantees believers of his commitment to do the same in and for them. It is because of the resurrected Savior that a counselor can assure Jessica of hope for change.

Jesus sits before the throne of the Father proclaiming the full, complete, finished work of the gospel. The resurrected Lamb, who takes away the sins of the world, is a perpetual sign for all the inhabitants of heaven and earth that the redemption of Christ's church has been fulfilled. Nothing can overturn it. "Who is to condemn? Christ Jesus is the one who died—more than that, who was raised—who is at the right hand of God, who indeed is interceding for us" (Romans 8:34).

The redemption of the church is at the heart of biblical counseling and spiritual healing. The guaranteed redemption of the church is the guaranteed redemption of individual people. Jesus is a sign that believers' transformation (including the deepest elements of our psychology) is inevitable. Consider what Paul wrote to Titus:

> For the grace of God has appeared, bringing salvation for all people, training us to renounce ungodliness and worldly passions, and to live self-controlled, upright, and godly lives in the present age, waiting for our blessed hope, the appearing of the glory of our great God and Savior Jesus Christ, who gave himself for us to redeem us from all lawlessness and to purify for himself a people for his own possession who are zealous for good works. (Titus 2:11–14)

Do you hear Paul's assurance? Do you hear the anticipation for present glory? God's grace, made available through Jesus's resurrection, is present and working in order to train believers for glory now. While Christians wait, while they battle, while they persevere, they can be confident that they will become zealous for good works because Jesus died and rose again in order to make it so. Jesus's precious grace is committed to this end—here and now—in this present age. A heart zealous for good and for the glory of God is a transformed, grace-filled, Holy Spirit empowered heart. Even when change comes slowly, counselors must encourage counselees again and again with this same confident assurance.

As we wait for this blessed return, the Redeemer of mankind ensured that his followers would not have to wait in isolation. Comforting his disciples, Jesus assured them that though he would be going away, he would send another—a Counselor, a Comforter who would apply his amazing work to all who place faith in him. Jesus promised the beloved Holy Spirit (John 16:7).

God the Spirit: Our Comforter and Counselor

If the Father has a plan and the Son has fulfilled the plan, then the Holy Spirit is executing the plan. The third person of the Trinity has claimed the terrain of human flourishing—whether mental, psychological, emotional, or behavioral. The Holy Spirit's awe-inspiring power brings forth this divine change. This completely relieves biblical counselors of the responsibility to enact change in the hearts of anyone. The Great Counselor, the Holy Spirit is far more committed to transforming hearts than any counselor could ever be (John 14:16–17).

The following are but a few ways the Holy Spirit is working in the lives of his saints:

- He regenerates God's people (John 3:5; Titus 3:5).
- He produces conviction of sin (John 16:8).
- He reveals truth through God's Word (John 16:13).
- He nurtures a believer's heart with the love of the Father (Romans 5:5).
- He helps believers in their weaknesses by interceding in prayer on their behalf (Romans 8:26–27).
- He dwells within the believer (1 Corinthians 6:19).
- He seals and guarantees a believer's salvation (2 Corinthians 1:21–22; Ephesians 1:13–14).
- He produces transformation within the believer's being (Galatians 5:22–23).
- He strengthens believers in power and helps them comprehend the love of Christ (Ephesians 3:14–19).
- He writes the laws of God upon believers' hearts and refuses to remember their lawless deeds (Hebrews 10:15–17).

The Holy Spirit is profoundly active in bringing forth the will of the Father in the lives of his people. He actuates spiritual life within dead hearts; he guides Christians in holy living; he convicts them when sin abounds. The Holy Spirit opens believers' eyes to see truth and transforms them into the likeness of Jesus so that they may love the truth they see. This transformational process reorients Christians' beliefs, thoughts, longings, desires, and hopes so that they more and more image the perfect mind of Christ.

Since the Holy Spirit is producing change in the human soul, there are major psychological implications. He empowers Christians to identify idolatry within their hearts while also creating within them a motivational core centered on the glory of God. This inner transformation produces new patterns of thought, new behaviors, and new perspectives of life and relationships.

Biblical counselors have the wonderful privilege of participating in this work to which the Holy Spirit is so committed. The Holy Spirit is producing change in counselees through the counseling process, but he is also producing change in the counselor (Philippians 2:12–13). As such, biblical counselors will continually need to consider and do the following:

- Seek the Holy Spirit to produce humility.
- Ask the Holy Spirit to search their hearts for selfish agendas or prideful attitudes.
- Ask the Holy Spirit to convict and bring repentance for any such attitudes.
- Pray for discernment regarding every situation brought before them.
- Ask the Holy Spirit to multiply love in their hearts for those they serve.
- Continually study God's Word since through it the Holy Spirit discerns the thoughts and intentions of the heart (Hebrews 4:12).
- Point counselees to the Scriptures, and encourage them to seek the Holy Spirit for discernment, guidance, and conviction.
- Remind counselees that the Spirit is in them and is committed to their change.
- Trust the Holy Spirit in his timely and active work within the hearts of the believer.

The Spirit breathes healing and life into the hearts of his people and actively works to produce good fruit in them (Romans 8:26–27; Galatians 5:22–23; Ephesians 2:4). Kevin DeYoung offers a wonderful summation of this magnificent work:

Though we must make effort in our growth and godliness (2 Pet. 1:5), the Spirit empowers through and through. The Bible is not a cheap infomercial telling us to change and then serving as an enthusiastic cheerleader: "You can do it!" We have already been changed. We are already new creations in Christ (2 Cor. 5:17) and have a new strength at work in our inner being (Eph. 3:16), producing gospel fruit in us by the Spirit (Gal. 5:22–23). The Bible expects that because God dwells in us by the Spirit, we can, by that same Spirit, begin to share in the qualities that are characteristic of God himself (2 Pet. 1:4).[8]

Once this transformation is initiated by the Holy Spirit, believers are catapulted into a spiritual war in which the remaining sin of their old selves continues to rage against a holy God. Since this war exists and is the terrain where human change occurs, biblical counselors will seek to enter the war zone armed with the sword of the Spirit, the Word. Biblical counselors serve their brothers and sisters by arming them with truth to navigate the battles sure to come. Ongoing prayer for the Spirit's direction in this process will be a regular practice for the counselor.

Beholding and Becoming

Being transformed into glory is not primarily about methods but about beholding the glory of God. If counselors fail to bring the splendor of God's activities to the awareness of counselees, then they will differ little from their secular counterparts. The process of change cannot be finally about counselees but about the God who created them. Paul emphasized the significance of God in people's transformation, "Now the Lord is the Spirit, and where the Spirit of the Lord is, there is freedom. And we all, with unveiled face, beholding the glory of the Lord, are being transformed into the same image from one degree of glory to another. For this comes from the Lord who is Spirit" (2 Corinthians 3:17–18).

If counselors are not careful, they can become prone to resting on methodologies from Scripture while forgetting the God of Scripture. They can emphasize idolatry to the exclusion of God's love, power, faithfulness, and grace. God is both the means and the ends of biblical counseling. By his grace and through the Holy Spirit, believers are empowered to change, and their change is rooted in becoming creatures captivated by God's glory. Paul says that in beholding the Lord while persevering through sin and suffering Christians are progressively transformed from one degree of glory to another. Counselors effectively prepare counselees to contemplate themselves by having them contemplate God. Citing John Newton, Tony Reinke writes:

> As we behold Christ's beauty by the eye of faith, we are transformed from one degree of maturity to another. As we behold the glory of Jesus, we increasingly participate in his image, transformed into his resemblance and his character. This transformation works incrementally as the Christian gazes deeper in the mystery of Christ's redeeming love. . . . In all of these acts of faith, the Christian becomes more deeply engaged in this "great business" of beholding Christ's glory.[9]

Reinke connects worship (beholding the glory of God) to being "transformed from one degree of maturity to another." Ultimately, ongoing transformation is rooted in God and a growing awe of him, not in human systems or methods of change. Each and every time counselors sit with people belonging to the family of God, this scene is ever unfolding in their lives—the Father has planned, the Son has fulfilled, and the Spirit is applying. If the entire Trinity is so committed to our good then we, of all people, have reason to hope.

Counseling Considerations

1. When counseling others, make sure to assess the beliefs they have adopted about God. Even though they may be avid churchgoers, they may hold erroneous views of God. Have

counselees list their initial impressions of God, then compare these to the attributes cited in the two previous chapters.

2. Do counselees believe they are experiencing problems because God is angry and seeking to get even with them? If so, how would you address this biblically?

3. Do counselees know how the present realities of the gospel are at work in their situation? How would you point them to the truths of propitiation, imputation, and the resurrection? Have them journal their response to these truths. There may be resistance or doubt. The purpose of this is to reveal to them the unfathomable love of the Redeemer.

4. What systems of redemption have they developed that distract them from the gospel?

5. How would you engender hope in the work of the Holy Spirit and his faithfulness to work in all things to conform believers into the image of Jesus Christ?

RESOURCES FOR FURTHER READING

- Chan, Francis. *Forgotten God: Revisiting Our Tragic Neglect of the Holy Spirit*. Colorado Springs, CO: David C. Cook, 2009.
- Frame, John. *The Doctrine of God: A Theology of Lordship*. Phillipsburg, NJ: P&R Publishing, 2002.
- Schaeffer, Francis. *The Finished Work of Christ: The Truth of Romans 1–8*. Wheaton, IL: Crossway, 1998.
- Sproul, R. C. *The Mystery of the Holy Spirit*. Wheaton, IL: Tyndale, 1990.
- Sproul, R. C. *The Work of Christ: What the Events of Jesus' Life Mean for You*. Colorado Springs, CO: David C. Cook, 2012.

CHAPTER NINE

· · · ·

HUMANKIND AND COUNSELING (PART 1)

In the distant future I see open fields for far more important researches.
Psychology will be based on a new foundation . . . Light will be thrown
on the origin of man and his history. —Charles Darwin[1]

The father of humanistic psychology, Abraham Maslow, once
made a remarkable assessment about the significance of one's
view of human nature. He said,

> When the philosophy of man (his nature, his goals, his
> potentialities, his fulfillment) changes, then everything
> changes, not only the philosophy of politics, of economics,
> of ethics and values, of interpersonal relations and of history
> itself, but also the philosophy of education, of psychother-
> apy and of personal growth, the theory of how to help men
> become what they can and deeply need to become.[2]

Maslow was right. How one conceptualizes the core of humanity
influences not only the individual, but it also shapes cultural views
and accepted norms. This is strikingly evident in a culture's attitude
on issues such as abortion, homosexuality, self-identity, mental illness, as well as mental health. Christians who will likely interact with
various literatures within psychology and counseling have a high
probability they will be confronted with many competing voices
about human nature. Most of them will claim the weight of science as
support. There are literally hundreds of different theories within psychology claiming they have arrived at the answer to the fundamental

question, Who are we? Most, if not all, find their streams of thought flowing from a single source—Darwinian evolution.

Counselors who operate from a biblical worldview must understand how prevalent this philosophy is within the field, especially when it comes to their own view of humanity. Thus, this chapter's overview of a biblical anthropology will begin with secularism's articulation of human nature.

The Influence of Darwinian Thought and Humanism

By and large, the theories of personality within classic secular psychology as well as more recent developments within neuropsychology tend to operate from a materialist perspective that is overwhelmingly influenced by the presuppositions of Darwinian evolution and humanistic philosophy. Stanton Jones expresses this point well.

> Introductory psychology textbooks commonly emphasize the empirical methods of study used in the field. . . . One subtle but important perspective offered throughout the field is the importance of analyzing all mental and behavioral phenomena in terms of their *function*; it is vital, it is argued, to analyze human phenomena in terms of their contribution to adaptation to the environment (survival) and to genetic propagation. Such a strategy is directly related to a Darwinian understanding of life, as Darwin emphasized natural selection of characteristics that served functional purposes.[3]

Such adherence to Darwinian evolution, humanism, and the prominent emphasis upon self undergirds the models of human nature developed by almost all foundational psychologies within the field and are purported by such individuals as Abraham Maslow,[4] B. F. Skinner,[5] Carl Rogers,[6] Joseph LeDoux,[7] Steven Pinker,[8] as well as proponents of pagan forms of spiritual counseling such as transpersonal psychologist Ken Wilber.[9] Since these researchers and theorists embrace materialistic presuppositions about people,[10] their interpretation of data and conclusions about human nature will be shaped by a philosophy that opposes biblical teaching.

Tension will emerge as Christians embrace the scientific research within psychology, in particular when such research speaks to the fundamental nature of people. Rival systems are created among the varying theorists, begging the question, who is right? With over one hundred voices weighing in, to whom should Christians listen? Most concerning, however, is that the majority of these systems fundamentally oppose the values and presuppositions of the Bible because they emphatically deny the immaterial or spiritual dimension of humanity.

The Implications of Human Nature[11]

The issue of human nature is critical for developing a model of counseling because it guides a person's diagnostic framework and prescriptive methods. For example, if I adopt a view of human nature influenced by a psychoanalytical framework, my diagnosis will always be shaped by constructs such as the unconscious (i.e., the interplay of the id, ego, and superego), some aspect of psychosexual development, and the myriad of defense mechanisms I believe are being employed by the patient. If my view of human nature leans in the direction of person-centered theory, I will tend to diagnose the problem as being unhealthy contexts in which my client's self-actualizing tendency is being thwarted.[12] Regardless of people's theoretical embrace, their view of human nature becomes the lens by which they evaluate the problem.

Likewise, people's view of human nature will influence their prescription for cure. For example, if I am psychoanalytically driven, I will utilize the method of free association so that my clients may tap into their unconscious, for according to this theory's view of human nature, it is in the realm of the unconscious that healing will be actuated. On the other hand, if I am operating as a person-centered theorist, my primary objective is to maintain a non-directional posture while exhibiting unconditional positive regard, empathy, and genuineness. This is because my view of human nature assumes that I must create the proper therapeutic environment in order to foster an experience wherein my client's innate self-actualizing tendency can thrive.[13]

While my view of human nature shapes my understanding of the problem, it also sets the stage as to how to make things right again. If we begin with a misguided understanding of who people are, this understanding will derail the process of cure. Which model is correct? Christian counselors seek to answer this question by first considering what Scripture reveals about the nature of humankind.

A Starting Place: Biblical Anthropology

A proper and biblical understanding of human nature begins with the affirmation that humankind has been created in the image of God—what theologians call the *Imago Dei*.[14] Concerning this doctrine, Ed Welch believes that it "determines the fate of every theology."[15] Dr. John Babler and his colleagues draw the conclusion that because humans are created in God's image it "sets man apart as unique in all creation."[16] A distinctive of the Christian faith is that humanity is a creation of a personal deity, not an extension of an impersonal life force or a complex material organism that has developed over millions of years by mere chance.

Humanity, therefore, exists in perpetual relationship to God.[17] This perspective reinforces a view of psychology that is utterly "theological because human beings are 'with-respect-to-God' creatures."[18] People are not autonomous, but they are continually operating "with respect to God" on a psychological level, often without any conscious awareness.

Contrary to secular thought, God's Word teaches that human autonomy is an illusion—a contrived strategy of Satan and the flesh that simply reinforces spiritual blindness (Genesis 3; Romans 1). If God is the infinite Creator and Sustainer, then people are completely dependent upon him for everything, including their very existence, even if they do not realize it. People are dependent upon God to breathe, think, perceive, relate, love, and survive. Jesus illustrated this dependence when he taught in the Sermon on the Mount.

> Therefore I tell you, do not be anxious about your life, what you will eat or what you will drink, nor about your body, what you will put on. Is not life more than food, and the body more than clothing? Look at the birds of the air: they neither sow nor reap nor gather into barns, and yet your heavenly Father feeds them. Are you not of more value than they? And which of you by being anxious can add a single hour to his span of life? (Matthew 6:25–27)

Jesus portrays humans as separate from other creatures, bearing a greater value to God than everything else he has made. Without diminishing the value of God's creation, the Bible affirms that humans hold a special place in the world because God values them to a greater degree than the rest of creation. Humanity is unique in the created order. This is clearly evident in the gospel story where Jesus enters the world, is crucified, and then raised again in order to redeem humankind from sin. His willingness to do this for humanity is direct evidence that Jesus possesses a special love for his most unique creatures (John 3:16; Genesis 1:26–28). This same love should emanate from the counselor to the counselee in every aspect of the counseling process.

Jesus also illuminates humanity's absolute dependence on the Creator. With exquisite logic, Jesus reveals the absurdity of worry and anxiety about one's life. Since the Creator is also sovereign Lord, it is futile to worry about the future because people cannot control it. Humankind is in the care of an infinite Creator for the provisions of daily life. Jesus stresses the love of the Creator for all creation—he feeds even the birds that never plant a single seed for harvest. Jesus then poses a question that brings warmth and comfort to the human soul, "Are you not of more value than they?"

People's identity as creature connotes dependence. Humans cannot flourish apart from God. This is true of all people, not just Christians. Every intellectual achievement, all artistic masterpieces, and any scholarly advancement emerged from human minds dependent upon God. The capacity to think, reason, and create is made possible on the condition that God exists and that he has granted such abilities to specific individuals through his creative power. Copernicus discovered the Earth's rotation around the sun on the condition that God enabled him through his intellect to do so. Einstein produced his *Theory of Relativity* by the common grace offered him by his Creator. Leonardo DiVinci's *Mona Lisa* or Michelangelo's *David* witness to the glory of God holding all things together with his mighty hand (Colossians 1:17). The millions of neurological connections required to produce such excellence exists because God forms and sustains them. Christian counselors initiate the counseling process with the presupposition that counselees are completely dependent upon and accountable to a holy, loving God.

The Bible teaches that when people fail to glory in their Creator and instead glory in their own perceived individualism, psychological disturbances begin (Romans 1). The ills of human psychological functioning have their ultimate origin in the separation or alienation from God. This alienation is intrinsic to the human condition and originates in the biblical account of the fall in which Adam and Eve, attempting to operate in the illusion of autonomy, rebelled against the counsel of their Creator (Genesis 3; Romans 5:12–14). The totality of Adam's and Eve's full inner lives were damaged tremendously from that point forward, and that damage continues to impact every human born into our fractured world (Romans 5:12). So, while humans are beautiful creatures designed in God's image, humankind is also infected with a spiritual disease that enslaves, distorts, and dismantles the human psyche.

This disease, however, is noticeably absent from the body of literature that has accumulated in the field of psychology. Far from being an empirical oversight, researchers have intentionally denied its influence as a psychological matter.

The Forbidden "S" Word

Embracing the creation account in Genesis produces a massive chasm between a biblical and humanistic view of human nature. Not only does biblical teaching oppose the claims of humanistic evolution, it also acknowledges the fall of humanity into sin and evil. Cornelius Plantinga Jr. has written,

People who believe in naturalistic evolution, for example, think that human concepts, values, desires, and religious beliefs are, like human life itself, metaphysically untethered to any transcendent purpose. Our lives and values are rather the product of such blind mechanisms as random genetic mutation and natural selection. In the view of such naturalist believers, there isn't any "way it's supposed to be" or anyone like God to sponsor and affirm this state of affairs. Thus there isn't anything like a violation of the "way it's supposed to be" or anything like an affront to God—hence there isn't anything that fits the definition of sin.[19]

In 1973, as he observed the decaying culture around him, renowned psychiatrist, Karl Menninger, also observed the dangerous influence of such naturalism—largely propagated by psychotherapy. He wrote,

Has the sense of morality vanished from the people? Has the rule of expediency, of success, of technological triumph replaced the necessity for moral integrity? Everything was "succeeding" for a while—progress was the order of the day. But now the new gods seem to have failed us, while the old God is said (by some) to be dead. Things are all wrong. . . . In all of the laments and reproaches made by our seers and prophets, one misses any mention of "sin," a word which used to be the veritable watchword of prophets.[20]

Menninger was concerned that the absence of sin as a psychological construct had heavily shaped modern culture as well as the basic ethics of psychiatry and psychology as it pertained to his culture's perspective of personal values—issues of moral right and wrong. His concerns have proven warranted. Today, the paradigm of naturalistic evolution has stripped the "ought" from the human experience so long as one person is not physically harming or violating another. Since this model asserts that humankind is the product of natural causes alone, humanity is left on its own to define morality. This is certainly prevalent in the arenas of professional psychology and counseling. As a licensed counselor, it could be considered counter-productive to the therapeutic endeavor for me to assert an "ought" within a counseling session. Most would consider it less than pro-fessional if I tell a husband he ought not to live promiscuously by sleeping with women other than his wife or that he ought to exhibit fidelity toward his spouse. Within this worldview there is no God, therefore, there is no "ought." Subsequently, there is no sin. The idea of sin has been banned from secular counseling. The irony innate to this philosophy is that the only way proponents may enforce it is to embrace an "ought"—the counselor ought to remain value neutral. The only means by which to enforce the myth of value neutrality is for proponents to draw from a particular value.

Furthermore, when secularists discuss sin, they are forced to make their own, often misguided, value judgments. Consider what one secular counseling textbook has to say on the issue, "Sin is a religious term, not a counseling concept . . . . Although it has well-intentioned and skilled followers, religious counseling is a contradiction in terms if practitioners intend, through their counseling, to save or convert their clients. Clients have a right to their personal values."[21]

I believe these authors articulate rightly the consensus of the secular field of counseling and psychology. However, to assert that sin is not a counseling concept seems both biased and nearsighted. Such a statement does not consider the reasonable worldview of Christianity.

Contrary to the authors' claims, Christians believe that sin is an aspect of human nature that cannot be ignored. Scripture is replete with examples of how sin impacts the human estate (Romans 1). The book of Proverbs offers an abundance of wise counsel as it pertains to sin and folly. Paul offers a transparent account of sin's impact upon the mind and motivations of the heart (Romans 7:11–25) while exposing the influence of sin upon one's behavior and emo-tions (Galatians 5:19–21). James points to the consequences of inner sin and its destructive force upon interpersonal relationships (James 4:1–4). All of these areas are counseling related, and none is excluded from sin's impact. To say that sin is not a counseling con-cept is to ignore Scripture's insight on sin's perpetual influence upon the human experience. Sin is a universal disease that taints and dis-figures every segment of the cosmos—the human heart (or psyche) included. But this is hardly conceivable unless one adheres to a faith that acknowledges a holy God.

Moreover, the authors' claim is discriminatory. For the secularist or materialist, sin is not a counseling concept because to them it is not a valid concept at all. Sin in a materialist universe is a meaningless term. Sin gleans its meaning from the concept of human beings who are responsible to God. Otherwise, the idea of sin (whether in counseling or casual conversation) is an absurdity. However, all people who seek counseling are not secularist or humanist. Many of them are people of faith, and of those, many are professing Christians. Research affirms that such individuals actually prefer counselors trained in applying Scripture to their counseling needs.[22] For them, sin is a construct that holds significant meaning and is believed to permeate many domains of their lives—the psychological included.

Sin Is a Valid Counseling Construct

Unlike secularists, biblical counselors recognize sin as a profoundly relevant counseling concept. I once wrote a document entitled, *Truths That (Should) Permeate Counsel,* where I outlined the intersection of psychology and sin.

> Our Biggest Enemy is the Enemy Within: A proper view of the psychology of Man acknowledges that humanity's greatest ill is sin. The active sinful desires that emanate from the human heart serve always to move individuals away from God. The hostile, deceptive agenda of such desires promote destruction and corruption within the heart and life of Man. Biblical counsel points counselees to the active Redeemer that they through Him might effectively confront and crucify the flesh.[23]

Sin is not exclusively behavioral. Behavior is a product of something deeper. Biblically, sin infects the heart—the motivational core of humanity (Luke 6:45). In fact, Christians believe that humans possess diseased hearts (Jeremiah 17:9). Puritan preacher Ralph Venning described sin's presence this way, "Sin is a loathsome thing. This is clear when we begin to consider that which sin resembles, unto which it is likened, as the most offensive and most loathsome diseases: a canker or gangrene (2 Timothy 2:17)."[24]

When Paul gives account of his own struggle with sin, he acknowledges, "So I find it to be a law that when I want to do right, evil lies close at hand. For I delight in the law of God, in my inner being, but I see in my members another law waging war against the law of my mind and making me captive to the law of sin that dwells in my members" (Romans 7:21–23). For Paul, sin was in part an inward issue.

James echoes these thoughts as well, "But each person is tempted when he is lured and enticed by his own desire. Then desire when it has conceived gives birth to sin, and sin when it is fully grown brings death" (James 1:14–15). With this in mind, biblical counselors will acknowledge the full impact of sin upon the lives of people, and they will avoid conceptualizing it as simply doing wrong. Rather, sin will be acknowledged as the driving reality that causes such wrong. Sin is an inner presence that perpetually influences the fallen human heart.

The Heart and Biblical Counseling

Concerning a biblical understanding of the heart, Herman Ridderbos has written, "Just as in the whole of the New Testament, so in Paul as well, heart is the concept that preeminently denotes the human ego in its thinking, affections, aspirations, decisions, both in man's relationship to God and to the world surrounding him."[25] In sync with the wisdom of Jesus as well as "the whole of the New Testament," the theological concept of the heart is abounding throughout the literature of Christian and biblical counseling. Scholars point to the fact that the word *heart* in Scripture refers to various aspects of people's makeup, including their desires, longings, thoughts, and perceptions.[26] Robert Roberts considers the "heart" as the seat of human functioning responsible for things such as "wishes, cares, intentions, plans, motives, emotions, thoughts, attitudes, and imaginings."[27] Psychologist Malcolm Jeeves writes that all motivation for human action and reaction finds its seat in the human heart.[28] Mark Talbot observes that, biblically, the heart is the "whole person—a person's inner life or character, the center of his or her personality."[29] Ed Welch refers to the heart as the "final cause" of human functioning.[30] Such descriptors, drawn from biblical teaching, place the core of human psychology within the heart.

The Scripture's robust insights on the heart help the Christian orchestrate an understanding of human nature unlike any model found within secular literature. Scripture elaborates on the psychological dimensions of the heart and provides perspective on the nature of the heart as continually operating before a holy God.

The Existential Either-Or

The Bible offers bountiful insights into human nature and existence not found within the secular literature. Prominent psychologists Bruce Narramore and John Carter have written, "The Bible, while not purporting to be a textbook on psychology, is filled with divinely revealed truths about the human psyche which cannot be ignored or relegated to giving us our purpose and perspective if we are to develop a comprehensive and accurate understanding of the human personality."[31] Scripture is the supreme source for revealing people's truest nature. It contains truths about the human mind that "cannot be ignored," and it reveals contrasting conclusions from secularism.

So what else does the Bible offer the counselor as it regards the question, Who are people and why do they do what they do? We will continue our pursuit to further understand human nature biblically by again reflecting on the words of the very architect of people's psyches, Jesus. He taught,

> For where your treasure is, there your heart will be also. (Matthew 6:21)
>
> No one can serve two masters, for either he will hate the one and love the other, or he will be devoted to the one

and despise the other. You cannot serve God and money. (Matthew 6:24)

Jesus touches on the central aspect of human motivation. Jesus depicts people as moral agents with active allegiances. These allegiances influence, even determine, people's motivations. What people treasure will master their hearts. "Treasure" is an issue of love and hate. This love-hate dynamic is a worshiping dynamic.

This dynamic says, "I will either be motivated by a love for God or a love for something else," and if it is the latter then by necessity it is also an act of hatred toward God. As people make choices in their marriages, their private lives, and their work, their hearts are shaped and motivated by what they treasure most in the moment. Every choice people make is rooted in what their hearts most value vis-à-vis God. People are dependent creatures—they must worship, trust, and find meaning. People's hearts are ever before God. It is a concept with which the psalmist was all too familiar, "Where shall I go from your Spirit? Or where shall I flee from your presence? If I ascend to heaven, you are there! If I make my bed in Sheol, you are there! If I take the wings of the morning and dwell in the uttermost parts of the sea, even there your hand shall lead me, and your right hand shall hold me" (Psalm 139:7–10). This places people within an existential reality in which their motives are either centered in glorifying God or committing cosmic war against him. Everything people do in the horizontal (life on earth) relates to the vertical (their relationship with God).

Therefore, when a husband is communicating sinfully with his wife because he does not get what he wants, it is important to bring to his awareness that he is making war against his Creator (James 4:4). Conversely, good counsel will also teach this husband that speaking words of kindness or doing merciful deeds toward his wife (who may have deeply offended him) is simultaneously loving his Creator (Romans 12:1). Life is worship.

Put simply, people live in an existential either-or. Either they are living motivated by a love for God or in opposition to him. This either-or includes the realms of thought, desire, words, and behavior. The crux of the human experience is that people's hearts always respond out of a treasure trove of loves. James K. A. Smith articulates this idea well, "we are talking about *ultimate* loves—that to which we are fundamentally oriented, what ultimately governs our vision of the good life, what shapes and molds our being-in-the-world—in other words, what we desire above all else, the ultimate desire that shapes and positions and makes sense of all our penultimate desires and actions."[32] These loves ultimately expose people's functional attitudes toward God.

People's psychology expresses itself in a loyalty to God or something else.[33] Paul Tripp unpacks this concept, "You don't divide human beings into those who worship and those who don't. Every human being is a worshiper and every act of a human being in some way expresses worship. Worship is who we are and what we do. Either I am living in proper covenantal relationship with God, or I am striking an idol covenant."[34] Tripp is formulating a theology of motivation rooted in active hearts of worship. This theology emphatically asserts that the heart is full of activity (Galatians 5:16–17).

Describing his own conversion experience, C. S. Lewis once echoed these same sentiments, "All my acts, desires, and thoughts were to be brought into harmony with universal Spirit. For the first time I examined myself with a seriously practical purpose. And there I found what appalled me; a zoo of lusts, a bedlam of ambitions, a nursery of fears, a harem of fondled hatreds. My name was legion."[35] Lewis understood that he was not a blank slate, but there was a war of loyalties raging within him. These loyalties, according to Scripture, are matters of worship. Jesus claims that loving one master is simultaneously hating a competing master—the moment-by-moment reality of man before God, either loving him or hating him, is glaring (Matthew 6:24).

This inner dynamic comprises the biblical concept of human motivation. The heart always pursues those desires that are in the moment most valued.[36] As such, the will (the seat of motivation) is not operating within a neutral space of freedom, but is enslaved by dominating desires.[37]

How might these ideas be implemented in counseling? Paul instructed believers of his day,

But that is not the way you learned Christ!—assuming that you have heard about him and were taught in him, as the truth is in Jesus, to put off your old self, which belongs to your former manner of life and is corrupt through deceitful desires, and to be renewed in the spirit of your minds, and to put on the new self, created after the likeness of God in true righteousness and holiness. (Ephesians 4:20–24)

Practical counseling steps from this passage might include the following points:

1. Highlighting the importance of putting off the old self—the counselees' core identity prior to salvation, their former selves and way of life
2. Identifying former enslaving desires that are producing corruption reminiscent of the old self (i.e., control, acceptance, approval, et cetera) while encouraging the counselee to put these desires in their rightful place. That place is always in subjection to God's glory, considering the call of the believer to love God and others
3. Identifying why such desires are deceitful (i.e., "I must have control" versus "I must live my life with a functional trust in God's sovereign control and redemptive purposes in this moment")
4. Teaching counselees how to practically renew their minds (i.e., This moment is not about me, but about God, his glory, and his redemptive purposes)
5. Helping counselees learn to operate from their new selves—a new Spirit-filled core that is proclaimed righteous and holy in Jesus and is designed to live out such holiness and righteousness progressively throughout the individual's remaining life span

After addressing the dynamics within the heart (i.e., the root of the issue), Paul then provides instruction regarding outward behavior (i.e., the fruit of one's life), such as putting away falsehood, speaking truthfully, not sinning in one's anger, refusing to steal, working honestly, not engaging in corrupt talk, speaking edifying words, not grieving the Holy Spirit, putting away bitterness, anger and slander, being kind to others, and forgiving others (Ephesians 4:25–32). Biblical counsel will mirror Paul's approach.

Scripture is clear that without grace, a person's dominating desires are naturally contrary to God (Ephesians 2:1–3). The psalmist renders people in this fallen condition from birth (Psalm 58:3) while the apostle Paul declares that all human hearts refuse to seek God in their natural states (Romans 3:10–18). Without divine assistance, mankind is incapable of possessing desires and longings motivated by a love for God and his glory. Helping believers recognize that their hearts were radically opposed to God prior to conversion sets the stage for deep, comforting dependence upon God as it pertains to the process of heart transformation. If God has been so loving and gracious to rescue them, from utter bondage to sin and enslaving desires, then he will be ever so faithful in the continued work of renewal throughout the remainder of their lives.

Counseling and the Christian life are about learning to rest upon God so that people may learn to respond in their sufferings and struggles with hearts driven, moment-by-moment, situation-by-situation, thought-by-thought, emotion-by-emotion, behavior-by-behavior with a relentless love for the Lord of creation. This is the overriding goal of all things biblical counseling. It is no wonder God's wisdom encourages, "Above all else, guard your heart, for everything you do flows from it" (Proverbs 4:23 NIV).

The Heart and Personal Responsibility

Blame shifting traces its roots to the first two people created (Genesis 3:9–14). However, if context or past experience serves as the root of causation, it becomes difficult to understand the rebellion of Adam and Eve who resided daily in an environment of perfection. No bad parenting or traumatic event or physical ailment explained their motives to disobey God's counsel, though each of them tried to place cause outside of themselves (Genesis 3:12–13). While the serpent used cunning schemes and false counsel to entice them, both Adam and Eve made individual choices driven by inner desires and beliefs (both issues of the heart), and God held them responsible for their decisions in spite of formidable influences. In an instant, Adam's and Eve's hearts no longer treasured God and his glory, but their passion degraded into a dark and evil delusion. They began to believe they could actually become like God—they assumed the illusion of autonomy. From this evil treasure, evil was produced—death and corruption soon followed (James 1:13–15).

A similar pattern is displayed in the book of Ezekiel. The Israelites were pointing to the faults of others as the reason for their own calamity. They were citing an old proverb that placed the cause of God's judgment upon the decisions and activities of their parents—a case of classic blame shifting. The prophet quickly set them straight.

> The word of the LORD came to me: "What do you mean by repeating this proverb concerning the land of Israel, 'The fathers have eaten sour grapes, and the children's teeth are set on edge'? As I live, declares the Lord GOD, this proverb shall no more be used by you in Israel. Behold, all souls are mine; the soul of the father as well as the soul of the son is mine: the soul who sins shall die." (Ezekiel 18:1–4)

Ezekiel warned the Israelites that they could no longer blame the past sins of their fathers for the judgment that was upon them. Instead, Ezekiel strongly emphasized the significance of personal responsibility.

Ezekiel then presents a scenario in which three generations of men, regardless of the behavior of the father, would be judged according to their own deeds. The first generation was represented as an obedient man who, according to his deeds, reaped life. His son, however, was disobedient and reaped death. Prior to death, that man eventually had a son who was obedient. He, unlike his own father, lived (Ezekiel 18:5–18). Individual obedience and repentance is critical in spite of one's upbringing or the lifestyle of an individual's parent. Blaming the family system was unacceptable to Ezekiel—and God.

Concluding his warning to Israel, the prophet appeals to the heart, "Cast away from you all transgressions that you have committed, and make yourselves a new heart and a new spirit! Why will you die, O house of Israel? For I have no pleasure in the death of anyone, declares the Lord GOD; so turn, and live" (Ezekiel 18:31–32).

A biblical understanding of human nature acknowledges the significance of the heart. Salvation and divine change require a renewed heart. The good news is that the healer of hearts, Jesus, came to give people new hearts, making it possible for them to cast away their transgressions as they seek to glorify God. Jesus has also sent the Holy Spirit, who has set believers free from the law of sin and death (Romans 8:2) so that they may worship God in a manner that corresponds with their original design.

COUNSELING CONSIDERATIONS

1. How does viewing people as creatures fashioned by a Creator, rather than a product of natural evolution, influence your conceptual understanding of human motivation? What are the implications?
2. Why is it important to consider sin as counselors seek to understand human nature?
3. What is considered the causal core or crucible of human motivation according to biblical counseling?
4. How does Ezekiel 8 support the idea of personal responsibility? Why is this important in counseling?

Resources for Further Study

- Edwards, Jonathan. *A Treatise Concerning Religious Affections: Affections in Three Parts*. Bedford, MA: Applewood Books, 1746.
- Owen, John. *Overcoming Sin and Temptation*. Ed. Kelly Kapic and Justin Taylor. Wheaton, IL: Crossway, 2006.

CHAPTER TEN

. . . .

Humankind and Counseling (Part 2)

Man is a universe within himself. —Bob Marley[1]

The gospel transforms human nature, literally rewiring people's psychology. The good news of the gospel is that God, in his mercy, has chosen to rescue those who had despised him and turned their backs on him (2 Timothy 1:8–10). One of the clearest accounts of this glorious liberation is found in Ephesians 2—a passage considered previously with regard to God's sovereign love. This chapter hones in on what Ephesians 2 exposes about people's nature.

New Heart, New Life

After explaining to the people of Ephesus that all humanity is by nature dead in their sins, Paul ushers in the only hope able to rescue them, "But God, being rich in mercy, because of the great love with which he loved us, even when we were dead in our trespasses, made us alive together with Christ—by grace you have been saved" (Ephesians 2:4–5).

Being dead, people cannot want or desire the Lord. This is the tragic effect of sin. People's natural state is fundamentally egocentric, and they do not possess the capacity in themselves to reach out to God. People can only reach out to him if something supernatural takes place; for example, as when God "made us alive together with Christ . . . and raised us up with him and seated us with him in the heavenly places" (Ephesians 2:5–6). Believers were dead; God made them alive. Dead means unresponsive, fixed in hatred, and incapable of movement toward God. Believers did not meet God halfway. Dead is dead. The only hope for the dead is for the magnificent grace of God to invade the desolate tomb of the soul and raise them to life. Luther writes, "When God works in us, the will is changed under the sweet influence of the Spirit of God."[2]

This revelation brings hope to both counselor and counselee. Being made alive by grace is one of the most profound moments of change that a human will ever experience. If God is able to actuate such radical change in the heart, is God not also capable and willing to bring about ongoing change according to his redemptive plan for the Christian? Knowing that God was faithful to save by his own mercy and of his own accord provides hope that he will also be faithful to sanctify the saint from the moment of salvation forward. Counselees did not will their way into the kingdom, and they are not left to will themselves toward conformity to the image of Jesus (Galatians 5:16–26). Scripture assures believers that the Spirit of God will be faithful to empower them to that end. Counselees will be desperate for this reminder again and again since this change impacts all aspects of their lives—the mental, emotional, psychological, behavioral, and relational.

When the change from death to life occurs, the Bible says that God gives his children a heart of living flesh where there was previously a heart of lifeless stone.[3] Within this new heart, the Spirit creates a new motivational core within believers—progressively multiplying their longings so that they are more and more rooted in an abiding love for God and others while empowering them with a new capacity to believe and receive truth from God. This act of divine salvation changes a person's mental makeup. Paul highlights this marvelous transition when he reminds Christians that before the Spirit moved upon their hearts, they were foolish, disobedient, slaves of passions and pleasures, malicious, envious, and hateful. When the Spirit initiated regeneration, they became more inclined toward submission to authorities, obedience, good works, more willing to avoid evil talk, quarreling, and having a willingness to extend gentleness, and courtesy to others (Titus 3:1–7). Christians can rejoice in the certainty that their psychological, emotional, and mental healing are unfolding within the redemptive purposes of God's amazing grace, and that these purposes are destined to be brought to utter completion according to the will of God (Romans 8:30).

God invites counselors to participate in this glorious process. They are privileged to assist others by reminding them of God's mercy and faithfulness in their initial transformation and new birth, aiding them to understand the old patterns of their hearts that produce corruption and emotional upheaval, and guiding them to live their lives centered on God's glory.

New Heart, New Battles: The Raging Inner War

When Christians are given new hearts, they are forced to contend with a new inner battle, one that did not exist in their hearts prior to their new life, since beforehand they were thoroughly enslaved by sin (Romans 6:6–7). The apostle Paul portrays the battle this way, "But I say, walk by the Spirit, and you will not gratify the desires of the flesh. For the desires of the flesh are against the Spirit, and the desires of the Spirit are against the flesh, for these are opposed to each other, to keep you from doing the things you want to do" (Galatians 5:16–17).

Notice Paul's use of the word *desire*. The Spirit is producing desires within the hearts of his people. The same is noted regarding a person's old self, the flesh. While the Christian is no longer enslaved by the flesh (Romans 6:14), the old domain of sin wields a continuing temptation and influence in a Christian's life.

Yet, Paul contends, "Therefore, if anyone is in Christ, he is a new creation. The old has passed away; behold, the new has come" (2 Corinthians 5:17). Believers, who are made new in Christ, reside in a new domain where they will never again experience the dominating slavery of the original state of their depravity (because of the faithfulness of the Father, the completed gospel work of Jesus, and the inner-working power of the Holy Spirit). Paul emphatically taught this when he offered another counseling insight, "For sin will have no dominion over you, since you are not under law but under grace" (Romans 6:14). Concerning this incredible declaration, John Murray explains, "Paul is not simply giving an exhortation. He is making an apodictic statement [beyond dispute] to the effect that sin will not have dominion over the person who is under grace. He gives exhortation in very similar language in the context, but here he is making an emphatic negation—'sin will not have dominion.'"[4]

What a stunning realization of divine hope to know that a Christian's renewed heart will never ultimately return to the life of the flesh. That life is gone. People of God are recovering from being under sin's domain and influence, but they are no longer sin's helpless slaves. Just imagine the impact of Paul's wisdom for believers struggling with addiction, whose experiences feel as though they are the very antithesis of this reality. They feel enslaved by their addiction. They feel dominated by their addiction when, in fact, in God's redemptive economy, their feeling is a profound distortion of God's divine reality—sin will have no dominion over them.

Paul also counsels that while Jesus has demolished sin, the persistent elements of the flesh still remain, "Now the works of the flesh are evident: sexual immorality, impurity, sensuality, idolatry, sorcery, enmity, strife, jealousy, fits of anger, rivalries, dissensions, divisions, envy, drunkenness, orgies, and things like these. I warn you, as I warned you before, that those who do such things will not inherit the kingdom of God" (Galatians 5:19–20). So while believers are no longer citizens of the old creation and no longer enslaved by sin, they will remain susceptible to the deceit of the crucified old self. The inner tension to serve God or something else still unfolds.[5]

Biblical counseling will encourage believers to maintain a growing awareness of their new citizenship, that Jesus ultimately defeated sin in them and calls them to be made new in the attitude of their minds, faithfully "putting on" the new self so they may actually become (in their daily lives) who Christ has already made them to be—holy and righteous. Paul stresses this in Ephesians 4:20–24, where he urges believers not to walk as they once did in the futility of their darkened minds when they were alienated from God. Instead, as believers made alive, Christians are to put off the deceitful desires of the old self that produce corruption, to be made new in the attitudes of their minds, and to put on the new self empowered to live in the reality of who they have become by God's grace.

Paul offers further insight on how to live out of this identity as God's new creations (2 Corinthians 5:17). Contained within Paul's instruction in Ephesians 4 above is an implicit warning about the heart's ongoing capacity to give way to futile thinking and deceitful desires reminiscent of the old world from which believers have been rescued. His divine counsel offers wisdom to protect them from believing in lies that may reinforce deceitful desires, and vice versa. The realms of desire and belief impact the experiential reality of people's emotions. Like a complex labyrinth, these automatic emotional responses tend to deepen a person's faulty beliefs and deceitful desires. Each of these heart functions is interrelated, each influencing and reinforcing the other.[6]

The remnants of the old self may impact the believer's psychology in the realms of belief, desire, and emotional experience. The chart below shows how desires and beliefs can be corrupted and leave familiar symptoms.

Deceitful Desire	Fleshly, Futile Belief	Corruption
Acceptance	People must like me. I should always be accepted. I'm unacceptable.	Fear of Man, Insecurity Anxiety, Depression
Security	I must be safe. I'm unprotected.	Fear, Elevated Need to Control, Insecurity
Control	Things must go my way. I should always get my way. I am sovereign.	Anger, Irritation, Frustration, Anxiety
Love	My sense of self depends on others loving me in meaningful ways. I'm unlovable.	Self-Centeredness, Insecurity, Frustration, Feelings of Worthlessness, Manipulative

It is important to note that not all the desires listed under "deceitful desires" above are wrong or sinful. Rather, a particular form of sin's deception is that it influences people to desire these good things to the point that they become evil.[7]

Those who have been made alive in Jesus must continue to put to death their original hostility toward God (Romans 8:7). Counselors will acknowledge that deep down, all people wrestle with wanting to be their own gods. The Bible reveals that one way this hostility manifests itself is in the form of idolatry—desiring something to the point of sinning to acquire it. Desiring something more than God is why Paul admonished the believer, "Put to death therefore what is earthly in you: sexual immorality, impurity, passion, *evil desire*, and *covetousness*, which is *idolatry*" (Colossians 3:5, emphasis added). Paul is writing to those who have been made alive in Jesus.[8] The Christian must, therefore, continue to put to death what is earthly while doing so as citizens of a new kingdom (Colossians 1:13) and as people who have been brought from death to life (Romans 6:13).

Paul writes, "If we live by the Spirit, let us also walk by the Spirit" (Galatians 5:25). His words remind believers of their new spiritually alive condition and encourage them to live in step with the Spirit by whom they are now empowered to obey. The biblical counselor would not say to the person struggling with alcohol, "I encourage you to live *by the Spirit by changing your habits of drinking.*" Instead, he would say, "*Since the Spirit has made you alive, you are now empowered* to live a life of self-control. You are now empowered to put away the lifestyle of drunkenness."

Consider this example:[9] A child is adopted from a bleak and barren orphanage in Russia where food was scarce and the ownership of anything was tenuous at best. Now, for the first time in a middle-class American home, the child is put into an environment with an abundance of food, multiple sets of clothes, and his own, real soccer ball. For months, he may still stuff food in his pockets, hide his clothes under his mattress, and hide his soccer ball in the corner of the basement. He is in a new healthy, safe environment, but his former life persists to a degree. It still has momentum.

Sin still has momentum in believers' lives. But they do not live in sin's bondage any longer. "He has delivered us from the domain of darkness and transferred us to the kingdom of his beloved Son" (Colossians 1:13). Believers are in a new place with new surroundings, under a new power. The problem in a fallen state is that it is difficult for believers to realize who they are and what they have in Christ. Biblical counseling will seek to help counselees deeply embrace their new identity, while encouraging them to walk according to new God-given spiritual desires (Galatians 5:16–18).

These truths should encourage Christians dealing with serious psychological problems who feel as though they will never overcome specific destructive habits influenced by sin. They may be comforted with the fact that Jesus has defeated the root of their habits (sin) and has made a way for overcoming such habits in their hearts and lives. Nonetheless, a battle remains, and that is why it is continually important to heed Paul's exhortation to put to death evil desires and coveting, both of which he equates to idolatry.

When Appropriate Desires Become Evil

By what standard does one judge an appropriate desire from an inappropriate, sinful one? How do Christians identify idolatry within the heart? Though not a contributor to the formal biblical counseling literature, Francis Schaeffer—a counselor in his own right—has provided a thorough explanation by which desires should be measured biblically. He wrote,

> However, eventually the Christian life and true spirituality are not to be seen as outward at all, but inward. The climax of the Ten Commandments is the Tenth Commandment in Exodus 20:17; "Thou shalt not covet thy neighbor's house, nor his maidservant, nor his ox, nor his ass, nor any thing that is thy neighbor's." The commandment not to covet is an entirely inward thing . . . Coveting is the negative side of the positive command "Thou shalt love thy Lord thy God with all thy heart and with all thy soul and with all thy mind; . . . and shalt love thy neighbor as thyself."[10]

Schaeffer then asks, "Does this mean that any desire is coveting and therefore sinful? The Bible makes plain that this is not so— all desire is not sin. So when does proper desire become coveting?

I think we can simply answer, desire becomes sin when it fails to include love of God or men" (Matthew 22:37, 39).[11]

Cornelius Plantinga Jr. echoes Schaeffer's assessment noting, "Idolatry violates both negative and positive law, both the first commandment's prohibition of idolatry ('You shall have no other gods before me'[Deut. 5:7]) and also the summary love command of the Deuteronomic code ('Love the LORD your God with all your heart, and with all your soul, and with all your might' [6:5])."[12]

These men are asserting that motivation is rooted in worship. They are confirming that sin is not just behavioral; it is systemic. Furthermore they affirm that motivation is deeply interpersonal since it shapes a relational transaction between people and their Creator.

Jesus made this very clear when he confronted the religious men who thought they were good practicing Jews for keeping the law outwardly. Jesus completely obliterated any form of works salvation by pointing out the sobering devastation of sin upon the heart, even if one is seemingly obeying the rules, "You have heard that it was said, 'You shall not commit adultery.' But I say to you that everyone who looks at a woman with lustful intent has already committed adultery with her in his heart" (Matthew 5:27–28). Jesus exposed the vanity of religion and humankind's desperation for a Redeemer. The emphasis upon the human heart again takes center stage in Jesus's teaching. Biblical counseling will follow suit.

If I conceptualize individuals as creatures crowned with glory whose active hearts of worship are designed to glory in another, my counsel will reflect this view. Desires and beliefs are either glorifying the Lord, or they are not. Biblical counselors will conceptualize people as creatures of worship and seek to engender this understanding in those they serve. Human hearts will serve something. Biblical counseling holds tightly to the hope that if human hearts have been made new by the grace of God and are being transformed by the redeeming power of the gospel, then redemptive change is certain. It is not based on the skill of the counselor or the determination of the client ultimately, but on God who has the power to raise the dead.

Counseling Considerations

1. To what do counselees attribute their problems? There are a myriad of theories that abound in the culture as to why individuals struggle in marriage, with anxiety, and with anger. What theory guides the mindset of your counselees?
2. What is the goal of counselee sin counseling—a better marriage, a more fulfilled life, better behaved children? Whatever the initial goal, this information will begin to reveal what their heart treasures.
3. How important is God's glory to the counselee? Press in with this question. Most Christians will say it is important. Ask for examples of how they are seeking his glory in the way they are thinking and dealing with their present issues.
4. What do your counselees want or think they need that may be creating the problems they are facing?

RESOURCES FOR FURTHER STUDY

- Powlison, David. "X-Ray Questions: Drawing Out the Whys and Wherefores of Human Behavior." *Journal of Biblical Counseling* 18, no. 1 (1999): 2–9.
- Tripp, Paul. "Identity and Story: A Counseling Transcript." *Journal of Biblical Counseling* (Winter 2004): 59–67.
- Welch, Ed. "Motives: Why Do I Do the Things I Do?" *Journal of Biblical Counseling* (Fall 2003): 48–56.

CHAPTER ELEVEN

. . . .

BIBLICAL COUNSELING AND CHANGE

If merely "feeling good" could decide, drunkenness would be the
supremely valid human experience. —William James[1]

Since we have these promises, beloved, let us cleanse ourselves from
every defilement of body and spirit, bringing holiness to completion in
the fear of God. —The Apostle Paul[2]

A new heart that can treasure God is the beginning of Christian
transformation, not the final end. Christian counselors not only
need a rich theology of motivation but also a vibrant theology of
change. Biblical counseling offers a theology of ongoing transformation that is situated in what theologians have termed progressive
sanctification. In this process, the gracious Holy Spirit faithfully con-
forms the whole of believers' beings into the image of Jesus Christ
throughout the totality of their lives.

The *Westminster Shorter Catechism* describes sanctification as
"the work of God's free grace, whereby we are renewed in the whole
of man after the image of God, and are enabled more and more to
die unto sin, and to live unto righteousness."[3] Sanctification is the
true means, context, and purpose of change. Dr. Powlison has provided a succinct conceptual framework for biblical change noting:

> We affirm that the growth process for which counseling must
> aim is conversion followed by lifelong progressive sanctifica-
> tion within every circumstance of life. Our motives, thought
> processes, actions, words, emotions, attitudes, values—heart,

soul, mind, and might—increasingly resemble Jesus Christ in conscious and evident love for God and other people.

We deny that there is any method of instantaneous or complete perfection into the image of Jesus Christ. The change process continues until we see Him face-to-face.[4]

Our Perfect Example

If counselors desire to help others move toward greater mental health, they need a construct of a healthy mind. That construct is realized in the person of Jesus Christ, the consummate display of psychological wellness. Though in every respect Jesus was tempted as people are and even suffered when being tempted, Jesus, however, was without sin (Matthew 4:1–11; Hebrews 2:18; 4:15). How many emotional and mental struggles would be avoided if people gave no room for sin in their lives? What if people could respond to stress the way their Lord did when in a boat he was confronted by a tumultuous storm, making him vulnerable to the crashing waves of the sea (Mark 4:35–41)? Unlike his disciples who were crippled by fear, Jesus exhibited a commanding peace. What if people's trust in God imaged Jesus's trust in the Father when faced with unbearable pressures, trauma, or even the loss of life (Luke 22:42)? Such faith would certainly foster a stable peace of mind. What if, in the face of betrayal and rejection, people could extend love and kindness to those who have hurt them while finding complete fulfillment in the joy of that love and the honor it brings to the Father (Matthew 15:6–15)? Gone would be the days when people allow acceptance, approval, loyalty, and fear to rule their hearts, producing despair, depression, and anxiety when friends fail to deliver on fulfilling their perceived, unmet needs.

These are the genuine characteristics of psychological health and transformative change—minds that are enabled to think, perceive, believe, and operate as Jesus did when he was upon the earth. This transformation culminates in the fruit of the Spirit: love, joy, peace, patience, kindness, goodness, faithfulness, gentleness, and self-control (Galatians 5:22–23).

People do not and could not develop the fruit of the Spirit on their own. Jesus did everything, even offering himself on the cross, by the Holy Spirit's power (Matthew 12:28; Luke 3:21–22; 4:1; 4:14, 18; John 1:32; Hebrews 9:14). Jesus has been given the Spirit without measure (John 3:34) and freely gives the Spirit to all who believe in him (John 7:37–39) so that now the character of Christ is increasingly manifested in believers' lives by that same Spirit (2 Corinthians 3:18; Galatians 2:20). That is why the produce of biblical change is described as the fruit of the Spirit. This is quite contrary to the assumptions of modern psychotherapy that describes healing as the alleviation of a particular symptom or an improved situation. Sanctification is rather understood as inner transformation that produces the character of Christ within the individual.

I have counseled people who have suffered from severe anxiety and depression for their entire lives. Many have taken various medications to help, but often nothing seems to bring relief. Others have participated in various forms of counseling and therapy only to be further discouraged when nothing seems to lift the darkness. To make things worse, some believe that if they cannot rid themselves of depressive symptoms it could be a sign that they are not authentic believers. Tragically, they even question their salvation.

The therapeutic concept that health equals comfortable emotions tends to focus attention on the wrong goal. If people's hope or sense of purpose is for depression to be erased from their hearts, then they are susceptible to setting themselves up for a continual cycle of despair and helplessness. The sad reality of living in a fallen world is that maybe the depression is not going to go away. What then? The idea of biblical sanctification rightly addresses this dilemma.

The biblical counselor, therefore, is tasked to help counselees connect their emotional turmoil to the theological foundations of suffering and change. Counselors must help counselees answer questions related to suffering in a manner that exceeds the goal of personal comfort.

Suffering Is Part of Sanctification

It is not uncommon for the authors of Scripture to conceptualize suffering as a vital part of sanctification, "Count it all joy, my brothers, when you meet trials of various kinds, for you know that the testing of your faith produces steadfastness. And let steadfastness have its full effect, that you may be perfect and complete lacking in nothing" (James 1:2–4). Some depression is associated with sin, but some depression occurs because people live in a broken and fallen world. Their bodies are broken. Their families are broken. Many depressed people who come to me for help dearly love Jesus. They are faithful in their walk. They simply have a chronic battle with emotional darkness that refuses to subside. This is where a healthy biblical anthropology that embraces the concept of the "embodied soul" is imperative. Science has verified that chronic depression has a devastating physiological impact in that it does in fact cause damage to the brain. Therefore, the physiological cannot be ignored. Those caught in this experience are definitely suffering and suffering terribly. To think otherwise would exhibit either a calloused or naïve heart.

James explains, however, that suffering of this type can also be an occasion for joy since suffering is often the crucible in which deep, divine change occurs. Suffering allows people to exercise faith in the truths they proclaim, though this can admittedly be a painstaking process. It is in the midst of such trying times that Matthew Henry reminds, "There must be a sound and believing of the great truths of Christianity, and a resolute cleaving to them, in times of trial."

Therefore, depression may actually be a potent variable God will factor into people's life experiences, inducing change that reaches the most intimate parts of their souls. Some possible aspects of this deeper inner healing may include:

- *A maturing trust in God's faithfulness.* Getting over depression is not the litmus test of being a faithful Christian. Instead, should depression persist, hearts must find rest in God's eternal faithfulness to sustain them in their weakness (Romans 8:26–39).
- *A focused searching and refining of believers' hearts.* While depression is not always caused by sin, its presence may make

someone more vulnerable to sin. Depression may provide an occasion to covet things like control, relief, and happiness. Depression may expose issues within people that otherwise would remain hidden. It may very well be the fire that refines the genuineness of their faith resulting in "praise and glory and honor at the revelation of Jesus Christ" (1 Peter 1:7b).

- *Finding joy and peace in fulfilling one's purpose in weakness.* Depression does not wield the power to prevent a Christian from loving God or neighbor. As a matter of fact, when Christians seek to love their Lord in a weakened physical or emotional state, God is pleased. Consider the application of Jesus's parable about the widow, "Jesus looked up and saw the rich putting their gifts into the offering box, and he saw a poor widow put in two small copper coins. And he said, 'Truly, I tell you, this poor widow has put in more than all of them. For they all contributed out of their abundance, but she out of her poverty put in all she had to live on'"(Luke 21:1–4).

    There is something precious and valuable in giving out of poverty. Certainly this applies monetarily, but it also applies spiritually. Depression depletes people's physical and mental strength. It makes them feel as though they have nothing to give. Yet, when operating from such a deficiency, the stage is set for even the smallest efforts to outweigh the seemingly great. Getting out of bed, showering, and fixing lunch for a child may seem like a small gesture in the kingdom, but it is greatly prized in the eyes of the Lord if it is done while gripped by the clutches of depression. God sees the poverty out of which such kindness emerged, and he whispers, "Well done, my good and faithful servant."

- *Developing a growing appreciation of the Holy Spirit's power.* When weakened, Christians are made more aware of their desperate need for the Holy Spirit. On their best days, believers often take for granted that the ability and wish to obey God comes from the Spirit of God (Ephesians 3:14–21).

Jesus Is Thoroughly Acquainted with Suffering

As counselees bear the weight of suffering, they do not suffer alone. Jesus was the God-man, meaning he was fully God and fully man. As a man, he suffered terribly, not just physically, but psychologically as well. One of the most stunning passages in the Bible reveals Jesus struggling in a genuinely existential way as he grappled with a deep sense of purposelessness.[5] The prophet Isaiah offers a glimpse into the heart of Christ during this crisis, "But I said, 'I have labored in vain; I have spent my strength for nothing and vanity; yet surely my right is with the LORD, and my recompense with my God'" (Isaiah 49:4). The Savior of the world actually lamented that his labors upon this earth felt as though they were for naught. His life was a waste. Jesus experienced a crisis of meaning and purpose, just as many people today experience. Yet, Jesus's faith amid such heaviness stands out. "Yet, surely my right is with the Lord, and my recompense with my God." When faced with mental duress as a result of profound rejection and slander, Jesus entrusted his life to the Father. Here, Jesus displays his perfect divinity. Peter gives account, "When he was reviled, he did not revile in return; when he suffered, he did not threaten, but continued entrusting himself to him who judges justly" (1 Peter 2:23).

The writer of Hebrews points out that, in part, Jesus subjected himself to such hardship in order to show mercy and sympathy toward believers when they are subjected to similar difficulty, "For surely it is not angels that he helps, but he helps the offspring of Abraham. Therefore he had to be made like his brothers in every respect, so that he might become a merciful and faithful high priest in the service of God, to make propitiation for the sins of the people. For because he himself has suffered when tempted, he is able to help those who are being tempted" (Hebrews 2:16–18). And again,

In the days of his flesh, Jesus offered up prayers and supplications, with loud cries and tears, to him who was able to save him from death, and he was heard because of his reverence. Although he was a son, he learned obedience through what he suffered. And being made perfect, he became the source of eternal salvation to all who obey him, being designated by God a high priest after the order of Melchizedek. (Hebrews 5:7–9)

It is also clear from Scripture that these hardships brought terrible anguish to Jesus, "My soul is very sorrowful, even to death" (Mark 14:34). Jesus's accounts of sorrow were not an exaggeration. What kind of sorrow must Jesus have suffered when he felt that his whole physical, emotional, and psychological being was going to give way? The Savior understands suffering.

When counselors highlight sanctification with counselees as being "conformed into the image of Jesus," this includes physical, emotional, and psychological anguish. Christ does not reject counselees because of that anguish. Jesus identifies with them, sympathizes with them, and enables them to walk with God. Jesus allows believers to manifest his character in the midst of tribulation. This process is not one of pristine piety, but one in which the battle scars of brutal spiritual warfare will no doubt be inflicted. The process is often riddled with pain and should never be taken lightly.

When struggles persist in the lives of counselees (and they often will) or change is slow to come, sanctification may still flourish. Barbara Duguid beautifully relates this wonder of wonders:

If you are in Christ you are cherished, you are washed, you are cleansed, and you are wrapped up tightly in the perfect robes of his goodness. Wherever you have sinned and continue to sin, he has obeyed in your place. That means that you are free to struggle and fail; you are free to grow slowly; you are free at times not to grow at all; you are free to cast yourself on the mercy of God for a lifetime. Repeated failure does not mean that you are unsaved or that God is tired of you and disappointed. It does mean that he has called you to a difficult struggle and that he will hold on to you in all of your standing and falling and bring you home safely.[6]

Counselors and clients must know the favor and intimate fellow-ship of God in the midst of protracted struggle and bitter suffering. The knowledge of Christ's own suffering can bring freedom to battle without fear or condemnation.

Transformation within the Context of the Gospel

D. Martyn Lloyd-Jones once noted,

> There is no aspect of life but that the gospel has something to say about it. The whole of life must come under its influence because it is all-inclusive; the gospel is meant to control and govern everything in our lives. If we do not realize that, we are certain sooner or later to find ourselves in an unhappy condition. So many, because they indulge in these harmful and unscriptural dichotomies and only apply their Christianity to certain aspects of their lives, are bound to be in trouble . . . We must realize the greatness of the gospel, its vast eternal span. We must dwell more on the riches, and in the riches, of these great doctrinal absolutes.[7]

God changes hearts so that people may glory in their Creator and Lord. As a counselor, I am well aware that this process of change can be very daunting. When I work with people struggling with ongoing marital strife, severe addictions, compulsive behavior, or chronic depression, I want to make sure that the process of change is conducted within the rich context of the gospel of Jesus Christ. Otherwise, I run the risk of those I serve trusting in methods, a system, or in me as the ultimate hope for change.

To avoid these tendencies, I seek to help people operate within the safety of the gospel. This pursuit often leads me to Galatians 5 where Paul writes,

> For freedom Christ has set us free; stand firm therefore, and do not submit again to a yoke of slavery. Look: I, Paul, say to you that if you accept circumcision, Christ will be of no

advantage to you. I testify again to every man who accepts circumcision that he is obligated to keep the whole law. You are severed from Christ, you who would be justified by the law; you have fallen away from grace. For through the Spirit, by faith, we ourselves eagerly wait for the hope of righteousness. (Galatians 5:1–5)

Paul's gospel-infused admonition is extremely pertinent to the change process. Believers who have ongoing struggles can begin to suffocate in the smog of self-condemnation. They may say things like, "I'm a terrible Christian because I had yet another panic attack in my car today." Or, "Last night I was very lonely and rather than reach out to someone I downed a fifth of Vodka. Maybe I'm not even a believer. I'm so pathetic." Sin and suffering are devastating. When the one, two, three-step programs published in many self-help books do not help, people begin to despair. They crumble under the burdensome yoke of shame. The enemy of their minds pours out condemnation upon them in their failures. The only hope in such moments is the gospel of Jesus Christ.

When counselors help their counselees process their failures and sins with the gospel in mind, two important realities emerge:

1. The biblical process of change is not mechanical but personal. It is not formulaic. Rather, the Holy Spirit tailors it.
2. Any setback in a believer's battles against sin and suffering is an occasion to glory in the cross.

In Galatians 5, Paul was not counseling addiction or obsessive-compulsive tendencies, but he was confronting a message that often resounds in the hearts of broken counselees. False teachers were teaching the Galatians, "If you're going to be a true and acceptable Christ-follower then simply believing by faith is not enough for you to be counted righteous. You must also partake in circumcision. You must offer some form of works." Counselees might say, "If I'm going to be a good and acceptable Christ-follower then simply believing by faith is not enough for me to be counted righteous. I must also be successful in my therapeutic endeavors. I must offer some form of works." This mindset is heavily influenced by at least three things: a legalistic understanding of Christianity, a heavy dose of psychology speak, and old-fashioned human pride. None can offer ultimate healing or hope.

Paul's words are glaring. They provide eternal messages essential for believers who find themselves in the throes of battle. Here are a few implications of his instruction:

- *For freedom Christ has set us free:* Freedom is purchased, complete, and finished. Christians' freedom is now as they wrestle against the sin in their hearts. No matter what people do, they cannot earn or attain any more freedom than what Christ has already provided in his life, death, burial, and resurrection.

- *Stand firm in our freedom:* The litmus test for a person's freedom is not the ability to overcome anxiety, depression, or addiction. The litmus test of freedom is Jesus. He has freed believers from the bondage of sin. Jesus has accounted to them his perfect record. Christians are to stand firm in his work and grace and praise him even in their weakness (2 Corinthians 12:7–10).

- *Do not submit again to a yoke of slavery:* Believers should not submit to the demands of the law as a means to earn God's favor. They cannot place superficial performance criteria around their necks in order to find acceptance from God. They cannot find hope in or define redemption as sobriety or self-control. To do so is to become enslaved by something other than the full, complete work of Christ upon the cross.

- *You are severed from Christ, you who would be justified by the law; you have fallen away from grace:* If people's sense of being acceptable to God rests in their being a perfect husband, wife, or Christian, they sever themselves from the blessings of Christ and the precious riches he offers through the gospel. If never looking at porn again is one's means of acceptance before the throne of God, then that person is in grave trouble. Relying on one's own performance as a means to gain God's good favor is one huge fall away from grace.

- *For through the Spirit, by faith, we ourselves eagerly wait for the hope of righteousness:* By faith, the righteousness of Jesus Christ has been accounted to believers. By faith, they hope for the righteousness that is to come when they are transformed into their glorified bodies. By faith, believers wrestle within their present righteousness (justification) as they also, by the power of the Holy Spirit, pursue holiness as a means to honor and glorify God (sanctification).

Paul emphasizes Jesus and his complete work upon the cross. Paul also allows believers to see his own desperation for the Redeemer as he vacillates between the law of God and the law of sin. Brilliant theologians have debated whether Paul references his life as a pagan (pre-conversion) or as a saint (post-conversion), but either way, Jesus alone is his final and only hope.

> I do not understand my own actions. For I do not do what I want, but I do the very thing I hate. Now if I do what I do not want, I agree with the law, that it is good. So now it is no longer I who do it, but sin that dwells within me. For I know that nothing good dwells in me, that is, in my flesh. For I have the desire to do what is right, but not the ability to carry it out. For I do not do the good I want, but the evil I do not want is what I keep on doing. Now if I do what I do not want, it is no longer I who do it, but sin that dwells in me. So I find it to be a law that when I want to do right, evil lies close at hand. For I delight in the law of God, in my inner being, but I see in my members another law waging war against the law of my mind and making me captive to the law of sin that dwells in my members. *Wretched man that I am! Who will deliver me from this body of death? Thanks be to God through Jesus Christ our Lord!* So then, I myself serve the law of God with my mind, but with my flesh I serve the law of sin. (Romans 7:15–25, emphasis added)

Jesus was Paul's only hope. Wise biblical counseling will vigorously encourage counselees to wage war against sin while wisely persevering in suffering. However, biblical counselors will help others do so in the refuge of Jesus Christ their Savior who has already won the battle on their behalf through the gospel.

CHAPTER TWELVE

. . . .

THE CHURCH AND COUNSELING

And he gave the apostles, the prophets, the evangelists, the shepherds
and teachers, to equip the saints for the work of ministry, for building
up the body of Christ. . . . —Ephesians 4:11–12

The empirical support for the effectiveness of lay counseling or
nonprofessional or paraprofessional helping in general is quite extensive.
—Siang-Yang Tan[1]

When some people think of counseling, they often have in
mind an individual lying back on a couch and simply talking.
I have had numerous people enter my office for an initial appoint-
ment, see the couch, and ask if they are supposed to lie down to
begin therapy. We typically chuckle, and move on, but the reality
is that this isolated, sterile image is what many envision when they
consider going to a counselor.

Biblical counseling will approach the issue of soul care quite
differently, however. While spiritual life and growth is certainly
individual, it is not merely individual. Biblical change is commu-
nal. Unlike Freud's isolationist analytical approach, Paul frequently
urged believers to embrace a community approach when faced with
personal struggles.

Brothers, if anyone is caught in any transgression, you who are
spiritual should restore him in the spirit of gentleness. Keep
watch on yourself, lest you too be tempted. Bear one another's
burdens, and so fulfill the law of Christ. (Galatians 6:1–2)

> Let the word of Christ dwell in you richly, teaching and admonishing one another in all wisdom, singing psalms and hymns and spiritual songs, with thankfulness in your hearts to God. (Colossians 3:16)

Unfortunately, the community of faith has not always been a safe place to struggle. Just open up about wrestling with a porn addiction, homosexuality, severe depression, or manic delusions and watch the room clear.

Christians have often been quick to judge or to utilize any "biblically validated" means possible to fix those things that are not orderly within the souls of fellow believers. In many cases, this has unfortunately reduced the community of saints to a religious Gestapo, eager to punish or ostracize anyone unable or unwilling to offer immediate conformity to a set of rules. Paul's instruction to restore with a spirit of gentleness is too often lost. When addressing the broken in their midst, believers have frequently deferred to the preposterous yet popular philosophy of Nike, expecting others to "Just Do It" rather than humbly walking with them.

Instead, Christians suffering together can continually point one another to God's mercy, grace, and commitment. They can remind each other of God's call to holiness, his willingness to transform lives, and his perfect timetable. Biblical counseling is a church endeavor, and it is imperative that pastors cultivate a culture within the church that allows parishioners the freedom advocated by pastors like Matt Chandler that "it's okay to not be okay."[2]

As a counselor, I am always encouraged when I work with churches that embrace this mindset because it fosters an open heart to the church's role in the work of sanctification. It de-stigmatizes the reality that Christians too struggle with sin. It is an inherent admission that Christians are not okay and that they too need continual support, help, confrontation, admonition, and love. Believers need Spirit-induced, community-driven help aimed at conformity to Jesus Christ, who presented this cataclysmic idea to the religious of his own day, saying, "Those who are well have no need of a physician, but those who are sick" (Matthew 9:12).

To follow Jesus's wisdom requires that the church allow the needy and sick to be so without the manipulation to perform to a certain standard. Instead, the church must show a willingness to jump into the muck and mire of the spiritual war that often manifests as intoxicating addiction, terrifying rage, paralyzing anxiety, and at times crippling depression. While it may certainly be uncomfortable when believers walk with the more broken among them, by doing so they enter the beautiful dance characterized by Scripture as "iron sharpening iron" (Proverbs 27:17)—the mutual transformation of the people of God. As believers, it will be important to come to grips with the fact that often such a process is difficult, even disturbingly messy, but it is a powerful context for God's amazing grace to thrive.

Mutual Transformation Is a Church-Wide Endeavor

Genuine biblical counseling cannot be effectively practiced in isolation from the church, even among those who hold a state license. Theologian R. B. Kuiper once noted,

> The supreme task of the Christian church is to bring to men the Word of God. That word is profitable for instruction, correction and a great many other things. It also contains an inexhaustible wealth of comfort. The glorious task of conveying that comfort to troubled souls belongs to the church.[3]

Kuiper's words are both convicting and encouraging—the church is called to be a refuge that offers wise instruction, helpful guidance, and inexhaustible comfort for the troubled soul.

The idea that the body of Christ is critical to the counseling endeavor may rub against the bent of modern, secular therapeutic ideology since it engenders the value of community as an essential element of maintaining psychological health. I have had pastors tell me things like, "Hey, the problems this couple are experiencing are so bad they need the confidentiality afforded them through professional counseling. I have no business infringing on their privacy." Pastors and church leaders have unfortunately surrendered so much territory to paganism as it relates to living honestly with their parishioners.[4] Feeling they are doing a good thing by adopting a pagan view of confidentiality, pastors keep a safe distance when issues (often counseling or psychology related) arise.

Confidentiality, as understood in therapy, is a secular construct profoundly influenced by a person-centered philosophy. It has the capacity to promote a context of isolation when believers face their darkest secrets of struggle. At times, it may even promote a context where sin can flourish in secrecy between counselor and client.

This conceptual idea pushes arrogantly against the wisdom of Jesus who said,

> If your brother sins against you, go and tell him his fault, between you and him alone. If he listens to you, you have gained your brother. But if he does not listen, take one or two others along with you, that every charge may be established by the evidence of two or three witnesses. If he refuses to listen to them, tell it to the church. And if he refuses to listen even to the church, let him be to you as a Gentile and a tax collector. (Matthew 18:15–17)

Or the instruction of Paul, "Brothers, if anyone is caught in any transgression, you who are spiritual should restore him in a spirit of gentleness. Keep watch on yourself, lest you too be tempted. Bear one another's burdens, and so fulfill the law of Christ" (Galatians 6:1–2). In the realm of sin and struggle, neither Jesus nor Paul leaves room for isolation. Both encourage interaction, accountability, confrontation, restoration, and community.

Jesus even goes a step further. He reveals the inevitable, unavoidable reality of community in that, "Where two or three are gathered in my name, there I am among them" (Matthew 18:20). When counseling Christians, confidentiality, as in "my life has hidden secrets of which only my counselor and I are aware," is an illusion. Jesus is always present. He is the counseling environment.[5] This is a very important fact to consider for the helper of souls in that all counsel, interaction, and community transpires in the presence of God.

One cannot read the Bible without coming away absolutely convinced that the church is the preeminent context for rich, personal, even psychological transformation. One participant in my dissertation study reflected upon the church's role in counseling, saying, "The church is about what counseling is about: Ephesians 4 describes all that we have said above. Human flourishing is the goal of what the church is, what the church is to become, and how the church gets there. Wise counseling is not individual self-improvement, but builds the community of faith and love."[6]

This participant was referencing the following words of Paul:

> And he gave the apostles, the prophets, the evangelists, the shepherds and teachers, to equip the saints for the work of ministry, for building up the body of Christ, until we all attain to the unity of the faith and of the knowledge of the Son of God, to mature manhood, to the measure of the stature of the fullness of Christ, so that we may no longer be children, tossed to and fro by the waves and carried about by every wind of doctrine, by human cunning, by craftiness in deceitful schemes. Rather, speaking truth in love, we are to grow up in every way into him who is the head, into Christ, from whom the whole body, joined and held together by every joint with which it is equipped, when each part is working properly, makes the body grow so that it builds itself up in love. (Ephesians 4:11–16)

These verses are given in direct reference to the responsibilities of the body of Christ. Paul clearly affirms the idea that God provides gifts to specific individuals (i.e., apostles, evangelists, pastors, teachers, et cetera) for the specified purpose of equipping the saints. The saints are to be equipped "for the work of ministry, for building up the body of Christ, until we all attain to the unity of the faith and of the knowledge of the Son of God."

The Bible does not set apart counseling, soul care, or discipleship as a special discipline exclusive to those who are state licensed. Biblical counseling—the one-to-one intimate ministry of the sacred Scriptures—is a community endeavor. Counseling is helping one another grow in the wisdom of God through his Word. This maturity in wisdom offers discernment for living and protects the people of God from false doctrines, foolish human philosophies, and carnal schemes. It fosters minds that are growing to reflect their Redeemer and operate as they were originally created.

Additionally, biblical counsel recognizes that individual well-being is part of the larger well-being of Christ's body. The health of each and every human being within the body of Christ is paramount since each and every person is a part of the other. Just as the health of my heart (a part of my body) is critical to my overall physical well-being, so is the spiritual well-being of my neighbor critical to the overall well-being of Christ's body, the church. Failing to minister to my neighbor is like ignoring the glaring symptoms of an imminent heart attack. Biblical emotional care is far from egocentric or individualistic as is often emphasized in secular models, instead it is organic. It is transpersonal (oriented toward loving God) and interpersonal (oriented toward loving one's neighbor). It is about taking care of Christ's body.

Finally, counseling tends to the body and in doing so aligns itself with the head of the body, Jesus. Paul said that it is Christ "from whom the whole body, joined and held together by every joint with which it is equipped, when each part is working properly, makes the body grow so that it builds itself up in love." The Redeemer is committed to growing the body so that believers become equipped to build one another up in love! Counseling is a community effort aimed at growing others in Christ so that they may more fully love one another for his sake. In the end, biblical counseling within the church is the culmination of a glorious story captured in Christ's priestly prayer, "I do not ask for these only, but also for those who will believe in me through their word, that they may all be one, just as you, Father, are in me, and I in you, that they also may be in us, so that the world may believe that you have sent me" (John 17:20–21).

As stunning as it may seem, counseling's glorious aim—transformed lives united in Christ—is the greatest evidence to the world that Jesus is indeed the Redeemer. Jesus prayed for the unity of his church so that others would believe that the Father sent him. May biblical counseling's work foster the unity of God's people and the health of his body so that the world may know that Jesus is indeed the Messiah!

Equipping the Saints

As the church is the epicenter of biblical care, equipping the saints for such work should be a preeminent task. Pastors often relegate the work of counseling to those holding a license in mental health care. Cultivating congregations that thrive in one-another ministry is often overlooked. However, during the past decade, I have witnessed many pastors who uphold the conviction that the most fruitful place for a Christian to receive soul care is within the body of Christ. In order to ensure quality care, these pastors provide ample training opportunities to equip members for this work. Organizations that offer exceptional training materials in order to support these churches include the Association of Biblical Counselors, the Association of Certified Biblical Counseling, and the Christian Counseling and Education Foundation. Each of these ministries is driven by a passion to assist pastors and parishioners in reclaiming their rightful places in the arena of soul care. If you are interested in developing your ministry of biblical counseling I highly recommend any of these resources.

Is There Room for Professional Counselors in the Body of Christ?

Biblical counselors are currently debating the question, *Does the Bible leave room for Christians to participate in what culture calls professional counseling and psychology?* This is a burning issue for scholars like David Powlison, and he poses significant concerns with the current status of professionalism among Christian counselors today. He says, "According to the Bible, caring for souls—sustaining sufferers and transforming sinners—is a component of the total ministry of the church, however poorly the contemporary church may be doing the job. There is no legitimate place for a semi-Christian counseling profession to operate autonomously from ecclesiastical jurisdiction and in subordination to state jurisdiction."[7]

Dr. Powlison's words were quite sobering for me, as a licensed professional who deeply admires him. They forced me to contemplate my own ministry and professional identity. I believe possible resolution on this matter may emerge from a specific phrase he employs, "semi-Christian counseling profession." What elements might bring a "semi-Christian counseling profession" into a fully-Christian counseling profession? I would pose the following brief suggestions:

- First, professional counselors need to possess a genuine, functional respect for the authority of the church as it regards the believer. When pastors refer someone from their flock to a professional counselor, the counselor is not the counselee's spiritual authority. There is not a massive separation between the spiritual and psychological. Anyone with experience as a professional counselor knows the inevitability that counseling will in some way overlap with issues spiritual in nature when working with those professing Christianity. Speaking from my understanding as a biblical counselor, there is really no issue of the human experience that is not in one way or another spiritually related. Inner struggles associated with depression, anxiety, paranoia, anger, addiction, and relational difficulties all touch upon biblical truth. Therefore, counselors must remain mindful that one referred by a pastor or fellow believer is not first and foremost "our client" or "our counselee." Instead, that individual is part of a larger body.

- Second, professionals must possess an in-depth, advanced working knowledge of Scripture's relevance to all things counseling. Currently, by and large, this is not the case. Many universities and seminaries are bound by state requirements concerning coursework that qualifies a student for licensure. Many counseling students may complete an advanced degree at an institution upholding evangelical values without ever taking a single course preparing them to use the Bible in a counseling setting. Many practitioners are extremely well versed in theory and research from the discipline of psychology, but they lack any formal understanding of how God's Word applies to counseling and psychology. This is unfortunate, but is an issue that I believe can be effectively addressed. Supervision is a critical component of counselor development. While universities and seminaries may be limited in their capacities to offer theological training to counseling students—training that connects theological constructs to counseling—supervisors possess an excellent opportunity to equip new professionals with practical theological application within the counseling context.[8]

- Third, professionals seeking a more authentic approach to Christian counseling will seek to gain a deep appreciation for what those in the church can offer counselees. Fellow parishioners possess a wealth of gifts that can benefit those in need. As a counselor, I am often limited to one or two hours per week with an individual or family. My counseling schedule also limits my availability. When a crisis emerges, one or two hours of weekly help are hardly enough. Counselors are often desperate for partners in the pew.

  Years ago, a crisis emerged with a couple I was counseling, but because of my busy schedule, I could only see them one or two hours per week. My pastor and his wife, on the other hand, spent in excess of fifteen hours a week offering their wisdom, guidance, support, and love to that same couple. Had they not been the boots on the ground, this couple would not have received the support they needed. There are many competent believers who can walk with those of us working in the professional realm—fellow Christians who are eager to offer time, energy, support, and personal investment in order to assist the suffering.

- Finally, university and seminary programs preparing students for professional licensure should train students to build their model of care upon specific and thoroughly outlined theological doctrines. Specifically, students must exhibit proficiency in articulating a robust theology of God, human nature, motivation, and the process of change.

While there are countless other changes that could be considered, I believe if counselors would begin by developing and implementing these basic principles, it would be a good start toward reflecting a more Christian approach to counseling. I concede that these recommendations are far from exhaustive, but I emphasize that they are nonetheless significant if the aim is to provide genuine Christian care to those in need.

Counseling Considerations

1. What voices of shame and fear may hinder counselees from living openly in community?
2. Assess counselees' community of faith. Do they attend a church where people are allowed to struggle or a place where struggling people are typically ostracized?
3. How are you utilizing the local church in conjunction with what you are doing as a counselor? How might the gifts and talents of fellow Christians supplement your service to believers?
4. Encourage counselees to disclose their issues with others they trust. Discourage the tendency to isolate.
5. If living in community is new to counselees, it may also provoke fear and resistance. It may prompt them to avoid counseling. If this is the case, be considerate of these concerns. Talk through these concerns. Appropriately validate these concerns. Consider having them keep a journal of their experience as they embark upon a new pattern in their lives. Review their experience with them regularly.

Resources for Further Study

- Garzon, Fernando L., Kimberly A. Tilley. "Do Lay Christian Counseling Approaches Work: What We Currently Know." *Journal of Psychology and Christianity* 28, no. 2, (2009): 130–140.
- Higbee, Garrett. *Uncommon Community: Biblical Soul Care in Small Groups,* DVD series.[9]
- Kellemen, Robert. *Equipping Counselors for Your Church: The 4E Ministry Training Strategy* (Phillipsburg, NJ: P&R, 2001).
- Tripp, Paul. *Your Walk With God Is a Community Project,* DVD or CD series.[10]

· · · ·

CHAPTER THIRTEEN

THE COUNSELOR AND COUNSELING METHODS

Knowledge speaks, but wisdom listens. —Jimi Hendrix[1]

I once counseled a husband who referred to me as Yoda. Yoda is a character in the famed *Star Wars* movies, and is portrayed in this sci-fi classic as the supreme Jedi of all Jedi warriors. Standing all of two feet tall, he possesses more power in his left pinky than all the other Jedi's combined. Yoda can catch electricity in his hands, wad it into a ball, and strike his opponents with stunning ferocity. He can simply stretch out his hand and lift incapacitated spaceships thirty feet into the air. To say the least, Yoda is one mean, green little dude. As a stellar Jedi, he also possesses the power to subject those around him to mind-altering realities known by fans as Jedi mind tricks. Yoda can manipulate an individual's mind in ways that can profoundly confuse an adversary. Yoda is portrayed as a master of the mind.

While initially my clients and I laughed about this nickname, I quickly realized that I needed to check my heart as well as set the record straight. During our meetings, the Holy Spirit was producing what I believe was supernatural healing and transformation. It was a situation far too broken for human effort to restore, but my clients and I were struck with amazement each time we met because we were witnessing nothing less than divine restoration.

As these progressive changes kept occurring, this husband began, somewhat tongue-in- cheek, to credit his experience of healing to my skills as a counselor. As embarrassed as I am to admit it,

I wanted him to believe I possessed such acuity. It would be easy to glory in the fantasy that I was such an amazing counselor. To do so, however, would be extreme blasphemy. It would have required me to have taken credit for a work that belongs exclusively to the power and grace of God (Philippians 2:13). Functioning in a genuinely biblical manner required I shed this illusion and point myself and my counselee to the one whose actual power dwarfs anything Hollywood sci-fi could ever produce. I was forced in that moment to remind myself that I was in no way the agent of change.

Christians Counselors as Farmers

As a practicing counselor, who am I? Biblical counselors must assume the role of a desperate (yet hopeful) farmer rather than a highly skilled guru of the psyche. They plant truth and wait. They accept the fact that actuating change in the hearts of others is far beyond their capacity. By coming to grips with this reality, biblical counselors affirm with the Scriptures that the human heart is far too sick, far too desperate for them or any other human to understand (Jeremiah 17:9). Yet, biblical counselors also recognize that they play a part in the journey of helping others acquire self-knowledge, even though they do not possess the power to assist them in reaching the destination of absolute knowing (Proverbs 20:5). Therefore, as a counselor I am both an active participant and a helpless conduit. I am an instrument that God is using. As Paul said of his ministry, "I planted, Apollos watered, but God gave the growth. So neither he who plants nor he who waters is anything, but only God who gives the growth" (1 Corinthians 3:6–7). Counselor and counselee are in the hands of a knowing, wise, and gracious God. He is their only hope. Both must never forget that.

The apostle Paul, as a preeminent counselor, exudes passion and dedication to influence the hearts and lives of people.

And when they came to him, he said to them: "You yourselves know how I lived among you the whole time from the first day that I set foot in Asia, serving the Lord with all humility and with tears and with trails that happened to me through the plots of the Jews; how I did not shrink from declaring to you anything that was profitable, and teaching you in public and from house to house, testifying both to Jews and to Greeks of repentance toward God and of faith in our Lord Jesus Christ. And now, behold, I am going to Jerusalem, constrained by the Spirit, not knowing what will happen to me there, except that the Holy Spirit testifies to me in every city that imprisonment and afflictions await me. But I do not account my life of any value nor as precious to myself, if only I may finish my course and the ministry that I received from the Lord Jesus, to testify to the gospel of the grace of God." (Acts 20:18–24)

Paul served with humility and endured horrific emotional turmoil for the sake of ministering to the hearts of those around him. He persevered in planting truth no matter the trial or challenge that raged against him. Paul even went to cities with the full knowledge and assurance that prison awaited him. He did not flinch in light of these revelations. Instead, Paul persisted. He loved. He declared. He persevered. Effective counseling ministry involves hearts as committed as Paul's, and counseling at times may be profoundly arduous, emotionally exhausting, and spiritually draining. The process can even test one's faith as the world's severe brokenness is on display.

Unlike the efficacy studies entrenching modern psychology, however, Paul's passion for helping others was not fueled by the results of ministry. Instead, Paul was motivated by a divine conviction to pursue the will of God—a call personally granted by Jesus Christ. This too should be the biblical counselor's driving motive and rationale. The counselor's cry must echo Paul's, who said he did not value his life but valued the significance of pleasing God with his life. Counselors will be diligent to minister well, but they will entrust the final results to God.

Biblical counselors are farmers, workers completely dependent upon God. To operate biblically, counselors will not commit themselves to service based on how many lives they may impact. They will commit themselves to service because it pleases God. Biblical counselors will leave the counselee in the hands of the Creator. They will submit to the role as planter because the Holy Spirit is the producer of the harvest. Biblical counselors will join others in working through the redemptive process while trusting that it is God who wills and works in lives for his own good pleasure (Philippians 2:12–13).

Paul encouraged believers of God's timing, "Do not be deceived: God is not mocked, for whatever one sows, that will he also reap. For the one who sows to his own flesh will from the flesh reap corruption, but the one who sows to the Spirit will from the Spirit reap eternal life. And let us not grow weary of doing good, for in due season we will reap, if we do not give up" (Galatians 6:7–9). The sowing and reaping principle is a prominent reality within the counseling process.

Both counselor and counselee alike must honor this law, learning what it means to sow in the Spirit. Counselors sow humility, gentleness, patience, love, and truth. Growing in these attributes, they assist counselees in sowing to the Spirit. Counselors will persevere with depressed people, modeling and teaching them to sow in faith and perseverance. Counselors will exhibit a trust in God while encouraging anxious people to sow within their own lives a growing trust in God. When working with the couple in a fractured marriage, counselors press them to sow love, kindness, gentleness, humility, and patience while they process with them the issues of the heart that create resistance to these new ways of relating. In each case, counselors teach others to sow new desires, thoughts, beliefs, and behaviors. Counselors help counselees plow up the field and plant new seeds in the spiritual journey. Counselors plant, and in faith, they wait. As God gives grace, counselors pray that counselees will walk in a new goodness—a reoriented life that gives themselves away more and more generously.

The activity of sowing while awaiting the harvest is sometimes exhausting. When methods do not produce instant change, counselors and counselees may face temptation to give up hope. Paul anticipated this reality and encouraged the Galatians to resist weariness in doing good and persevere until the harvest blossoms. Just as farmers are not guaranteed to reap the exact number of seeds they have sown, counselors must learn to submit to and accept the crop that the Spirit cultivates. Maybe the wife will sow love in her marriage, hoping her husband will become more loving. Counselors would join her in this hope, but they would not stop there. The Spirit of God may choose to multiply her love for God and her husband as the husband's apathy in the marriage persists. However the Lord chooses to work in the harvest, counselors must humble their hearts to the results of that work. Counselors and counselees reap what they sow, but both must trust the Spirit for the type and timing of the harvest.

Counselors Who Sow to the Spirit

Counseling is a practice of learned dependency. Counselors and counselees both will learn that the process of change is one in which they are subject to the wisdom of the Holy Spirit and how he chooses to work in the process. This dependency is not a blind dependency; it is a faith dependency. God's revelation in the Bible promotes trust and faith in his omniscience and omnipotence. As counselors sow to the Spirit, they do so with an assurance that God's purposes are good, wise, perfect, loving, and sure. This presupposition is vital if they hope to encourage others. It fosters a hope in God's work of harvest as seeds of faith are being planted.

What are the specific seeds counselors will sow as they walk with others? Consider again Paul's words.

I therefore, prisoner for the Lord, urge you to walk in a manner worthy of the calling to which you have been called, with all humility and gentleness, with patience, bearing with one another in love, eager to maintain the unity of the Spirit in the bond of peace. There is one body and one Spirit . . . (Ephesians 4:1–3)

Let no corrupting talk come out of your mouths, but only such as is good for building up, as fits the occasion, that it may give grace to those who hear. (Ephesians 4:29)

Have this mind among yourselves, which is yours in Christ Jesus, who, though he was in the form of God, did not count equality with God a thing to be grasped, but made himself nothing, taking the form of a servant, being born in the likeness of men. And being found in human form, he humbled himself by becoming obedient to the point of death, even death on a cross. (Philippians 2:5–8)

Counselors Will Sow Humility

Witnessing the sin and suffering of others can be an occasion for self-righteousness. Counselors must resist such deceit. Biblical counselors must diligently seek the Holy Spirit to empower them with humility. When they sit across from the broken, they must recall their own capacity to sin. Counseling the adulterer in one respect reminds me of my own potential, apart from God's grace, to do the same and far, far worse. Additionally, humility is offering counsel based on the finished work of Christ alone and not upon my own "having it together" as the counselor. Humility is also appropriate self-disclosure, should sharing my own struggle be beneficial to my client.

Counselors Will Sow Gentleness

The struggles and issues of others may push emotional buttons within counselors that tempt them toward a myriad of harsh responses. When I see a spouse speaking abusively to another spouse, my inner judge is awakened, and I am sometimes tempted to answer such abuse with my own hateful words. However, the Word of God has proven true over and over again when I am confronted with these situations in that a gentle answer really does temper wrath (Proverbs 15:1). Gentle resolve has a tendency to disarm the insecure, fearful, and angry while calming tension pervading the air so that truth may be heard and embraced.

Counselors Will Sow Patience

Counselors must be willing to bear with others in love. The Holy Spirit holds the timetable of change within his hands. Sometimes, he brings about transformation immediately while other times, it feels more like a slow, grinding process. Either way, counselors must exhibit patience and perseverance. Counselors exhibit an attitude that pushes against a microwave, instant dinner mentality. Instead, counselors and counselees may have to simmer and marinate in truth for quite some time before actual evidence of consistent change arises.

Counselors Will Sow God's Wisdom

Counseling is not about the counselor's agenda. Counselors must make themselves nothing as a means to glorify God as sovereign. They enter the process prayerfully seeking the Lord for understanding and guidance. They do not encourage counselees to hope in them, but in God. Counselors are not offended when people resist their counsel, instead they seek to understand what fears or concerns are driving such resistance. Counselors genuinely acknowledge such fears. They incarnate the love of Jesus continually.

Counselors Will Sow Service

Counselors are called to operate with the heart of a servant. By God's grace, their love and concern will be tangible, encouraging, and comforting. Counselors are open to questions and doubts if they are present. They are serving counselees' needs, not their own. Counselors seek to alleviate counselees' questions and doubts. In church settings, counselors make themselves available even when it is not convenient. Counselors seek to love counselees with Christ's love.

Counselors Will Sow Obedience

The supreme authority under which the biblical counselor works is God. Counselors' words, actions, thoughts, and counsel should always honor the Lord and all he has revealed in his Word. If encouragement is offered, it corresponds with God's Word.[2] If confrontation is necessary, the means by which it is offered corresponds with the character of God. As God transforms counselors, their obedience in the counseling session will be radical and patterned after Jesus, who obeyed to the point of death. Such obedience is what it means to love one's neighbor.

Sowing by What Means?

What methods might biblical counselors employ as they sow into the lives of others? A cursory survey of biblical counseling literature reveals a variety of methodologies—each derived from the Bible. Below is a brief list of such methods:

- *Instilling hope centered in the gospel of Jesus:*[3] There is no power to biblically change outside of Jesus and the gifts he offers through the gospel. Counselors will continually and repeatedly assist counselees in practically applying the gospel to the here and now struggles of life.

    For I am not ashamed of the gospel, for it is the power of God for salvation to everyone who believes, to the Jew first and also to the Greek. For in it the righteousness of God is revealed from faith for faith, as it is written, "The righteous shall live by faith." (Romans 1:16–17)

- *Helping counselees develop a structured or disciplined way of life:*[4] There is wisdom in developing structured patterns in life (though not legalistically). Considering with counselees areas of their lives that are chaotic, out of control, or constantly strained while collaborating with them to develop patterns of life that include organization and discipline is applying wise biblical truth.

    The soul of the sluggard craves and gets nothing, while the soul of the diligent is richly supplied. (Proverbs 13:4)

    If you put these things before the brothers, you will be a good servant of Christ Jesus, being trained in the words of the faith and of the good doctrine that you have followed. Having nothing to do with irreverent, silly myths. Rather train yourself for godliness; for while bodily training is of some value, godliness is of value in every way, as it holds promise for the present life and also for the life to come. (1 Timothy 4:6–8)

- *Utilizing church discipline:*[5] The church community is a vital aspect of counseling. If unrepentant sin is involved, counseling may require church discipline. Such discipline is always aimed at restoration for the saint and is to be motivated by love. Church discipline, appropriately applied, is often used by God to foster redemptive purposes.

If your brother sins against you, go and tell him his fault, between you and him alone. If he listens to you, you have gained your brother. But if he does not listen, take one or two others along with you, that every charge may be established by the evidence of two or three witnesses. If he refuses to listen to them, tell it to the church. And if he refuses to listen even to the church, let him be to you as a Gentile and a tax collector. (Matthew 18:15–17)

• *Identifying a person's habitual response patterns and encouraging new habits:*[6] Sin and obedience possess habitual qualities. Sin begets sin and obedience encourages obedience. In a real sense, the heart is profoundly impacted by habits of sin or habits centered in God's glory. While transformation is not to be considered mere behavioral modification, modifying behavior is to be considered an aspect of biblical change.

But that is not the way you learned Christ!—assuming that you have heard about him and were taught in him, as the truth is in Jesus, to put off your old self, which belongs to your former manner of life and is corrupt through deceitful desires, and to be renewed in the spirit of your minds, and to put on the new self, created after the likeness of God in true righteousness and holiness. (Ephesians 4:20–24)

• *Teaching authoritatively for purposeful obedience:*[7] Counselees, even those who have been faithful church attendees their entire lives, benefit from solid biblical teaching. Given the myriad of voices, theories, and ideas that shape the culture's perspective on counseling, depression, anxiety, addiction, marriage, parenting, and other counseling related issues, sound teaching that reorients individuals toward a biblical conceptual framework is essential. Counselors must connect biblical teaching to purposeful obedience motivated by love and for the glory of God. They want to protect counselees from translating doctrinal teaching to that of dead, futile legalism.

All Scripture is breathed out by God and profitable for teaching, for reproof, for correction, and for training in righteousness, that the man of God may be competent, equipped for every good work. (2 Timothy 3:16–17)

Be doers of the word, and not hearers only, deceiving yourselves. For if anyone is a hearer of the word and not a doer, he
is like a man who looks intently at his natural face in a mirror.
For he looks at himself and goes away and at once forgets what
he was like. But the one who looks into the perfect law, the law
of liberty, and perseveres, being no hearer who forgets but a
doer who acts, he will be blessed in his doing. (James 1:22–25)

- *Radical amputating*:[8] When a person is battling deeply embedded sin patterns, they must learn to exhibit an attitude of
violence toward such sin. If something or someone is influencing sin or making it more difficult to resist, wisdom would
encourage ridding one's self of that thing or person in appropriate God-honoring ways. Likewise, as we war against the
sins of the heart, our attitudes must reflect that of a soldier in
hand-to-hand combat, seeking to destroy a dangerous adversary. We must be militant against our common enemy of sin.

And if your eye causes you to sin, tear it out. It is better for
you to enter the kingdom of God with one eye than with two
eyes to be thrown into hell. (Mark 9:47)[9]

For if you live according to the flesh you will die, but if by
the Spirit you put to death the deeds of the body, you will live.
(Romans 8:13)

- *Praying*:[10] Prayer is vital to counseling. Counselors should pray
for themselves that God would grant them wisdom, discernment, guidance, compassion, courage, boldness, and love.
Counselors should pray for those they counsel that counselees
would be healed, conformed to the likeness of Christ, freed from
sin, humbled for God's glory, captivated by God's love, infused
with love for others, and comforted by the abiding love of Jesus.

And so, from the day we heard, we have not ceased to pray
for you, asking that you may be filled with the knowledge of
his will in all spiritual wisdom and understanding, so as to
walk in a manner worthy of the Lord, fully pleasing to him,
bearing fruit in every good work and increasing in the knowledge of God. May you be strengthened with all power, according to his glorious might, for all endurance and patience with
joy, giving thanks to the Father, who has qualified you to share

in the inheritance of the saints in light. (Colossians 1:9–12)

- *Gathering data:*[11] Counselors will diligently gather all data pertinent to the counselees. Such data includes physical/medical histories, information about family of origin, current stressors, and perceptions and assumptions held by counselees related to the issues at hand, as well as their hopes and goals for the counseling process.

The purpose in a man's heart is like deep water, but a man of understanding will draw it out. (Proverbs 20:5)

- *Fostering insight and understanding:*[12] Counselors will seek insight and understanding for counselees by locating strongholds that create distortions, demolishing pretensions—destroying false assumptions about situations, self, God, and others, and helping them take every thought captive to Christ.

The heart is deceitful above all things, and desperately sick; who can understand it? I the LORD search the heart and test the mind, to give every man according to his ways, according to the fruit of his deeds. (Jeremiah 17:9–10)

For the weapons of our warfare are not of the flesh but have divine power to destroy strongholds. We destroy arguments and every lofty opinion raised against the knowledge of God, and take every thought captive to obey Christ. (2 Corinthians 10:4–5)

- *Assigning appropriate homework:*[13] Counselors will utilize homework that orients people toward God and his ways. The homework should engender an accurate perspective of self. Examples include reading biblical narratives that emphasize God's sovereignty, studying people in Scripture who experienced similar forms of suffering, or assigning exercises that help identify and replace deceit within the heart.

Finally, brothers, whatever is true, whatever is honorable, whatever is just, whatever is pure, whatever is lovely, whatever is commendable, if there is any excellence, if there is anything worthy of praise, think about these things. (Philippians 4:8)

- *Examining motives (the heart):*[14] Counselors will assist others in wisely considering the motives and intentions of the heart as conceptualized by Scripture. What desires rule the heart and influence behavior? What belief systems are dominating the way a person views and experiences God, life, others, and certain situations? What emotions may be overwhelming the individual in need?

For the word of God is living and active, sharper than any two-edged sword, piercing to the division of soul and of spirit, of joints and of marrow, and discerning the thoughts and intentions of the heart. (Hebrews 4:12)

- *Understanding feelings:*[15] Counselors recognize that emotions and feelings are a part of the human experience and are sensitive to the fact that such emotions have significant influence on a person's life. Counselors seek to develop and exhibit compassion, kindness, and encouragement to those struggling with difficult feelings.

   For we do not have a high priest who is unable to sympathize with our weaknesses, but one who in every respect has been tempted as we are, yet without sin. (Hebrews 4:15)

- *Developing an accurate self-image:*[16] Counselors help others develop a self-image that is rooted in God.

   I praise you, for I am fearfully and wonderfully made. (Psalm 139:14)

   For by the grace given to me I say to everyone among you not to think of himself more highly than he ought to think, but to think with sober judgment, each according to the measure of faith God has assigned. (Romans 12:3)

   For we are his workmanship, created in Christ Jesus for good works, which God prepared beforehand, that we should walk in them. (Ephesians 2:10)

- *Teaching with illustrations:*[17] Following the example of Jesus, counselors are creative in their methods of teaching designed to help counselees understand and implement biblical wisdom.

   And which of you by being anxious can add a single hour to his span of life? And why are you anxious about clothing? Consider the lilies of the field, how they grow: they neither toil nor spin, yet I tell you, even Solomon in all his glory was not arrayed like one of these. But if God so clothes the grass of the field, which today is alive and tomorrow is thrown into the oven, will he not much more clothe you, O you of little faith? (Matthew 6:27–30)

- *Training in spiritual warfare:*[18] Counselors seek to train counselees in spiritual warfare so they may implement biblical methods and effectively engage in the battle.

  For we do not wrestle against flesh and blood, but against the rulers, against the authorities, against the cosmic powers over this present darkness, against the spiritual forces of evil in the heavenly places. Therefore take up the whole armor of God, that you may be able to withstand in the evil day, and having done all, to stand firm. (Ephesians 6:12–13)

- *Training counselees to use the Bible as an offensive weapon:* Counselors will help counselees develop wisdom, knowledge, and practical skill in utilizing Scripture in spiritual warfare . . . and take the helmet of salvation, and the sword of the Spirit, which is the word of God . . . (Ephesians 6:17)

- *Following through with commitments:*[19] Building a trusting relationship is very important in counseling. Therefore, counselors will work diligently to follow through with commitments, modeling for counselees what they should do in their own lives.

  It is better that you should not vow than that you should vow and not pay. (Ecclesiastes 5:5)

- *Checking one's own attitude and life:*[20] Counselors continually assess their own hearts and motives within the counseling process. Selfish agendas do not belong in a process where the Holy Spirit is implementing his perfect plan. If admonition or rebuke is necessary, then such counsel should be centered in a love for God and others.

  Search me, O God, and know my heart! Try me and know my thoughts! And see if there be any grievous way in me, and lead me in the way everlasting! (Psalm 139:23–24)

  Clothe yourselves, all of you, with humility toward one another, for "God opposes the proud but gives grace to the humble." (1 Peter 5:5b)

- *Reading and studying the Bible:*[21] Ongoing study of the Bible is imperative for the Christian counselor. Counseling sessions should include frequent reading of Scripture.

How can a young man keep his way pure? By guarding it according to your word. With my whole heart I seek you; let me not wander from your commandments! I have stored up your word in my heart, that I might not sin against you. (Psalm 119:9–11)

Do your best to present yourself to God as one approved, a worker who has no need to be ashamed, rightly handling the Word of Truth. (2 Timothy 2:15)

- *Exercising sensitivity and flexibility:*[22] Counseling is a process, not a program. Ongoing dependence upon the Holy Spirit and sensitivity to his work are important. Personal interaction is favored over mechanical, dogmatic interaction. Awareness of the demeanor, body language, and mood are also key elements in order to exhibit sensitivity regarding the counselee's experience.

Brothers, if anyone is caught in any transgression, you who are spiritual should restore him in a spirit of gentleness. Keep watch over yourself, lest you too be tempted. Bear one another's burdens, and so fulfill the law of Christ. (Galatians 6:1–2)

A friend loves at all times, and a brother is born for adversity. (Proverbs 17:17)

- *Dialoguing with peers:*[23] Wise counselors glean from the wisdom, experience, and expertise of their colleagues. Participating in ongoing peer supervision facilitates growth in Christ as well as continued counselor development.

Where there is no guidance, a people falls, but in an abundance of counselors there is safety. (Proverbs 11:14)

- *Engaging secular literature:*[24] Knowledge of secular literature promotes a detailed, rich understanding of particular emotional, mental, and familial issues while serving as ancillary resources to Scripture, so long as such literature is interpreted through a biblical lens. Familiarity with the research literature may strengthen one's study of Scripture as it relates to the same subject matter and promote fluency for counselors in the language of the culture—the language of psychology and psychiatry with which many counselees may be well versed.

As for these four youths, God gave them learning and skill in all literature and wisdom, and Daniel had understanding in all visions and dreams . . . And in every matter of wisdom and understanding about which the king inquired of them, he found them ten times better than all the magicians and enchanters that were in all his kingdom. (Daniel 1:17, 20)

- *Assessing skillfully*:[25] Counselors go to great lengths to assess people and situations rightly. Obtaining all pertinent information to inform wise guidance is critical to the counseling process. It is helpful to consider areas such as relationship with God, understanding of the gospel, knowledge of Scripture, family history, physical influences, presence of shame, belief systems, relational dynamics with others, history of trauma, emotional influences, desires, longings, and body language.

    Do not judge by appearances, but judge with right judgment. (John 7:24)

- *Listening compassionately*:[26] One of the most important skills a counselor must develop is the ability to listen with sincere ears. People's stories are important. Their fears, despair, and pain are often comforted by the compassionate attunement of the counselor's heart. Quick answers and reckless attempts to solve problems before taking time to listen can be devastating.

    Blessed be the God and Father of our Lord Jesus Christ, the Father of mercies and God of all comfort, who comforts us in all our affliction, so that we may be able to comfort those who are in any affliction, with the comfort with which we ourselves are comforted by God. (2 Corinthians 1:3–4)

- *Offering words of hope*:[27] Developing the ability to offer biblical hope while avoiding shallow platitudes is vital to good counseling. Hope in God's faithfulness and love are most important for the believer.

    The hope of the righteous brings joy . . . (Proverbs 10:28)

- *Speaking redemptively*:[28] Conversation and counsel will be saturated with themes of redemption such as God's sovereignty, grace, forgiveness, mercy, faithfulness, and love, as well as our hope in Christ.

    My flesh and my heart may fail, but God is the strength of my heart and my portion forever. (Psalm 73:26)

- *Conceptualizing problems carefully:*[29] Counselors will employ every means available to rightly conceptualize a counselee's problems. This will include continual prayer for understanding, study of Scripture as it applies to the issues, consulting research, peer supervision, openness to new information, willingness to admit error in the assessment process, and ongoing examination.

  If any of you lacks wisdom, let him ask God, who gives generously to all without reproach, and it will be given him. (James 1:5)

- *Stressing the Lordship of Jesus:*[30] Jesus is Lord over all, and his plans and purposes for his people will not and cannot be thwarted. His church and his kingdom will flourish according to the counsel of his will. All of life and all of Scripture point to Jesus, and he is the portrait of holiness and health. Exemplifying Jesus in all faculties, by his grace, is the final aim of biblical counsel.

  He is the radiance of the glory of God and the exact imprint of his nature, and he upholds the universe by the word of his power. After making purification for sins, he sat down at the right hand of the Majesty on high, having become as much superior to angels as the name he has inherited is more excellent than theirs. (Hebrews 1:3–4)

While Scripture offers more methods for the counselor, this list provides a good starting point for building a toolbox to implement effective, genuine biblical care.

Counseling Considerations

1. Be mindful of any tendencies towards pride. Does your role as a counselor elevate you in your own mind above those you serve? Do you rely too much on your skill or intellect to prompt change in others?
2. Are you relational in your counseling (i.e., humble, kind, patient, genuinely interested) or does the pressure to perform distract you? Are you more concerned about loving those

you serve or having the best answer or best biblical verse to address the issues at hand? Be present, be attentive, and be compassionate.

3. Are there experiences in your life or your past that might make certain issues difficult to counsel? Have you been abused or did you experience your parent's divorce when a child? Is there hidden sin in your own life? Seek counsel from others if you believe anything in your life would hinder you as a counselor.

4. Do you get discouraged if people are not getting better? If so, what might this reveal about your heart regarding the work of God in your counselee's life? How might Jeremiah 17:5–9 apply to you as the counselor?

5. Do you allow others to evaluate you as a counselor? Do you allow them to sharpen you in areas where you may not be as developed? If not, consider finding someone to walk with you in this regard.

RESOURCES FOR FURTHER STUDY

- Adams, Jay. *Helps for Counselors: A Mini-Manual for Christian Counseling.* Grand Rapids, MI: Baker Books, 2001.
- Powlison, David. "How Healthy Is Your Preparation?" *Journal of Biblical Counseling* 14, no. 3 (1996): 2–5.
- Powlison, David. *Power Encounters: Reclaiming Spiritual Warfare.* Grand Rapids, MI: Baker Books, 1995.
- Scott, Stuart, and Heath Lambert, Eds. *Counseling the Hard Cases: True Stories Illustrating the Sufficiency of God's Resources in Scripture.* Nashville, TN: B&H Academic, 2012.
- Tripp, Paul David. *Instruments in the Redeemer's Hands: People in Need of Change Helping People in Need of Change.* Phillipsburg, NJ: P&R Publishing, 2002.

CHAPTER FOURTEEN

. . . .

HOLISTIC AND CONTEXTUALIZED UNDERSTANDING

Who can explain madmen? Who can explain evil? —Dan Rather[1]

A biblical approach to counseling will be open to consulting much of the research in psychology. However, biblical counseling also affirms the delicate reality outlined by Abraham Kuyper when he wrote the following:

> The distinction between the true science and the false science lies not in the arena where people perform their investigations, but in the manner with which they investigate, *and the principle from which people begin to investigate.* Sin has not only corrupted our moral life, but has also darkened our understanding. The result can only be that anyone attempting to reach scientific knowledge with that darkened understanding is bound to acquire a distorted view of things, and thereby reach false conclusions (emphasis added).[2]

Biblical counseling welcomes empirical data, but with one caveat—the interpretation of such data is not neutral. Kuyper's phrase, "the principle from which people begin to investigate" largely points to a person conducting science with either an awareness of God or a blindness toward him. Science is interpreted through one of two very specific lenses—theism or atheism. As such, biblical counselors will first need a solid understanding of biblical theology in order to interpret the scientific data in such a way that is consistent with the universe God created. This is most glaring in an understanding of the age-old issue of nature versus nurture.

The Role of Biology: Nature

Consider the realm of genetics, biology, and physiology—aspects of development people often refer to as nature. Theologian Anthony Hoekema once urged, "man must be understood as a unitary being. He has a physical side and a mental or spiritual side, but we must not separate these two. The human person must be understood as an embodied soul or a 'besouled' body."[3]

This traditional view of the body opens the door for biblical counselors to consider how the physical nature of humanity influences and interacts with one's cognitive, emotional, and behavioral dimensions. It encourages a holistic view of people. How do biblical counselors approach such data in a manner that does not detract from their biblical presuppositions?

Consider a case from the world of neuroscience. Neuroscience is pioneering some of the most impressive discoveries today. Brain research is booming. For this, believers can be grateful since such research offers an impressive array of information regarding the biology of mental functioning. However, brain research is typically conducted in a closed system—a context in which God is not considered. Therefore, when scientists interpret the spectacular data they gather, the conclusions drawn rarely reflect the idea that the brain is an amazing organism designed by God. Most leading researchers tend to view the human brain as a highly complex product of Darwinian evolution.[4] This presupposition creates a need for careful scrutiny on the part of Christians engaging with psychological research.

Researchers Andrew Newberg and Mark Robert Waldman have written an interesting book highlighting recent neurological findings on God and the brain.[5] They write, "The moment we encounter God, or the idea of God, our brain begins to change."[6] As a biblical counselor trained in psychology, I found this statement to be fascinating. I was captivated by the idea that modernism was actually giving a nod to the Creator.

My captivation was short-lived, however, as I quickly realized that these men were not referring to the God of Scripture as they relayed their scientific results. Instead, they were approaching the idea of God with an as-if mentality. A god may be there or may not, but if people live, think, and meditate as-if a god exists and as-if this god is benevolent rather than angry, then positive outcomes may be expected in the brain for those who pray to this benevolent being. God was portrayed as a mere construct of human thinking and was reduced to a means to an end, ideally offering a mental status of personal peace. God's literal existence and his actual interaction with humanity were not the pressing issues for the authors. Contrary to my hopes, their methodology reflected what Francis Schaeffer addressed years ago as he surveyed the changing culture around him.

> Whenever men are saying they are looking for a greater reality, we must show them at once the reality of true Christianity. This is real because it is concerned with the God who is there and who has spoken to us about Himself, not just the use of the symbol god or Christ which sounds spiritual but is not. The men who merely use the symbol ought to be pessimists, for the mere word god or the idea god is not a sufficient base for the optimism they display.[7]

As Newberg and Waldman interpreted their data, God was not an objective reality, but he was a subjectively formulated construct. From this reference point, God became nothing more than a placebo able to produce brain-altering results. Whether God actually exists and whether he literally interacts with people was of no genuine concern. While the book was quite fascinating, I was forced to transpose the data in order to utilize it within a biblical framework.

So, did the authors' failure to validate a literal God require that I throw the book to the side and forget anything written within its pages? No, it did not. In many ways their exceptional research simply reinforced eternal presuppositions offered me in the Bible. For example, they discovered the neurological impact of anger and worry in that "if you obsess on your doubts and worries, your emotional limbic system will slow down those parts of the frontal lobe that generate logic, empathy, and pleasure. Again, it's a simple seesaw effect. Love goes up, and fear goes down. Anger goes up, and compassion goes down."[8] They cited meditation and prayer as a means to elevate a sense of love and compassion and to engage the parts of the brain that stabilize obsessive fears or hard-to-control rage. These conclusions closely parallel the inspired wisdom of Scripture, "There is no fear in love, but perfect love casts out fear" (1 John 4:18).

The neurological interactions cited by the researchers were certainly interesting, and they hold potential to help me better explain the physiological impacts of anger and fear to those I counsel. I was encouraged how their results affirm the Scriptures in that when one's mind becomes fixed on the supernatural desires of the Holy Spirit—loving God and others—life and peace follow (Romans 8:5–6). Conversely, when the mind is set on the passions of the flesh, corruption follows (Ephesians 4:22). Their science did not alter my views, even though they approached their research outcomes with very different views about God than I hold. On the contrary, much of their data simply affirmed what Scripture has already revealed. I simply had to engage the task of reinterpreting their results through the lens of the Bible.

While reading research with a mind made alive by the amazing grace of God, I was captured all the more by the psalmist's proclamation that only a personal, brilliant God possesses such wisdom, power, and creativity to knit together the complex structures of every synapse in my neurological makeup. I was moved to affirm once again that when people are given the opportunity to observe God's handiwork in real time via modern technology, they witness in detail how they are fearfully and wonderfully made (Psalm 139:13–14). These brilliant facts, theologically understood, pointed me to God.

Did I, therefore, need this research to point counselees to God's magnificence? No, the Bible does that sufficiently. At the same time is it joyful to celebrate God's greatness as he provides intricate details of his creativity through general revelation? Absolutely, and I will engage the research and literature to capture the wonder of God's fingerprints upon every facet of existence. Biblical counselors should utilize such data (in reinterpreted form), if they believe it is helpful to minister truth to their counselees.

Newberg and Waldman's data validated the mind/brain relationship of human functioning through secular research methods, and when viewed from a biblical frame of reference, I did not have to exclude or minimize in any way actual spiritual or physical realities related to psychological functioning. As I read through the book, I applied the philosophy of a dear friend and pioneer in Christian soul care who once told me the craft of biblical counseling is not one of separatism (avoiding every piece of data that is not Christian), but it is redemptive (interpreting all information through a biblical reality).

Operating from this position makes it unnecessary for me to avoid every secular piece of information. It also keeps me from the futile task of separating the secular and the sacred. Instead, I am challenged to formulate a robust theology of care that will equip me to navigate secular research in such a way that God is honored. Physician and biblical counselor, Mike Emlet, explains, "We are simultaneously body and soul. There's never a time we're not spiritually engaged. And there's never a time we are not bodily engaged."[9] Counseling from this perspective not only fosters a holistic approach to human functioning, it also promotes a genuinely biblical view of people by recognizing the importance of both their inner and outer beings. Schaeffer again reminds us, "The things of the body are not to be despised when compared with the soul."[10] Newberg and Waldman's research offered me a physiological picture of worship and provided insight on how the neurology of anger and anxiety impact one's capacity to relate to God. This information did not drive my understanding, but it helped me better understand people.

The Role of Personal History: Nurture

Another realm of human development that psychology addresses is nurture. Simply stated, this approach seeks to gain an understanding of how one's social, familial, experiential, and relational histories may have impacted one's psychological makeup.[11] Wise biblical counseling will not exclude personal history from the process of assessment.

On the contrary, biblical wisdom encourages listening, probing, and understanding. The book of Proverbs wisely compels believers toward these activities:

> A fool takes no pleasure in understanding, but only in expressing his opinion. (Proverbs 18:2)
>
> If one gives an answer before he hears, it is his folly and shame. (Proverbs 18:13)
>
> An intelligent heart acquires knowledge, and the ear of the wise seeks knowledge. (Proverbs 18:15)

Biblical counselors will work diligently to walk in wisdom, learning about the soul to whom they are ministering. If they do not, they imitate fools and bring shame upon themselves, and even worse, bring shame upon the Lord. Knowing counselees means biblical counselors patiently listen to their story and help them consider how the experiences interwoven into that story may have shaped certain beliefs and responses in their lives.

If I am counseling someone whose father was abusive, I will acknowledge (as does the Bible) that such behavior has a devastating impact on the one abused (Proverbs 12:18). If I counsel someone reared in a home of drunken parents, I acknowledge (as does the Bible) that such an experience destroys not only the individuals who abuse alcohol but also those under their care (Isaiah 5:11–13). I understand that calloused rejection and ridicule from a close childhood friend has a tendency to set off a spiral of retaliatory sins that become patterns of relating over time. Hearts devastated by such evil desperately need the guidance of God's light to overcome pain invoked by others. Healing will occur as counselees grow, by his Spirit, to engage in relationships with love, mercy, and compassion (Romans 12:14–21).

Dr. John Bettler offers important points to remember when counselors consider the impact of their counselee's past on current emotional struggles:

1. We believe that a counselee's personal past has a significant influence upon his development and manner of life. We do not

believe that the counselee is a helpless victim whose manner of life is determined by his past.

2. We believe that a person creatively interacts with and interprets past events and incorporates his interpretation into his manner of life. We do not believe that a counselee so constructs his past that it has no necessary existence in history. Just as God acts and explains or interprets his actions, so the person interprets the actual events in his life.

3. We believe that the Christian should seek to interpret his past as coming from God and for God's glory; the unbeliever will distort the event with an explanation that does not honor God's truth. He will resist the truth and endeavor to believe the lie.

4. We believe that a counselee is not always aware of the assumptions, values, and habits that shape his manner of life. We do not believe there exists within the person an "unconscious," i.e., an unexplored and largely unexplorable entity which drives his behavior.

5. We believe that exploration of a person's past may help to reveal to himself his manner of life. We do not believe such exploration is always necessary to produce biblical change.

6. We believe that change occurs in the present. It involves repentance for the distorted values and habits of false manner of life, and the putting on of godly values and behavior patterns in the present. We do not believe that change occurs in the past through the reliving of past experiences or through emotional release of stored-up emotions (a process commonly called catharsis).

7. We believe that God is sovereign over all the events of a person's life and works providentially through those events to make Christians more like Christ. [12]

I would add that biblical counselors also seek to enter the brokenness and devastation that painful or traumatic past life experiences bring. Counselors will not only consider the values and thought processes that have been shaped by one's past, but also any emotional devastation experienced by the counselee. In other words, counselors seek the Lord for compassion as they carefully listen to the stories of those they serve. Counselors ask questions to learn about the psychological experiences counselees may have encountered during the more difficult moments of their lives. Imitating Jesus, counselors seek to understand and sympathize with those devastated by the curses of a fallen world. Consider again what Hebrews tells us:

> Therefore he had to be made like his brothers in every respect, so that he might become a merciful and faithful high priest in the service of God, to make propitiation for the sins of his people. For because he himself has suffered when tempted, he is able to help those who are being tempted. (2:17–18)
>
> For we do not have a high priest who is unable to sympathize with our weaknesses, but one who in every respect has been tempted as we are, yet without sin. (4:15)

These passages illustrate a particular work of Jesus—that he subjected himself to the trials and temptations of humanity. Jesus overcame each with perfect obedience and righteousness so that he might serve as the perfect and great high priest. These passages are also a powerful example of ministry. Just as Jesus entered the broken world as a means to love and sympathize with his people, counselors should be willing to enter the broken worlds (past or present) of counselees. Biblical counselors should not stand on a pedestal of self-righteousness or counsel from a sterile position of religiosity. Instead, counselors should enter in with those whose stories are filled with grief and pain so that counselees may be known intimately.

Unlike Jesus, however, counselors will relate to counselees as fellow redeemed saints desperate for God's grace in the midst of their own weaknesses. Counseling is a place where the stories of counselees and counselors interact in many ways. The pain and suffering that counselors have experienced allows them to connect with counselees who are suffering. Their mutual stories of failure and pain should provide occasion to point toward comfort in the Father of mercies and God of all comfort. Consider Paul's wisdom in 2 Corinthians.

Blessed be the God and Father of our Lord Jesus Christ, the Father of mercies and God of all comfort, who comforts us in all our affliction, so that we may be able to comfort those who are in any affliction, with the comfort with which we ourselves are comforted by God. For as we share abundantly in Christ's sufferings, so through Christ we share abundantly in comfort too. If we are afflicted, it is for your comfort and salvation; and if we are comforted, it is for your comfort, which you experience when you patiently endure the same sufferings that we suffer. Our hope for you is unshaken, for we know that as you share in our sufferings, you will also share in our comfort. (1:3–7)

Life stories matter. Paul's stories of sufferings were intended to engender deeper faith in God. Life stories (good and bad) should lead people back to God. This is precisely what the Bible itself does. It contains many honest (often brutal) life stories of real people with feet of clay. Their stories point to God. Their stories were inspired by God for this very purpose—that as believers read of his interaction with people who were weak, people who were abused, people who were traumatized, people who were prey to sin, they would be granted the honor of witnessing his mercy, grace, holiness and love as he related to them. As counselors listen to the details of suffering, pain, and sin within the narratives of their counselees, they should experience a deeper love for others and a deeper awareness and awe of God.

Biological and social influences are not to be ignored if one's aim is to treat people biblically. Biblical counselors will be both holistic and contextual in their assessments. Theology informs them in this regard. It tells biblical counselors that they live in a fallen world in which both their biology and sociology have gone awry (Job 1–2). As such, counselors will consider family of origin as well as physiological and neurological dysfunction. They will assess how these spheres interact and contribute to the presenting issues of their counselees.

Biblical counselors will differ substantially from many of their secular counterparts in that they will consider these influences within the context that humans are ultimately responsible to their Creator (Ezekiel 18:1–20). Biblical counselors will embrace the reality that the final cause of a counselee's functioning does not reside in the exterior or material, but within the inner workings of the soul (Matthew 15:17–20). Therefore, they will genuinely validate the suffering of others while carefully working to help them conceptualize their life story, their belief systems, and their motivations in light of God's divine truth (Hebrews 4:12).

Counseling Considerations

1. Ensure your intake form contains a section that assesses basic medical history. Include questions pertaining to current prescribed medications and the reasons for such medications.
2. Assess the history of those you serve. What traumas or experiences may have shaped their current struggle? Be patient and take great care to show interest in their story.
3. Be wise and refer people to a medical professional if the situation merits such a referral. Recommend physicals to rule out organic possibilities. If a person is unable to function well, recommend a trusted psychiatrist.
4. Challenge yourself to read secular literature on issues such as anxiety, anger, and addiction. Practice and develop the skill of reinterpreting the information through Scripture. Be mindful that all counseling books are written with presuppositions about God, man, and the world. There will be times when reinterpretation is the appropriate method. There will be other times when the information is so skewed it will not be helpful to use. Learn to know the difference.
5. The Bible is the final authority. Never diminish its value, no matter what problems are presented to you by counselees.

RESOURCES FOR FURTHER STUDY

- Emlet, Michael. *Descriptions and Prescriptions: A Biblical Perspective.* Greensboro, NC: New Growth Press, 2017.
- Frances, Allen. *Saving Normal: An Insider's Revolt against Out-of-Control Psychiatric Diagnosis, DSM-5, Big Pharma, and the Medicalization of Ordinary Life.* New York: William Morrow, 2013.
- Jeeves, Malcolm. *Minds, Brains, Souls, and Gods.* Downers Grove, IL: IVP Academic, 2013.
- Pinker, Steven. *The Blank Slate: The Modern Denial of Human Nature.* New York: Viking Penguin, 2002.
- Thomson, Rich. *The Heart of Man and the Mental Disorders: How the Word of God Is Sufficient.* Alief, TX: Rich Tomson, 2004.
- Welch, Ed. *Blame It on the Brain: Distinguishing Chemical Imbalances, Brain Disorders, and Disobedience.* Phillipsburg, NJ: P&R Publishing, 1998.

Part Three

Future

CHAPTER FIFTEEN

. . . .

THE SUFFICIENCY OF SCRIPTURE AND THE USE OF EXTRA-BIBLICAL DATA— THE ISSUE OF EPISTEMOLOGY

The sufficiency of Scripture does not mean the Scripture is all we need to live obediently. To be obedient in the sciences we need to read science and study nature. —John Piper[1]

The founder of modern biblical counseling, Jay Adams, frames the discussion of the Bible and extra-biblical data:

> The conclusions of the book [*Competent to Counsel*] are not based upon scientific findings. My method is presuppositional. I avowedly accept the inerrant Bible as the Standard of all faith and practice. The Scriptures, therefore, are the basis, and contain the criteria by which I have sought to make every judgment. Two precautions must be suggested. First, I am aware that my interpretations and applications of Scripture are not infallible. Secondly, I do not wish to disregard science, but rather I welcome it as a useful adjunct for the purposes of illustrating, filling in generalizations with specifics, and challenging wrong human interpretations of Scripture, thereby forcing the student to restudy the Scriptures. However, in the area of psychiatry, science largely has given way to humanistic philosophy and gross speculation.[2]

Biblical counseling has never been anti-science. That may not be the case among particular individuals ascribing to biblical counseling, but the leadership within the movement has never endorsed an anti-science protocol.

Adams's epistemology ultimately rested in the Bible, not science. Epistemology, the source of knowledge, is especially relevant to this particular discussion. Epistemology asks, *Is Scripture or science the fundamental source of knowledge?* Biblical counseling would affirm the former, but not to the exclusion of utilizing the latter. Biblical counseling's epistemological base, the Bible, will shape and interpret all other data.

From its inception, pioneers in biblical counseling have not viewed their work as a scientific endeavor, but a theological one. Heath Lambert reminds, "Biblical counselors have not argued that the Bible is adequate as a scientific text. They have argued that the Bible is adequate *as it is.*"[3] This standpoint undergirds biblical counseling's understanding of Scripture's sufficiency. Nonetheless, the concepts of the sufficiency of Scripture and the integration of science are far from precise.

Ambiguity of the Terms *Integration* and *Sufficiency*

When I began my doctoral dissertation, I thought I had the issue of integration and the sufficiency of Scripture figured out fairly well (integration being the art of utilizing scientific data within a biblical counseling framework). But, when I presented the following questions to several of the most accomplished minds in Christian psychology, biblical counseling, nouthetic counseling, and Christian counseling, I was intrigued by their answers, and aware I had much work to do in gaining a clear understanding of these concepts. I admit that initially I was quite bewildered. It all began when I submitted this question:[4]

1. Which of the following best describes your philosophy of counseling?
   • I believe that true biblical counseling requires one to embrace the idea that *the Bible is sufficient* to develop a comprehensive model of counseling, therefore finding no

need to integrate secular theory into one's philosophy and methods of counseling.

• I believe that true biblical counseling does not require one to embrace the idea that the Bible is sufficient to develop a comprehensive model of counseling, therefore finding the need to *integrate secular theory* into one's philosophy and methods of counseling.

While most panelists chose answers I would have expected, given my understanding of the sufficiency of Scripture and integration at that time, several panelists refused to circle either answer, but instead provided some thoughtful feedback for me to consider. One of the panelists on the biblical counseling panel offered the following:

Neither of these options reflects my position, nor am I able to select a "best" one, since each one would grossly misrepresent my position. A comprehensive model of counseling can be developed from Scripture, which allows for and even suggests recognition of truth wherever it might be found. . . . Putting it another way, I believe that true biblical counseling requires one to embrace the idea that the Bible is sufficient to develop a comprehensive model of counseling, therefore finding a compelling need to engage secular theory (as Daniel engaged Babylonian wisdom) into one's evangelistic ministry and methods of counseling.[5]

As days passed, and I awaited other panelists to respond, a Christian psychologist in my study sent me this feedback:

The framing of your statements using "sufficient," "secular," and "philosophy" forces those who would not take a nouthetic stance to opt for the second statement and to move toward integrating secular theory into one's philosophy of counseling. That is not at all satisfactory or particularly sensible. Theory stands after philosophy. The forced choice is between a weak nouthetic formulation and an insufficient alternative. I suspect "neither of the above" is a better answer.[6]

The comments from Christian psychology continued to pour in. Another panelist wrote:

> Sufficiency of Scripture is a complex topic and there are different ways one can interpret it. I believe the Bible is sufficient for knowing God, salvation, morality, and how to live the Christian life. However, I don't believe that it is sufficient for the science of psychology (e.g., it does not discuss neuropsychology). At the same time, biblical counseling focuses on the Bible, so the Bible is sufficient for biblical counseling. My own view, however, is Christian psychology, and (following Calvin and others) I am open to learning from non-Christians about psychology, but I do not want to "integrate secular theory into my philosophy and methods of counseling." On the contrary, when reading and interpreting modern/secular psychology I make it my objective to transplant/translate/transpose the truth of secular psychology into a God-centered Christian scheme, so that its secularism is eliminated.[7]

One Christian counselor also expressed his struggle with the wording I had chosen:

> I truthfully have a hard time using the word *integrate* to describe the type of counseling I do. I believe in the inerrancy and authority of Scripture and believe everything should be filtered through it. I also believe there are techniques and counseling practices used for various types of mental illnesses that we should use to enhance and inform how we help people.[8]

I realized, upon receiving these concerns from highly skilled thinkers in Christian soul care, that my conceptual framework for the sufficiency of Scripture and integration may have been too rigid as evidenced in the wording of my initial study question. Honestly, as these individuals began to express concerns, I felt a bit panicked. I thought the conclusions on these issue were far more cut and dry.

My confusion only amplified with the second question on my questionnaire. It read as follows:

2.   Circle the comment below that most reflects your philosophy of counseling.
   •   I am a counselor who integrates secular theory into my model of Christian counseling.
   •   I am a counselor who does not integrate secular theory into my model of Christian counseling.

Answers should have been pretty straightforward, right? Not so fast. As was the case for the initial question, several participants offered comments. More than any others, these comments forced me to step back and reconsider my own understanding of integration and the sufficiency of Scripture. For example, the same biblical counselor who expressed concerns for my first question did the same with question two. He stated,

> I am a biblical counselor who, like Daniel (1–2), engages the wisdom of the secular, and like Paul (I Cor. 9), seeks to speak Stoic to the Stoics, Epicurean to the Epicureans, Roman to the Romans, Greek to the Greeks, and Law to the Jews, all governed by and resting on the inerrancy, sufficiency, and sole or singular final authority of the Word of God. I do not integrate or add to Scripture, I follow the instruction and model of Scripture in engaging, evaluating, and utilizing research and theory.[9]

This time, however, another biblical counselor (a person highly respected in the biblical counseling community) chimed in, and it was this answer that really forced me to step back and rethink my own thinking. He said "The word *integrate* is, of course, ambiguous, and there are definitions of the word that make it acceptable and even desirable to integrate from a belief in Scripture's sufficiency."[10]

Muddying the waters even more (for me), comments from Christian psychology continued to come in:

> I do not integrate secular theory into my model of Christian counseling. To do so would make it secular counseling, not Christian counseling. I realize this happens all too often in integration literature, but that is antithetical to the goal of a Christian psychology. As a result, I would wish that a third response were available in the questionnaire that would articulate a position closer to Christian psychology.[11]

A colleague of this particular panelist added, "My preference would be to say that I utilize empirical research into my counseling work. There are, of course, theoretical assumptions within the research."[12]

I read over these responses with a certain sense of perplexity. I had biblical counselors (very respected ones at that) responding that a proper understanding of integration makes it desirable to engage secular literature. Then I had Christian psychologists (again, very respectable) responding that they believed in the sufficiency of Scripture (rightly defined) while strongly resisting the concept of integrating secular research into their model of care. I soon realized I had oversimplified the various camps of soul care—especially as it centered on the issues of sufficiency of Scripture and integration. My hunch is that many reading this book, without realizing it, may have done the same.

There are still elements within the field that would pressure people to embrace an either-or mindset when it comes to the Bible and outside sources. I believe it is imperative that Scripture serves as the comprehensive lens, authority, and source—upholding the sufficiency of Scripture. I also find value in consulting extra-biblical literature. I hope to illustrate this idea in the following pages. While I hold this perspective, I also believe that outside sources are not essential for me to provide rich, transformative biblical counsel. To begin unpacking what may feel convoluted at this point, I want to hone in on the issue of the sufficiency of Scripture.

The Sufficiency of Scripture

The most ardent pioneer of the sufficiency view, Jay Adams, once wrote, "And God doesn't duplicate in general revelation (creation) what He gives us by special revelation (the Bible). That is not common grace."[13] By this, he was setting the stage for his nouthetic model in which it is believed that the Bible is utterly sufficient for the work of counseling. Powlison summarized this sentiment well, stating, "Nouthetic counseling was founded in the confidence that God has spoken comprehensively about and to human beings."[14] Elsewhere, Powlison adds, "The scope of the Scripture's sufficiency includes those face-to-face relationships that our culture labels 'counseling' and 'psychotherapy.' The content? The problems, needs, and struggles of real people—right down to the details—must be rationally explained by the categories with which the Bible teaches us to understand human life."[15]

Powlison has offered a summation of this concept that tends to most reflect what is found in current biblical counseling literature, "Scripture is sufficient, not in that it is exhaustive, containing all valid knowledge, but in that it rightly aligns a coherent and comprehensive system of counseling that is radically at odds with every atheistic model."[16] He adds, however, that the honest observers of this ideal will also "want to gain what knowledge they can, both theoretical and applied, from the social sciences and other fields."[17]

As such, the sufficiency view advocated by Powlison and others does not necessarily imply what Johnson has referred to as "absolute sufficiency" in which any source other than the Bible is virtually ignored. While Johnson rightly affirms that there are some on the Christian counseling spectrum who hold this view, it is not the view of many who served on my research panel, nor is it the view I want to promote.[18] So, in an attempt to clarify what is meant by the phrase "sufficiency of Scripture" as it relates to counseling, consider the question, *For what is the Bible sufficient within the counseling endeavor?*

For What Is the Bible Sufficient?

The Bible as spectacles idea utilizes the Scriptures as a lens rather than a topical encyclopedia. In so doing, it removes the logical necessity for the Bible to be exhaustive regarding all labels found within counseling, psychology, and psychiatry. The caveat to this perspective, however, is that this lens must be well developed through careful study of God's Word. I will tackle this enormous issue by illustrating a potential counseling situation.

A person walks into my counseling office and begins to share the following symptoms:

- He is having intrusive thoughts about losing his salvation.
- He experiences intense guilt when he commits common offenses such as going one mile-per-hour over the speed limit or failure to turn on a blinker when changing lanes on the highway. He obsesses over this offense and repeatedly begs God to forgive him.
- He fears God is angry with him and is going to abandon him.
- He spends hours a day performing compulsive acts of penance for his sins as a means to alleviate his obsessive guilt.
- He suffers from constant anxiety.
- He suffers from severe depression due to his inability to perfectly please God.
- He has been diagnosed with obsessive-compulsive disorder (OCD) by a psychiatrist, and has been on medication for years. He experiences positive changes initially, but over time, the obsessions and compulsions return. As a result, two months ago he decided to cease all medical treatment as he believes it has proven ineffective.

Is it imperative to rely on secular theory or research to effectively counsel this individual biblically? Please note the word *imperative* as it is a dividing line when it comes to a proper understanding of sufficiency of Scripture. In my view and experience, the answer to the above question is no. I do *not* believe it is imperative to consult secular research in order to address this person's underlying symptoms or to counsel him.

Nonetheless, would I consult research literature from the secular community as a means to better understand the physiological and sociological aspects that might be at play here? I certainly would. I recognize that such consultation will provide important data to consider in my efforts to counsel this individual wisely.

Although it does not use the modern term, the Bible addresses complex diagnoses such as that of OCD. The Scriptures are very clear that people's hearts are deceitful and therefore produce inaccurate thoughts, beliefs, fears, desires, perceptions, and more (Isaiah 55:8–9; Jeremiah 17:9; Romans 1:18–23; 1 Corinthians 13:12; Ephesians 4:22). People have an innate propensity to rely on their own reason or experience to formulate their concepts of reality, all the while rejecting the reality set forth by God's wisdom. The person in the case study above is doing the same thing. He is relying on his own reason, shaped by mistrust and perpetuated by futile, compulsive rituals. In the process, he is rejecting actual reality constructed by the gospel of Jesus Christ, and he is therefore missing the peace Christ brings. His own physiological experience of anxiety and his faith in his own system of redemption are usurping reality set forth by God.

Now, as I am helping this person, I understand that there may be something physiological that makes his challenge to believe truth more difficult than mine. Something in his brain may reinforce his tendency to ruminate on fearful obsessions. Yet, I also seek to instill hope that God's faithfulness in the midst of my counselee's weakness is his greatest refuge for solace, not his own ability to obliterate his obsessions (though I also believe the Spirit will assist him in this goal as well).

One aspect of counseling will aim to help him accept the fact that the very sin for which he is trying to compensate via penance is actually far more invasive and expansive than an occasional moral failure. It is an infectious virus that will perpetually influence him to believe lies. Only within this narrative will his obsessive fears be understood for what they really are—deceitful cognitions produced and shaped by a flesh that will always resist God.

Paul, in Ephesians 2, explains that God alone can rescue people from spiritual death caused by sin. People in the state of spiritual death are not longing for God nor do they have the ability to do so (Matthew 11:27). They are not concerned about pleasing God, and they cannot see their need for him (Romans 3:11–18). This is encouraging news for my counselee struggling with OCD. If he is genuinely longing to honor God in his conduct, then those longings have emerged due to a sovereign work of redemption in his life. His dead heart has literally been resurrected by grace, and he now possesses longings to please God. Without the Lord working in his life, such longings would not be present. If he is wrestling to please God then he is doing so with a heart made alive by God. He must accept that his good conduct did not get him into the door of relationship with God; rather, it was God alone who initiated this loving process.

Accepting this truth will also be a divine work of the Holy Spirit. Freedom comes as this counselee experiences his helplessness so that he might rest in the loving, faithful work of his Redeemer. As his counselor, I must encourage him, by grace, to accept the inspired words Paul wrote, "So then it depends not on human will or exertion, but on God, who has mercy" (Romans 9:16). As things stand in the counselee's current state, part of his problem is that he has made God very small and his own self-designed plan of salvation very, very big.

This counselee may offer a rebuttal by arguing, "OK, I can accept that God made me alive, but what if I commit a sin that causes him to reject me—you know, the unpardonable sin." Well, the Bible is sufficient to answer this deceitful obsession too. Jesus declared, "All that the Father gives me will come to me, and whoever comes to me I will never cast out. For I have come down from heaven, not to do my own will but the will of him who sent me. And this is the will of him who sent me, that I should lose nothing of all that he has given me, but raise it up on the last day" (John 6:37–39).

Jesus issues strong all-or-nothing statements. Whoever has been given to Jesus will come to him. Whoever comes to Jesus will never be cast out. It is God's will that of all who have come to him none will be lost. Jesus promises to consummate his act of faithfulness in that those who were given to him in eternity past will be raised up on the last day to be with him forever in eternity future. In the mind of God, actualities of the predestined, called, justified, and glorified are already complete—irreversible (Romans 8:30). In the heavenly places, God's redemptive work is done—it is finished. Overcome by these glorious truths, Paul responded, "If God is for us, who can be against us?" (Romans 8:31b).

Additionally, since the counselee is genuinely concerned about committing the unpardonable sin against God, his worry is evidence that he has been made alive by God's mercy. He may take comfort in this since unregenerate hearts do not seek after God nor are they concerned about committing an unpardonable sin against him (Romans 3:10). Louis Berkhof has written,

> In those who have committed this sin we may therefore expect to find a pronounced hatred to God, a defiant attitude to Him and all that is divine, delight in ridiculing and slandering that which is holy, and absolute unconcern respecting the welfare of their soul and the future life. In view of the fact that this sin is not followed by repentance, we may be reasonably sure that they who fear that they have committed it and worry about this, and who desire the prayers of others for them, have not committed it.[19]

OCD often consists of a complex labyrinth of thoughts, beliefs, and rituals in which a significant underlying motive is control. People who struggle with OCD may tell themselves, *If I can just stop these intrusive doubts, then I can experience security in God. If I can manage my sin better I will be acceptable to God, and therefore never be rejected. If I repent passionately enough and often enough, I will experience assurance in my salvation. If I wash my hands enough, I will rid myself of germs.* These thoughts and rituals dictate the conditions of safety and security and form a reality in which neither will ever be achieved. It matters not whether the obsession is fear of losing one's salvation, fear of germs, hoarding, or any other obsessive manifestation, each resides in the illusion that control will guarantee a sense of emotional peace and security. The illusion of power in control dominates and destroys.

The gospel message will rush in upon these lies and offer a powerful alternative rooted in God, exposing helplessness and centering this counselee in the fact that control is a commodity beyond his grasp. Salvation is not to earn and control but a gift that believers humbly accept. Persevering in these truths will be imperative since the counselee's mind, with these tendencies, will not give up the lies easily (even if he genuinely desires to do so). The good news is that Jesus, by grace, is working in the counselee so that he will become zealous in participating in good works (Titus 2:11–14). This is a supernatural phenomenon. Such works would consist, in part, of Jesus personally helping the counselee believe the truths of the Bible rather than the deception of his heart. Patience, prayer, and unending encouragement will need to be steady companions.

While a plethora of other truths will inform my work with this counselee, to cover them all in detail would require an entire book. The following truths are a few to consider:

- The Bible is sufficient to gain understanding about God. What is the counselee's view of God? Does he conceptualize God through projections of his own father (who may have been emotionally distant, angry, demanding, or abusive)? Or, does the counselee conceptualize God as he has revealed himself in the Bible? Offering this counselee truth from Scripture here will be vital. If I want to encourage trust in God, I must help him construct a biblical view of God.

- The Bible is sufficient to help me partly understand the inner workings of the counselee's heart. He likely covets control. Coveting is a component of motivation. If the counselee continues to do this, it will only further corrupt his soul (Ephesians 4:22). This is a matter of worship. I would want to patiently hear his life story and consider if there are any significant events that may have shaped a perceived need for control. Issues of abandonment, rejection, or trauma may be variables. I would listen compassionately to his life story and refuse to minimize his painful experiences. In time, I would help him learn that these events shaped his struggle, but did not cause them (Mark 7:21–23; James 1:13–15).

- The Bible is sufficient to assist me in understanding my role in the process of helping. I will take seriously my call to "bear one another's burdens" (Galatians 6:2) and will love and encourage the counselee as my brother. I will incarnate the faithfulness of Jesus in my relationship with him no matter how difficult the path toward healing may become.

- The Bible is sufficient to reveal that the Holy Spirit is committed to producing alternative desires in his heart that glorify God (Romans 8:5–8).

- The Bible is sufficient to provide me understanding about living by faith. The counselee's obsessions and compulsions are not necessarily going to disappear. Intrusive thoughts may be a part of his life for some time. My role as counselor is to help him learn experientially what it means to walk in faith, "the assurance of things hoped for, the conviction of things not seen" (Hebrews 11:1). Walking in faith provides a freedom from feeling threatened when obsessive fears present themselves.

- The Bible is sufficient to offer biblical methods of change. By grace, the counselee will need to pray for the ability to comprehend and exercise the instructions and principles of Scripture as they pertain to his struggle (Deuteronomy 8; Ephesians 4:22–24; Colossians 3; Titus 2:11–14).

- The Bible offers effective principles such as sowing and reaping to apply to the counselee's thought life as well as to his desires. His job is to wait and trust God for the ultimate harvest (Galatians 6:7–8).

- The Bible offers sufficient truth to help the counselee trust the sovereign work and timetable of God in healing him in this process (Galatians 6:9).

- The Bible is sufficient to develop a gospel-centered definition of healing that is captured in an abiding faith in the trustworthiness of God for salvation and transformation. A mind that believes and loves God in the midst of suffering is a mind that reflects mental healing (2 Corinthians 12:9–10). Healing will not necessarily mean my counselee's obsessions will forever be gone. The battle of the flesh and Spirit will rage on in some form (Galatians 5:16–17).

- The Bible offers sufficient truth to help the counselee replace the objectives of becoming acceptable via his rituals or ridding himself of obsessions. A robust theology of suffering understands that despite this person's struggle, the Father has designed a profound redemptive plan (Hebrews 12:7–10; James 1:2–4). Maybe the symptoms are a necessary part of his redemptive story.

- The Bible offers sufficient truth to help this counselee rest in the freedom of the gospel and not in his ability to execute biblical methods or free himself from symptoms (Galatians 5:1–12).
- The Bible is sufficient to expose sin that is driving the counselee's thoughts (Hebrews 4:12).
- The Bible offers sufficient truth to help the counselee learn to live with and address the noise of the flesh that manifests in deceitful thoughts. He can learn to squelch these thoughts from his mind with the beautiful melodies of the gospel.

These truths and more from Scripture have provided amazing help and healing to many I have counseled who were diagnosed with OCD. Most of the time, these truths have equipped counselees to live fruitful, joyous lives.

The Bible offers sufficient revelation to do great good to the soul tormented by obsessive worries, issues of control, and relentless fear. It comprehensively informs why the person is obsessing, how to address such obsessions, and with what expectations to engage the process of change. Biblical counseling purposes to pursue change that transcends the temporal alleviation of symptoms. The wealth of wisdom it possesses about the human soul far exceeds any theoretical model produced by man. While the Bible does not cover every mental disorder cited in the *Diagnostic and Statistical Manual of Mental Disorders*, learning to conceptualize these descriptive categories from a biblical vantage point is an imperative task for the provider of Christian soul care.

This approach relieves the tension between utilizing God's Word as my conceptual lens and my choice to consult outside scientific literature on OCD. My embrace of the sufficiency of Scripture does not forbid me to engage and utilize the secular research, nor does it hold that the Bible is exhaustive on every issue relevant to counseling. As a matter of fact, the Bible tells me that all things exist for the service of God (Psalm 119:91), and it is my duty as a Christian to utilize all God's gifts to love my neighbor. Scripture proclaims God's common grace in that even in sin, man continues to demonstrate aspects of God's wisdom and insight. God's common grace rests on all people to some degree (Acts 14:16–17).

As I peruse the literature, much of the data may have to be rejected or require significant reinterpretation, but much of it will prove quite helpful. Biblical counselors seek "to hold faithfully to the categories of biblical truth *and* to grow case-wise about diverse human beings."[20] This approach substantiates a very specific view of the sufficiency of Scripture that allows for interaction with outside sources in the pursuit of understanding people while biblical categories drive such interaction. Interaction with psychological research requires the skilled biblical counselor to appreciate, redeem, and reframe "the culture of even the most godless men and women."[21]

This task is impossible if one does not first possess a robust theology of care formulated from the Bible alone. Licensed Psychologist Dr. Stephen Farra poses the following, "A question to those who say they want to practice a Christian psychology: Instead of starting with a Freudian, Jungian, Skinnerian, or Rogerian model, and then trying oh-so-hard (yet, oh-so-ineffectively) to adapt it to Christian practice, why not start with the biblical understanding of the human being, and then look for and develop methods of therapy, guidance, and counseling built upon this foundation?"[22]

I could not agree more. In order to accomplish this, however, Christian psychology, theology, and counseling departments will need to require more practical theology courses within their programs to ensure they are offering the world a psychology that is distinctively biblical in application. This is the only way Christians will wisely engage the vast amounts of secular literature at their fingertips.

It is common knowledge that a person does not learn to identify a counterfeit by studying counterfeits but by becoming an expert in identifying the original. The original and authentic source to understand the soul (the psyche) is Scripture. Any and all attempts to define humanity without this source as the starting point and authority is an undeniable counterfeit. It is my deep conviction that to become a wise interpreter of secular psychological data requires becoming a wise student of the Bible and all that it offers pertaining to the disciplines that the culture refers to as counseling and psychology.

Johnson references something similar in his analysis of this issue. He recommends that Christian psychologists "should use *all* the means at their disposal that will yield the greatest amount of relevant information about individual human beings, regardless of their previous assignment to a separate discipline," and he warns that such a process is "a *discipline-in-constituting* activity, rather than a post-hoc activity conducted after psychology has already been formed (by modernism)."[23] The biblical counselors' task, should they choose to survey the research, is to ensure that biblical presuppositions regarding human nature, motivation, and change serve as their interpretive lens in considering such extra-biblical data—not the other way around.

Biblical Reliance: Propositional vs. Functional

It is important for counselors to assess their hearts regarding their functional worldviews. For Christians, their epistemological allegiances will determine their understanding of people and problems. The following questions may promote honest self-assessment:

1. When working with individuals with complex issues cited by psychiatry such as OCD, bipolar disorder, or ADHD, what determines your view of such a person's fundamental nature and struggle? Is your first consideration that which is asserted by research and theory or by what the Bible claims about humanity?

2. Is your model of counseling dominated by theoretical assumptions or theological truth? Who has more to offer as it regards psychology, human motivation, and the process of change: Rogers, Ellis, Madanes, the scientific researcher, or Jesus? To whom do you turn when seeking to understand people fundamentally?

3. Do you possess a rich theology of human motivation derived from the Bible?

4. Do you possess a rich theology of human change derived from the Bible?

5. Do you possess a rich theology of human nature derived from the Bible?

6. If there were no extra-biblical data offered in psychology (theory and research) regarding relational, emotional, and mental problems, have you developed a system of theology that would effectively address these issues? Would you be able to offer more than a verse and a prayer?

7. As a counselor, psychologist, or psychiatrist are you more competent in applying theoretical methods informed by secular models than you are the truths of the Bible as they apply to mental, emotional, and relational problems?

8. When seeking to become a better counselor, psychologist or psychiatrist, which of these excites you most: growing in your wisdom of Scripture as it applies to the practical struggles of life or reading the latest book on psychology?

9. Which is more reliable in diagnosing human dysfunction: the Bible or the *DSM*? Which of these do you rely on most to understand those you serve?

10. How much training have you had in richly applying the Bible to the myriad of psychological issues present within the culture and world?

These ten questions help me often as I continue to develop as a counselor. They keep me grounded, and always remind me, amid the vast literature in my field, where my foundation lies when it comes to understanding people.

I believe biblical counselors have a long way to go in helping people understand the categories of the sufficiency of Scripture and integration in a manner that is balanced and well informed. I experienced this firsthand in my own doctoral study. I do not underestimate the importance of this discussion, but I now realize I held assumptions about both biblical counselors (which I am) and Christian psychologists that were not altogether accurate. I was operating from a fairly entrenched, naïve bias. I believe counselors are all susceptible to the same mistake. This bias leads to creating and perpetuating unnecessary caricatures of those who do not fit in a particular camp.

I also believe biblical counselors have much work ahead to prepare future counselors for operating from a rich biblical framework. Counselors, psychologists, psychiatrists, pastors, or soul care workers within the body of Christ, may often propositionally believe Scripture is superior, but what is the case functionally in their work and practice? According to Drs. Ron Hawkins, Ed Hindson, and Tim Clinton of Liberty University, "Christian counseling is deficient in its theological roots and spiritual practices."[24] May biblical counselors take this assessment seriously, and for God's glory, do their part to stem this tide and seek to shape the future of Christian soul care by making the comprehensive, robust nature of the Bible the center of all they do in both their professed propositions and their functional practices.

Counseling Considerations

1. Most important, be a diligent, passionate student of God's Word—the Bible. You identify counterfeit not by studying counterfeits but by becoming a scholar of truth.

2. Reread the questions in "Biblical Reliance: Proposition vs. Functional" in this chapter. How do you measure up to these questions? Consider classes or training that may help you become more reliant on Scripture in your counseling practices. The Association of Biblical Counselors' certification process would serve this purpose well. You may find out more on ABC's training by visiting www.christiancounseling.com.

3. Read a good systematic theology book and take notes on the following questions:

4. How does God actively operate in the life of the believer?

5. How do themes of redemption (creation, fall, redemption) apply to your counselees' specific issues?

6. What theological ideas can you develop and apply in a practical way?

7. Who is man? How does this book inform my view of human nature?

8. What is the process of change? What are the elements of such change? How is God involved in such change?

9. How might I apply these truths in a counseling context?
10. Do you feel equipped to read secular literature and interpret it from a biblical reference point? How might you enhance your skills in this regard?
11. When you are assessing and conceptualizing a counselee's issues or situation, learn to ask the question, *what does my theology say?*
12. Seek to build authentic friendships with colleagues outside your camp. Refuse to restrict your friends to those who celebrate your ideas. Find other believers with differing views regarding Christian soul care and engage in honest, respectful conversations—even on the most dividing issues. This will help you grow in your own thoughts while potentially protecting you from debating truth from the perspective of caricatures.

RESOURCES FOR FURTHER STUDY

~ Hindson, Ed, and Howard Eyrich. *Totally Sufficient: The Bible and Christian Counseling.* Great Britain: Christian Focus, 2004.
~ Johnson, Eric. *Foundations of Soul Care.* Downers Grove, IL: IVP Academic, 2007.
~ Johnson, Eric. *Psychology and Christianity: Five Views.* Downers Grove, IL: IVP Academic, 2010.
~ Powlison, David. "Critique of Modern Integrationists." *Journal of Biblical Counseling* 11, no. 3, (1993): 24–34.
~ Powlison, David. "How Do You Help a 'Psychologized' Counselee?" *Journal of Biblical Counseling* 15, no. 1 (1996): 2–7.

CHAPTER SIXTEEN

. . . .

THE ROAD AHEAD

These times are so hard, and it's getting even harder. —Eminem[1]

The needs of our world call for true spiritual warfare to be reclaimed.
—David Powlison[2]

Everyone, even the secularist, operates from a particular theology—a specific belief system about God. While the counseling wars of the 70s and 80s consisted primarily of debates regarding the sufficiency of Scripture and integration—debates essential to biblical counseling—the emphasis that all counselors must first develop a robust theology was sparse. Theological understanding was certainly a major highlight of the formal biblical counseling movement, but within the broader disciplines of Christian soul care (Christian psychology and Christian counseling) a focus on theology was not adequately emphasized.

I witnessed the fruit of this oversight while participating on a panel at a recent national conference hosted by one of the most established professional organizations within Christian soul care. During the Q&A portion of the presentation, one of the attendees—a professor of psychology at a very prominent evangelical university—raised her hand, and with concerned voice noted, "It is very difficult to utilize Scripture in counseling courses because the vast majority of my counseling students have an elementary understanding of theology at best." Counseling and psychology students attending a Christian university or seminary are often faced with one of two crises:

1. The degree program does not emphasize expertise in theology, but rather focuses on counseling or psychology courses required by the state for licensure.
2. If theology is stressed it occurs within the theology department, leaving a massive disconnect on how such theology applies to the counseling experience.

To offer a form of Christian counseling or psychology that most genuinely honors Scripture, anyone entering these fields must first become a wise theologian while simultaneously connecting such theology to the counseling process. Becoming a wise practitioner of care does not begin with learning secular theory or honing one's skills in reading the research literature. The process of integration becomes a dangerous practice when conducted by a theologically anemic person. Those offering Christian care need to develop a robust theological framework— of God, man, motivation, change, suffering, abnormal psychology, and relationships—before attempting integration. Only with such a foundation are people competent to consider complex secular data.

As licensed professionals, counselors' ethics require adequate training in order to offer help in a specialized area. If the profession requires special training and competence in areas such as trauma, eating disorders, obsessive-compulsive disorders and the myriad of psychiatric labels, should biblical counselors not be even more diligent in becoming competent stewards of Scripture if they choose to offer counsel under the name of Christianity? I believe there is no other way if they are seeking to honor God and love people well.

The Church, the Counselor, and the Rise of Secularism

Proposing theological truth for the purpose of counseling creates occasion for significant controversy. Secularism exerts a tyrannical hold on the fields of counseling, psychology, and social work. Theoretical assumptions, empirical investigation, and ethical guidelines are ruled by secular thought. A humanistic worldview births a form of relativism centered in the values of the subjective self. Self is now the accepted social measure of right and wrong, and this has profoundly changed the cultural ethos within the United States.

One of the most seismic shifts in Western culture has recently been witnessed in the Supreme Court's ruling on same-sex marriage. The broader issue of homosexuality is undergoing a radical social transformation among the perspectives of Americans that will present new challenges to Christians seeking to minister biblically.

This single issue exposes a critical need for biblical counselors within the church. For decades, Christians have embraced the notion that trained professionals are necessary for people seeking to receive any form of in-depth psychological care. There is a crisis brewing in this arena, however, and Christian professionals are now being challenged on complicated moral issues.

Laws are currently being passed in various states that prohibit licensed professionals from counseling minors who identify as homosexual, unless their counsel embraces the person's homosexuality. Imagine a sixteen-year-old Christian male who comes to a counselor in California seeking help handling this struggle while honoring his faith, which views homosexuality as sin. The counselor is not allowed to offer counsel that would coincide with such a young man's faith. It is illegal to counsel him on resisting such urges, even if this is his desperate desire. Instead, the practitioner may only provide counseling that teaches the young man to accept and embrace who he is at his core—a homosexual. Only gay affirmative therapy is permitted. While this law exists in only a handful of states, it seems inevitable that it will become the law of the land very soon.

While not a national law, the American Psychological Association, the American Counseling Association and the American Psychiatric Association have all formulated public stances supporting only gay affirmative therapies while ascribing to the idea that any therapeutic intervention that does not affirm one's homosexual identity is potentially dangerous and damaging to the client. Should this stance become law in all fifty states, then many individuals currently licensed may face enormous ethical challenges—keep the license and honor the ethic of gay affirmative only counseling or terminate the license and continue to provide biblical help to those struggling with homosexuality? While other options may emerge, there is no doubt an increasing complexity will develop as Christians seek to navigate their way through a thoroughly secular field.

Where will believers go if pressure mounts for Christian professionals to exclusively provide gay affirmative treatment? Hopefully,
believers within the field would hold their ground and refuse to
provide such treatment. However, should they choose to keep their
license while seeking to adhere to biblical teaching, their hands will
be tied. Their mouths will be silenced as it regards biblically helping
people who struggle with homosexuality. Sadly, this is not the only
issue where Christians will face hardline resistance. I anticipate resistance on many fronts simply because we choose to uphold the Bible
as the sacred Word of God.

Should this scenario transpire, the only place a person will be
able to receive authentic biblical ministry on such an issue is the
church. Cultural trends may very well force Christians back to their
roots where soul care was a familiar form of ministry among believers. The providence of God in allowing these societal transformations
may serve to nudge the church to once again be the church. All
believers should ask themselves, "Am I prepared to help my neighbor
apply Scripture in a helpful and meaningful way when it comes to
significant relational, emotional, and mental difficulties?" Ironically,
the church may be finding itself again forced to answer the same call
elicited by Boisen more than eighty years ago:

> It seems truly an astounding situation that a group of suf-
> ferers larger than that to be found in all other hospitals put
> together, a group whose difficulties seem to lie for the most
> part in the realm of character rather than in that of organic dis-
> ease, should be so neglected by the church. Notwithstanding
> the fact that the church has always been interested in the
> care of the sick and that the Protestant churches of America
> have been supporting 380 or more hospitals, they are giving
> scarcely any attention to the maladies of the mind.[3]

Thankfully, God has used various ministries to spur on biblical
counseling, and the church is further down the road than it was when
Boisen initially penned these words. Yet, there is still much to be done,
and it will take committed believers from all denominations to walk in
their roles as disciple-makers to apply the truth of God's Word faithfully, thoughtfully, and prayerfully to the broken hearts around them.

Broadening Our International Reach

While it is imperative that Christians wisely address issues within the Western culture, it is equally imperative to recognize the amazing opportunities and challenges in other countries as well. One of the most heartbreaking realities I have encountered in recent years is that the modernist influence of the West has now infiltrated every corner of the globe. As my colleagues and I have traveled to places like Zambia, Sudan, Russia, Mexico, and India, we have witnessed the titanic influence of Western secular psychology upon the citizens of these and other countries. I was taken aback when I was told that the dominant theoretical model in many South American countries is Freud's psychoanalysis. Secularism in the form of psychological orthodoxy is on the move and the most viable alternative to materialist dogmatism is biblical truth. As biblical counselors consider their roles and purposes, they cannot limit their mission to the United States alone. They cannot rest in their own comforts while people around the world are being indoctrinated by humanistic ideology as the means to care for their ailing souls. Just imagine the implications of missionaries being trained in biblical counseling, and the impact it would have on the regions to which they have been called.

The Association of Biblical Counselors (ABC) witnessed this critical need when some of its friends and representatives began traveling to Zambia, Africa to train pastors and laity in the ministry of biblical counseling. The primary options with which the wonderful people of Zambia were most familiar to address the traumatic issues they were facing (such as murder, rape, incest, and death from HIV) were either the heretical teachings of the prosperity movement, the spiritual approaches of native shamanism, or secular psychology. These precious people were starving for an answer that adequately met the deep needs of their wounded souls, and they were left wanting—that is until they learned how the riches of Scripture apply to their most difficult emotional, mental, and relational traumas.

Today, hundreds of individuals in Zambia have been trained in biblical counseling through ABC's initiative, Equip the Nations. ABC has helped equip Zambians to replace the empty self-help models of the West with a God-glorifying approach that encourages them to locate their experiences within the narrative of redemption. Where there was once hopelessness and purposelessness in their sufferings, the people of Zambia are learning to rest in the amazing grace of God as he works personally and intimately in the midst of their circumstances to bring about the beauty of his will in their lives.

ABC has not only witnessed this powerful work in Zambia but in various countries around the globe. As it forges ahead in its mission, it continues to ask how its message will translate to the unique struggles of brothers and sisters who reside around the world. How will it work to equip others in a manner that is sensitive to specific cultural norms? Conversely, how will it compassionately address cultural norms that do not square with Scripture? How will it challenge itself to create resources that most effectively suit the people it is ministering to? Advancing its message to others across the globe is an extremely exciting opportunity, and it will require ABC (and all biblical counselors) to image God creatively as it seeks to serve others for the sake of his eternal glory.

Spiritual Warfare

When they choose to minister in parts of the world where spirituality has been a major thread in the culture's fabric, biblical counselors must be mindful of how modernism has influenced them unaware. Biblical counselors must be careful not to minimize the unseen spiritual realities. This will require theological balance and cautious aversion to extremes.

Biblical counselors must resist the extreme idea that spiritual warfare requires the dramatic. It is not evidenced in a person's head rotating 360 degrees when Scripture is being read or by holy water being an essential tool to drive out an unwanted spirit. Biblical counselors will discard the notion that a cross is needed to ward off a stubborn demon or that exorcism must be performed by specialized priests who have at their disposal an anointed manual to exorcise the demonic. Hollywood will not serve as a reference point in conceptualizing spiritual warfare.

On the other hand, biblical counselors will avoid concluding that demonic activity is a thing of the past. Biblical counselors will discerningly resist the notion that all manifestations of psychosis are exclusively explained by bio-physiological malfunctions. Instead, they will leave room for the possibility of spiritual influence on such behavior. Biblical counselors will heed the words of Peter who warned, "Be sober-minded; be watchful. Your adversary the devil prowls around like a roaring lion, seeking someone to devour" (1 Peter 5:8). Biblical counselors will also embrace the wisdom of Paul who wrote, "Finally, be strong in the Lord and in the strength of his might. Put on the whole armor of God, that you may be able to stand against the schemes of the devil. For we do not wrestle against flesh and blood, but against the rulers against the authorities, against the cosmic powers over this present darkness, against spiritual forces of evil in the heavenly places" (Ephesians 6:10–12).

Spiritual warfare is a pervasive reality of the human experience. Demons exist. Satan is real. A dark agenda seeks to destroy. David Powlison brilliantly articulates, "Christians—in fact all human beings—take sides in a world war. God and God's people face off against adversaries in this world under malign spiritual rule. This world war had a beginning, has a middle, and will have an end. We are now in the midst of a fire fight. We are 'in action,' actors in the theater of war."[4]

Moving forward, I believe it would be helpful for individuals within biblical counseling to create resources that outline practical approaches to engage in spiritual warfare—resources that uphold biblical orthodoxy. In other words, as the movement spans the globe, biblical counselors need resources that will help educate those in other countries to embrace a view of spiritual warfare that reflects biblical teaching while not minimizing the significance of spiritual realities in specific cultures.

Pursuing Collaboration in Christian Soul Care

Ongoing interaction with experts who span the spectrum of Christian soul care sparked the idea for this book. While conducting research, I was given the opportunity to converse with many colleagues both within and outside the formal biblical counseling movement. Some exchanges were more challenging than others, but overall, every exchange was fruitful. Where there was agreement, I was encouraged in my position. Where there was disagreement I had the opportunity to grow in my understanding and perspectives.

Through this experience, I learned that one of the greatest antidotes to unfair caricatures is building relationship with others who do not necessarily hold my views. I gleaned wisdom from many who disagree with me, and my correspondence with them tended to promote a new humility as well as a genuine respect for many of their thoughtful perspectives. Something I appreciated most about every participant in my study was the deep love for God and the church they each exhibited.

There will always be differences in approaches and perspectives within the arena of Christian soul care. Some of these differences are significant and will likely be irreconcilable. However, I believe that among the diversity of individuals on the spectrum of soul care, many possess nuggets of wisdom and knowledge within their respected disciplines that may sharpen others. I hope everyone will be open where such openness is appropriate. I was certainly refined as I engaged with individuals holding differing opinions. Humility does not require compromise. It simply affords the opportunity to love others well even in the face of disagreement. Loving interaction exhibits something divine to others. Whether it is the watching world or a newcomer to Christian soul care, how counselors interact with one another matters. Honest, respectful dialogue is profoundly important as counselors grow in their development as professionals and Christians.

Upholding the Splendor of God's Word

God's Word contains everything humanity needs for life and godliness. The God of Scripture has counseled humankind since creation, and he has chosen to speak into the universe through the prophets, disciples, the apostles, and his own incarnation. Jesus made himself nothing and entered the fractured mess of the world, and he has given people record of his life and revelations in the Scripture. No book, no empirical discovery, no theoretical idea, no human method will ever hold a candle to the radiance that shines forth from Scripture as it pertains to the human experience. My prayer is that pastors, parishioners, and professionals within the body of Christ would aim to become wiser stewards of God's Word as it applies to the mental, emotional, and relational maladies of others.

The Bible is relevant to the questions of psychology: Who are people? Why do they do the things they do? How do they change? Until counselors seek to answer these questions from the perspective of Scripture, I do not think they are well equipped to consider ideas proposed outside its sacred pages—ideas that are extra-biblical in nature. My prayer is that biblical counselors will always prioritize becoming wise stewards of God's Word, and that they will relentlessly seek to grow in applying what they learn to the here and now realities of life—both to others and to themselves. There are many competing voices within the culture that oppose biblical truth. The church needs believers who are able to offer wise and gentle alternatives to these voices that resonate with the deep afflictions and besetting sins of those within the family of God. God has spoken, and what he has said matters. This has been the primary presupposition of biblical counseling since its inception, and may it continue to be its resounding anthem forevermore.

Appendix A

Biblical Counseling and the Non-Christian[1]

As I speak throughout the country, one of the most common questions I receive is, How does this biblical counseling thing work when the counselee does not profess faith in Jesus? Scripture speaks to this matter. One of the greatest privileges biblical counselors receive is when God brings non-believers into their counseling office.

When counseling non-Christians, remember that this relationship did not happen by accident. God has sovereignly orchestrated the encounter. Therefore, biblical counselors will not minimize what God may be doing in the individual's life, but they will view it as an opportunity to extend the gospel creatively throughout the counseling experience.

This interaction with a non-Christian is a situation where the counselee is actually brushing up against the edges of God's kingdom through the counseling conversation. Who biblical counselors are and what they say throughout the counseling process may be the closest a counselee comes to experiencing the love and wisdom of God. Biblical counselors will seek to walk within the tension of human responsibility and God's sovereignty. Christians have a responsibility to bring forth the gospel in their relationship with counselees, but counselors must also submit to the reality that only God has the power to give people "eyes to see" and "ears to hear" (Matthew 13:10–17).

Walking in Wisdom with an Unbeliever

Paul offers the following instruction regarding non-Christians, "Walk in wisdom toward outsiders, making the best use of the time. Let your speech always be gracious, seasoned with salt, so that you may know how you ought to answer each person" (Colossians 4:5–6). One of the best uses of time with unbelievers is to listen well. Through listening, counselors are able to enter in to the particular turmoil of counselees and understand how the gospel is relevant to the particular pain that they experience. This is a time to consider counselees more significant than oneself (Philippians 2:3). This is a time to hear the wounded state of another and ask the question, "How might I speak into this with gracious, redemptive words?" This will look differently than it would with a Christian because the unbeliever has not yet embraced Jesus and the gospel.

For example, Ken is a thirty-two-year-old man who has realized how his bitterness and lack of forgiveness toward his mother seems to shape some of his interactions with his wife. His best friend (who is a believer) recommended that Ken seek out biblical counseling since it might shed a different light on his struggle than what he has thus far been exposed to in secular therapy. Ken's previous therapist tended to focus excessively on how his relationship with his mom has impacted him, but Ken was given little, if any, direction on what to do about it. Ken is now seeking help in another direction.

Ken begins the first session by sharing his story, that of a young boy raised in an authoritarian home where his parents (especially mom) were profoundly overbearing, critical to the point of abuse, and hypervigilant in following the rules of their faith. Ken hardly remembers any nurturing from his mother, only persistent demands to live for Jesus with a cold demeanor of disgust when he expressed any interest in things like baseball or movies. Ken's mother was so opposed to anything outside the church that she and Ken's father withheld any financial support for him to pursue college (though they were very wealthy) because they did not want him exposed to the filth taught and experienced in higher education. This left Ken to find a career on his own where he has been able to work his way up the ladder in the corporate world. While he has a sense of accomplishment for his successes, he is also bearing the weight of some major marital problems. Currently, Ken's wife has separated from him, citing that his constant criticism and anger are more than she can bear. At this point, Ken is so overwhelmed with emotion that he breaks down in tears and is almost inconsolable.

To make the most use of my initial meeting with Ken, it is extremely important that I connect with him in his current sorrow. Personally, I deeply respect and marvel that he has sought out a person of faith when his experience with Christianity has been so traumatic. This must have taken extreme courage, and I want to be very sensitive to his past experience as we move forward. Speaking gracious words seasoned with salt might sound something like this:

- Ken, it is very clear you are in tremendous pain, and I will do my best to walk with you in this difficult season of your life.
- Ken, from your perspective it sounds like Mom was really tough on you and used her Christianity as a way to control you. Tell me more about this experience.
- Ken, tell me more about the pain you're experiencing because of your wife leaving you.
- Ken, you made it very clear that you do not pursue God in your struggles. Does your past influence this decision, and if so, how?
- Ken, how do you best think I can serve you?

If counselors succumb to the Western evangelical pressure to immediately ask the question, If you died today, do you know how you would enter the kingdom of God? it might feel like a cheap, insensitive "quick fix" to the counselee. To rush in with a call to repentance could unintentionally mirror the feel Ken had with his legalistic mother. As a counselor, I would want to ensure that Ken brushes up against the kingdom through our conversation and that he experiences a genuine love and compassion for his current situation. All the while, I will be praying that the Holy Spirit would soften Ken's heart and provide opportunity through our growing relationship to speak more overtly about how God and his gospel weigh in on Ken's devastating pain.

Respond with Humility, Gentleness, Kindness, Respect, and Grace

My hope is not only that I would be used as an instrument of grace in Ken's life, but that he would also be used as an instrument of grace in mine. Working with an unbeliever who is feeling the blows of living in a fallen world is a profound context for humility. Ken's current predicament is a reminder that outside of God's amazing grace, I, too, would be enslaved by resentment, bitterness, an unforgiving spirit, and hopelessness (or worse). It reminds me of Paul's teaching in Titus where he says, "For we ourselves were once foolish, disobedient, led astray, slaves to various passions and pleasures, passing our days in malice and envy, hated by others and hating one another. But when the goodness and loving kindness of God our Savior appeared, he saved us, not because of works done by us in righteousness, but according to his own mercy" (Titus 3:3–5a).

As I recall my own heart prior to Jesus, I am prepared to counsel Ken lovingly as a fellow human created in the image of God. My attitude will reflect kindness, courtesy, and respect. My conversation with Ken during our first meeting should engender empathy for someone, who in many ways, is just like me.

As counseling progresses and we begin to explore the specifics of his struggles in a more detailed manner, I may experience resistance, even anger, from Ken. When we press into his resentment, Ken may respond with more exaggerated anger. Our conversation may look something like this:

> *Counselor:* Ken, you have made it clear that you believe you harbor major resentment against your mother, yet you also know this needs to change. What resentments do you need to release?
>
> *Ken:* Don't start preaching at me! I know it's wrong for me to feel resentment toward my mother, but you know what, she deserves it. You Christians are nothing but a bunch of self-righteous lunatics. I'm not sure this is the right place for me!
>
> *Counselor:* Ken, I know we are nearing some painful places in your heart when it comes to considering forgiveness,

and I know that a part of that struggle is that forgiveness is associated with Christian teaching—something you have historically experienced as oppressive and judgmental. I am also aware that you know I am a Christian, and I take this into consideration for you. Rather than push you to forgive, I want to be respectful with your current state of being. Why was my initial question about letting go of resentments so provoking for you? It is clear that was a difficult question to start with today.

Responding in this manner, as a Christian, pushes against the legalism with which Ken was raised. Rather than drop a list of dos and don'ts on Ken, I stay engaged with what brought him to counseling in the first place. He is in pain. Whereas his comments were actually pretty judgmental, I do not respond in like manner or feel the need to be defensive. I patiently and gently continue my journey into Ken's broken heart.[2] This approach is also exercising an abiding trust in the Holy Spirit in that, as I engage with Ken, I know the Spirit will be the one to change Ken's heart, and the Spirit will hopefully soften Ken to hear about a different path to take regarding his mother (and God).

Speak Honestly but Not Argumentatively

Paul repeatedly reminds Christians that they "must not be quarrelsome" (2 Timothy 2:24), are "not be argumentative" (Titus 2:9), are to "avoid quarreling" and to "speak evil of no one" (Titus 3:2), and "let no corrupting talk come out of your mouth" (Ephesians 4:29). In correspondence with my pastor on counseling the unbeliever, he articulated, "The counselor must not be 'primed for battle' with an unbelieving client, not 'ready to move in for the kill,' not 'out to prove the client wrong.' A counselor may technically believe in grace while communicating only rejection, bitterness, and disdain. The counselor must 'adorn the doctrine of our Savior' (Titus 2:10) not mask it or distort it or pervert it."[3]

While I want to avoid a self-righteous, oppositional demeanor with Ken, I am also obligated to be honest with him regarding the limitations, even dangers, of extracting counsel from me without embracing the whole of my counseling approach (i.e., the gospel of Jesus Christ). I may be able to extend wisdom from the Proverbs or convince him of the power inherent in walking in forgiveness. These may actually help Ken let go of bitterness, become more sensitive to his wife, and decrease his anger responses toward her. Since Ken is created in the image of God, he has a limited capacity to embrace such virtues.

However, I will also want to let him know of my particular beliefs and experiences when dealing with similar issues. I will find moments to share how fellowship with Jesus creates a deeper and richer context for change and forgiveness and how the experience of God's forgiveness in Christ enables me to forgive those who have wronged, hurt, and abandoned me. This helps me temper my anger and criticism. I will also share how Jesus creates a love for the God who is slow to anger; how I realize that he has been slow to anger with me. I will confess that God has forgiven me in Christ and accepted me and that his full and constant favor is now upon me. The realization and experience of God's patience, forgiveness, and love nourishes and sustains my forgiveness and patience toward others.

I will share how Jesus brings me into fellowship with God, giving me knowledge of his constant presence to know me. Jesus embraces me and helps me, empowering me to change through the Holy Spirit—all of which gives me great hope in tackling my anger. I will share how Jesus creates new fellowship with his people, which encourages me, excites me, and comforts me as fellow believers worship and serve this gracious God in a communion of joy. I will share how Jesus gives me hope in my final rescue from judgment, in the final resurrection of my body, and in my living forever in the new heavens and the new earth. This hope further strengthens me in my capacity to persevere in obedience. I might begin such a conversation this way:[4]

> *Counselor:* Ken, it has been a privilege to walk with you as you seek help with your bitterness toward your mother as well as your tumultuous relationship with your wife. It is wonderful to hear that your wife is beginning to move toward you again in relationship, and that it seems your heart has truly been broken by the way you have treated her. I feel like we've

grown closer in this journey. I wanted to share a bit of my own experience, and how the gospel has actually transformed me so that I may walk in the kind ways of Jesus more consistently. I want to share why the gospel is so important on those days I don't do so well in relating sensitively to my wife. Would you be open to hearing some of that today?

Ken may respond with an eagerness to hear my thoughts, he may offer a reluctant yes to my question, or he may completely reject me. My heart's position, from the moment I met Ken, was that the Lord would use our time together as a means of drawing his heart to the Lord. Regardless of Ken's initial response, however, I would want to emphasize my genuine concern for his well-being and my love for him. If he completely rejects my request, I might follow up with exploring why as well as provide the intent of my request. I also want him to know that there is so much more for him in the gospel, and that without it, I fear we have only placed a Band-Aid over his gaping wounds. Ken and I have addressed some symptoms, but have yet to nail the true heart of the problem.

If I am not in a professional setting, I would likely press even harder. If I am doing life with Ken, I will continue to pursue and befriend him. Whether in a professional setting or not, so long as I have done all I am able to bring the gospel to Ken, I will rest contently in the words of Paul, "So neither he who plants nor he who waters is anything, but only God who gives the growth" (1 Corinthians 3:7). I will definitely continue to pray that the God of salvation would bring life and growth to Ken by saving him and transforming him to the uttermost.

Three Principles for Walking with Unbelievers

Operate with Honorable Conduct

Beloved, I urge you as sojourners and exiles to abstain from the passions of the flesh, which wage war against your soul. Keep your conduct among the Gentiles honorable, so that when they speak against you as evildoers, they may see your deeds and glorify God on the day of visitation. (1 Peter 2:11–12)

- How Christians operate with others and before others is important. One aspect of their witness to the watching world is that their lives reflect holiness and obedience.
- Christians honor others by keeping their commitments, showing up on time, and extending genuine concern. They have been given a divine mandate to honor those who do not necessarily agree with them.
- Christians' lives, conduct, demeanor, and words should be an aroma that draws others toward the gospel of Jesus Christ (Matthew 5:16).
- While these are principles Christians would also exercise with believers, we must be mindful of their evangelistic implications when working with unbelievers.

Remember Humanity Bears the Glory of God

When I look at your heavens, the work of your fingers, the moon and the stars, which you have set in place, what is man that you are mindful of him, and the son of man that you care for him? You have made him a little lower than the heavenly beings and crowned him with glory and honor. (Psalm 8:3–5)

- It is always good for Christians to check their attitudes when it comes to those that do not share their faith. Do Christians judge others or view them as glorious?
- Christians should remind themselves that every person they counsel, Christian or not, drug addicted or not, homosexual or not, adulterer or not—any type of sinner or not—is crowned by the Creator with majestic glory. Each has been created in the image of God, and God expects Christians

to treat each individual with absolute respect and honor (James 3:9–10).

- From this starting point, Christians will engage others in ways that make their interests and lives a priority. The agenda is not to save others but to love them. Christians will trust God alone as they do his will to love others.

Remember the Gospel Invitation Is for Everyone

The Spirit and the Bride say, "Come." And let the one who hears say, "Come." And let the one who is thirsty come; let the one who desires take the water of life without price. (Revelation 22:17)

How then will they call on him in whom they have not believed? And how are they to believe in him of whom they have never heard? And how are they to hear without someone preaching? And how are they to preach unless they are sent? As it is written, 'How beautiful are the feet of those who preach the good news! . . .So faith comes from hearing, and hearing through the word of Christ. (Romans 10:14–15, 17)

The wind blows where it wishes, and you hear its sound, but you do not know where it comes from or where it goes. So it is with everyone who is born of the Spirit. (John 3:8)

- The call to relationship with Jesus goes out to all humanity—to every single person Christians counsel. Counselors invite everyone to the same banquet table of redemption where they themselves have been graciously invited.
- Christian counselors take seriously Jesus's command to go into the world and make disciples. They are zealous to take part in Jesus's redemptive purposes.
- The Scriptures encourage Christians as they bring the good news to those who have not heard. How beautiful are the feet of those who bear such news (Isaiah 52:7).

Christians should be honored that God has given them such a profound privilege.

- Being born again is completely dependent upon the work of the Holy Spirit. Counselors are not responsible to make people born again. This is an impossible task. Counselors are responsible only to bring the good news. The way the Lord chooses to work through counselors is a mystery known only to him. Some will be saved, others will not. That is ultimately a work of God's sovereign grace, not human efforts. Methods of counseling do not change hearts, only the effectual power of the Holy Spirit will produce such transformation. Counselors will trust God in this work, as they faithfully love others. This will hold whether a person places faith in Jesus or not.

When counseling non-Christians, counselors are forced into a place where their dependence on God is profoundly glaring. Dr. Ian Jones aptly describes this,

The Bible shows us that we should start where people are located in their spiritual, mental, emotional, and physical lives. We may be part of a larger plan for the person in need whereby we will be used of God to give someone a glimpse of the ultimate healing possibilities found in Christ, or we may be fortunate enough to participate directly in presenting the message of salvation. If a person accepts Christ, discipleship and counseling can work hand in hand as the process of sanctification or growth in Christ begins. If not, then the Christian counselor should continue to pray for the person and seek to be used by God as a means of planting seeds of grace through the healing encounter.[5]

Appendix B

Secular Psychology and Biblical Soul Care: Parallel Pursuits

In chapters one and two I offered a brief history of counseling as understood in church history. Sometimes, this history gets lost in the stories of Freud, Darwin, Maslow, Nietzsche, and others. That is why I think it might be helpful to gain perspective regarding the overlapping interests of the early church fathers, the Reformers, and the Puritans discussed in chapter one with many of the modern thinkers of psychology that followed them centuries later. The questions of modern psychology are not original to that discipline. These two worlds have shared the same turf for quite a long time.

Similar to Luther, Calvin, and Edwards, psychology's early personality theorists were also interested in the subjects of the will and human motivation. One of the most famous was Abraham Maslow whose hierarchy of needs continues to wield significant influence in the field of psychology and counseling.

Maslow believed people are ultimately motivated by "desire or want or yearning or wish or lack."[1] His concepts on this point were similar to the early church fathers, Reformers, and Puritans but were distinctively slanted toward the ideals of humanism.[2] Maslow postulated that intrinsic to human nature are specific innate needs. He identified them as "safety, belongingness, love, respect, and self-esteem."[3] He also put forth the idea that people have an innate tendency to fulfill these needs in order to achieve an inner "unity, integration or synergy" culminating in a fully actualized self—something he and others refer to as the self-actualizing tendency.[4]

The ultimate task for the individual, therefore, is to choose those qualities that will perpetuate the self-actualizing tendency (the innate force that exerts a natural inertia toward human potential) while resisting those desires that would impede this process. Maslow noted,

> Therefore we can consider the process of healthy growth to be a never ending series of free choice situations, confronting each individual at every point throughout his life, in which he must choose between the delights of safety and growth, dependence and independence, regression and progression, immaturity and maturity. Safety has both anxieties and delights; growth has both anxieties and delights. We grow forward when the delights of growth and anxieties of safety are greater than the anxieties of growth and the delights of safety.[5]

He adds, "Of course this growth-through-delight also commits us to the necessary postulation that what tastes good is also, in the growth sense, 'better' for us. We rest here on the faith that if free choice is really free and if the chooser is not too sick or frightened to choose, he will choose wisely, in a healthy and growthward direction, more often than not."[6] Maslow's faith in human potential is powerfully captured in the final sentence above. He strongly assumes—all things being considered—that if the conditions are ideal humans will typically choose the healthy choice. This edification of humanity should come as no surprise since Maslow was one of the prominent leaders in what has been referred to as third force, humanistic psychology. This approach is centered in the potentiality of humanity and resists any assertions of innate evil in mankind. It was, in part, a reactionary model that arose in opposition to the determinism of Freudian psychoanalysis and Skinnerian behaviorism. It was a system of therapy in which people's capacity to transition toward a self-actualized state depended on their freedom to choose that which would fulfill the appropriate needs essential for an optimal integrated self.

Maslow was seeking to answer the identical questions that Augustine, Luther, Calvin, Edwards, and Owen considered, but his reference point for understanding was humankind instead of God. Such an approach makes it impossible to understand human nature accurately. Humankind is a profoundly deficient reference point to comprehend the psyche at the deepest levels.

Moving forward from Maslow it is clear that the priority of acquiring deeper knowledge of the human will did not die with him and early theorists in psychology. Today, such knowledge is considered an important piece in developing a viable understanding of humanity's psychological makeup. Many current authors reflect Maslow's interests, one of which is the distinguished professor of psychology at Harvard University, Steven Pinker. Dr. Pinker notes, "Science is guaranteed to appear to eat away at the will, *regardless* of what it finds, because the scientific mode of explanation cannot accommodate the mysterious notion of uncaused causation that underlies the will."[7] As such, he concludes, "Either we dispense with all morality as an unscientific superstition, or we find a way to reconcile causation (genetic or otherwise) with responsibility and free will."[8]

Pinker, like many today, is developing an understanding of human psychology while properly balancing the age-old dilemma of free human agency and personal responsibility. Luther and Maslow were doing the same. This simple comparison evidences that developing models of human nature inherently concerned with why people do what they do continues to preoccupy the most gifted researchers in psychology. Pinker offers a robust, scholarly argument supporting his theory of human nature. I am deeply fascinated and entertained by his high level of intellectual analysis and his winsome style. I also deeply respect his scholarship. Yet, without divine wisdom, his model remains deficient. Followers of Jesus cannot afford to sit silently in the ongoing debate and development of these ideas.

From Augustine to Pinker, it is quite clear that as far as pursuing an understanding of psychology goes, not much has changed in several thousand years (though the conclusions drawn may be vastly different). Luther, an accomplished theologian and Reformer, Owen, a prominent Puritan scholar, Maslow, a renowned humanistic theorist, and Pinker, a modern-day advocate of the computational theory of mind are each addressing the same basic questions. What motivates the will, what causes behavior, and why is it so important?

For the authors of Scripture, the church fathers, the Reformers, and the Puritans, it was a question centered in God and his perspective of humanity. This perspective included themes such as sin, grace, and sanctification. Maslow, on the other hand, approached the concept of free will from the laws and presuppositions of humanistic orthodoxy—a man-centered system that sternly dismissed any allusion to Christian doctrine. Unlike any of the former, Pinker denounces all "archaic conceptions of the mind"[9] and offers a model deeply grounded in biological evolution—"a psychology of many computational faculties engineered by natural selection."[10] He regards this approach as "the best hope for a grasp on how the mind works that does justice to its complexity."[11]

Biblical counselors will be confronted with similar competing voices today. We must pray the Lord grant us the grace and wisdom to confront these voices as articulately and courageously as did our forefathers in the faith.

ENDNOTES

Dedication

[1] Acknowledgment of these individuals in my doctoral study does not necessarily infer their agreement with the study's final results, nor does it assume they endorse the contents of this book. Permission was granted by each individual to publicly acknowledge him or her as a study participant in my dissertation.

[2] In order to honor confidentiality agreements associated with my research, some participants chose to forego being named specifically in this section. While not mentioned by name, these individuals were equally significant in helping me complete my PhD study.

Chapter One

[1] Franz Delitzsch, *A System of Biblical Psychology*, 4th ed., trans. Robert Wallis (New York: Scribner and Welford), 3.

[2] Friedrich Nietzsche, *Beyond Good and Evil: Prelude to a Philosophy of the Future*, trans. Walter Kauffmann (New York: Vintage Books, 1989), 32.

[3] Online Etymology Dictionary. https://www.etymonline.com/word/psychology, accessed November 25, 2017.

[4] B. R. Hergenhahn, *An Introduction to the History of Psychology*, 2nd ed. (Pacific Grove, CA: Brooks/Cole Publishing Co., 1992), 81.

[5] John Henderson, *Equipped to Counsel: A Training Program in Biblical Counseling* (Bedford, TX: Association of Biblical Counselors, 2008), 22.

[6] Jay Adams, *More Than Redemption: A Theology of Christian Counseling* (Grand Rapids, MI: Zondervan, 1979), 1.

[7] For an in-depth exposition on this passage see Jay Adams, *From Forgiven to Forgiving* (Amityville, NY: Calvary Press, 1994), 14.

[8] Eric Johnson, "Whatever Happened to the Human Soul? A Brief Christian Genealogy of Psychological Terms," *Journal of Psychology and Theology* 26 (1998): 16–28.

[9] Eric Johnson, *Foundations of Soul Care* (Downers Grove, IL: IVP Academic, 2007), 52.

[10] Morton Hunt, *The Story of Psychology* (New York, NY: Double Day Publishing Group, 1993), 52.

[11] Rebecca Konyndyk DeYoung, *Glittering Vices: A New Look at the Seven Deadly Sins and Their Remedies* (Grand Rapids, MI: Brazos Press, 2009), 9.

[12] Ibid., 40.

[13] Ibid.

[14] More will be offered pertaining to the specifics of Luther's and Calvin's theology in the realm of soul care in later chapters.

[15] Tim Keller, "Puritan Resources for Biblical Counseling," *Journal of Pastoral Practice* 9, no. 3 (1988): 11–44.

[16] Ken Sarles, "The English Puritans: A Historical Paradigm of Biblical Counseling," in *Introduction to Biblical Counseling: A Basic Guide to the Principles and Practice of Counseling*, eds. J. F. MacArthur & W. A. Mack (Dallas, TX: Word,1994), 21–43.

[17] Jonathan Edwards, *The Freedom of the Will* (Morgan, PA: Soli Deo Gloria Publications, 1996), 13.

[18] Jonathan Edwards, *The Religious Affections* (Carlisle, PA: The Banner of Truth Trust, 2001), 29.

[19] Kelly Kapic and Justin Taylor, eds., *John Owen's Overcoming Sin and Temptation* (Wheaton, IL: Crossway, 2006), 124.

[20] Ibid., 27.

[21] John Owen, *The Holy Spirit: His Gifts and Power* (Scotland, UK: Christian Focus Publications, 2004), 21.

[22] J. I. Packer, *A Quest for Godliness: The Puritan Vision of the Christian Life* (Wheaton, IL: Crossway Books, 1990), 64.

[23] Johnson, *Foundations of Soul Care*, 62.

[24] I am indebted to Dr. Ian Jones who provided me each of these titles (and more) through personal correspondence.

[25] To grasp an idea of how secular psychology has always sought to cover the very same questions as the church fathers, the Reformers, and the Puritans, see Appendix B.

[26] Johnson, "Whatever Happened to the Human Soul?," 16–28.

[27] Erik Erikson, *Young Man Luther: A Study in Psychoanalysis and History* (W. W. Norton & Co.: New York, 1958), 64–65.

[28] S. Rosenzweig, *The Historic Expedition to America (1909): Freud, Young, and Hall the King Maker* (St. Louis, MO: Rana House, 1994), 82–85.

[29] Johnson, *Foundations of Soul Care*, 67–71.

[30] S. B. Narramore, "Perspectives on the Integration of Psychology and Theology," in *Psychology and Christianity: Integrative Readings*, eds. J. R. Fleck and J. D. Carter (Nashville, TN: Abingdon, 1981), 27–45.

[31] John Bettler, "CCEF: The Beginning," *Journal of Pastoral Practice* 9, no. 3 (1988): 46.

[32] David Powlison, "What do You Feel?," *Journal of Pastoral Practice* 10, no.4 (1992): 50–61.

[33] Anton Boisen, *The Exploration of the Inner World: A Study of Mental Disorder and Religious Experience* (New York, NY: Harper and Brothers, 1936), 221.

[34] G. R. Collins, "The Pulpit and the Couch," in *Psychology and Christianity: Integrative Readings*, eds. J. R. Fleck and J. D. Carter (Nashville, TN: Abington, 1981), 46–53.

[35] Anton Boisen, *The Exploration of the Inner World*, 221.

[36] Ibid., 221.

[37] Ibid., 236.

[38] Hobart Mowrer, *The Crisis in Psychiatry and Religion* (Princeton, NJ: D. Van Nostrand Co, 1961), 73.

[39] John Carter and Bruce Narramore, *The Integration of Psychology and Theology* (Grand Rapids, MI: Zondervan, 1979), 33.

[40] John Rea Thomas, *A History of "Clinical Training" and Clinical Pastoral Education in the North Central Region*: 1932–2006, accessed September 22, 2017, http://ncracpe.org/history&research/ncrhistory.pdf.

[41] Eric Fromm, *Sigmund Freud's Mission: An Analysis of His Personality and Influence* (New York: Grove Press 1959), 101.

[42] Carl Rogers, *On Becoming a Person: The Therapist's View of Psychotherapy* (New York: Houghton Mifflin Co., 1989), 23–24.

[43] John Carter and Bruce Narramore, *The Integration of Psychology and Theology*, 34.

[44] E. T. Charry, "Theology after Psychology," in *Care for the Soul: Exploring the Intersection of Psychology and Theology*, eds., M. R. McMinn and T. R. Phillips (Downers Grove, IL: IVP Academic, 2001), 122.

[45] S. B. Narramore, "Perspectives on the Integration of Psychology and Theology," 33.

[46] Chris Evans, *Søren Kierkegaard's Christian Psychology* (Grand Rapids, MI: Zondervan, 1990).

[47] David Powlison, "Modern Therapies and the Church's Faith," *Journal of Biblical Counseling* 15, no.1 (1996): 35.

[48] Hobart Mowrer, *The Crisis in Psychiatry and Religion*, 52.

[49] Ibid., 73.

[50] Ibid., 60.

[51] Karl Menninger, *Whatever Became of Sin?* (New York, NY: Hawthorn Books, 1973), 38–49.

[52] Thomas Szasz, *The Myth of Mental Illness* (New York, NY: Harper Perennial, 1974), 32–47.

[53] Willian Glasser, *Reality Therapy: A New Approach to Psychiatry* (New York: Harper and Row, 1975), 5–41.

[54] Eric Johnson and Stanton Jones, eds., *Psychology and Christianity: Four Views* (Downers Grove, IL: InterVarsity Press, 2000), 33.

[55] For more information on the Christian Association for Psychological Studies, see http://caps.net/.

[56] R. E. Larzelere, "The Task Ahead: Six Levels of Integration of Christianity," in *Psychology and Christianity: Integrative Readings*, eds. J. R. Fleck and J. D. Carter (Nashville, TN: Abingdon, 1981), 54–65.

[57] Clyde Narramore, *The Psychology of Counseling* (Grand Rapids, MI: Zondervan, 1960).

[58] Bruce Narramore, *Someone Special* (Grand Rapids, MI: Zondervan, 1978).

[59] Gary Collins, *Search for Reality: Psychology and the Christian* (Santa Ana, CA: Vision House, 1969); Gary Collins, *The Rebuilding of Psychology* (Wheaton, IL: Tyndale, 1977).

[60] Larry Crabb, *Effective Biblical Counseling: A Model for Helping Caring Christians Become Capable Counselors* (Grand Rapids, MI: Zondervan, 1977).

[61] Frank Minirth & Paul Meier, *Counseling and the Nature of Man* (Grand Rapids, MI: Baker Book House, 1982).

[62] See Appendix A for a brief comparison between the church fathers, the Reformers, and Puritans and secular theorists and researchers.

Chapter Two

[1] Jay Adams, *Competent to Counsel: Introduction to Nouthetic Counseling* (Grand Rapids, MI: Zondervan, 1970), 21.

[2] Francis Schaeffer, *The Great Evangelical Disaster* (Wheaton, IL: Crossway, 1984), 48.

[3] John Carter and Bruce Narramore, *The Integration of Psychology and Theology*, 54.

[4] Ibid.

[5] Ibid.

[6] Collins, *The Rebuilding of Psychology*, 116.

[7] John Carter and Bruce Narramore, *The Integration of Psychology and Theology*, 54.

[8] Gary Collins, *Psychology and Theology: Prospects for Integration* (Nashville, TN: Abington, 1981), 18.

[9] Bruce Narramore and John Carter, "On Straw Men, Autonomous Spheres, and the Integration of Psychology and Theology: A Reply to Cole," *Journal of Psychology and Christianity* 19, no. 1 (2000): 72.

[10] Larry Crabb, *Effective Biblical Counseling: A Model for Helping Caring Christians Become Capable Counselors*, 47.

[11] Ibid., 48.

[12]   John Carter and Bruce Narramore, *The Integration of Psychology and Theology*, 9–27; Gary Collins, *Psychology and Theology*, 49; Larry Crabb, *Effective Biblical Counseling*, 31–56.

[13]   Richard Ganz, *Psychobabble: The Failure of Modern Psychology and the Biblical Alternative* (Wheaton, IL: Crossway, 1993), 61; William K. Kilpatrick, *Psychological Seduction: The Failure of Modern Psychology* (Nashville, TN: Thomas Nelson, 1983), 144; Ed Bulkley, *Why Christians Can't Trust Psychology* (Eugene, OR: Harvest House, 1993), 231; David G. Myers and Malcom A Jeeves, *Psychology Through the Eyes of Faith* (New York: Harper Collins, 1987), 11.

[14]   Martin Bobgan and Deidra Bobgan, *Psychoheresy* (Santa Barbara, CA: Eastgate, 1987), 3–25.

[15]   David Powlison, *The Biblical Counseling Movement: History and Context* (Greensboro, NC: New Growth Press, 2010), 51–71.

[16]   Adams, *Competent to Counsel*. Find out more regarding Dr. Adams's revolutionary model and current opportunities for training at www.nouthetic.org.

[17]   Ibid., xiii.

[18]   Adams, *Competent to Counsel*; O. Hobart Mowrer, *The Crisis in Psychiatry and Religion*, 40–46.

[19]   Adams, *Competent to Counsel*, xix.

[20]   Adams, *More Than Redemption: A Theology of Christian Counseling*, 8.

[21]   Ibid., 44.

[22]   Jay Adams, *The Christian Counselor's Manual* (Phillipsburg, NJ: P&R Publishing Co., 1973).

[23]   David Powlison, *Competent to Counsel? The History of a Conservative Protestant Anti-psychiatry Movement* (Unpublished doctoral dissertation, University of Pennsylvania, 1996), 175.

[24]   Ibid., 174–76.

[25]   Adams, *More Than Redemption: A Theology of Christian Counseling*, 11.

[26]   Robert Roberts, "Parameters of a Christian Psychology," in *Limning the Psyche: Explorations in Christian Psychology*, eds. R. C. Roberts and M. R. Talbot (Grand Rapids, MI: William Eerdmans, 1997), 76.

[27]   Johnson, *Foundations of Soul Care*.

[28]   Powlison, *Competent to Counsel?*, 114.

[29]   Powlison, *The Biblical Counseling Movement: History and Context*, 63.

[30]   John MacArthur & Wayne Mack, *Introduction to Biblical Counseling: A Basic Guide to Principles and Practice of Biblical Counseling* (Dallas, TX: Word, 1994).

[31]   Lou Priolo, *The Heart of Anger: Practical Help for the Prevention and Cure of Anger in Children* (Amityville, NY: Calvary Press, 1997).

[32]   David Powlison, "Crucial Issues in Contemporary Biblical Counseling," *Journal of Pastoral Practice* 9, no. 3 (1988): 53–78; David Powlison,

"Integration or Inundation?" in *Power Religion : The Selling Out of the Evangelical Church?*, ed. M. S. Horton (Chicago, IL: Moody Press, 1992), 191–218.

[33] Ed Welch, "Sin or Sickness? Biblical Counseling and the Medical Model," *Journal of Pastoral Practice* 10, no. 2 (1990): 29–39.

[34] Elyse Fitzpatrick, "Helping Overeaters," *Journal of Pastoral Practice* 11, no.1 (1992): 51–56.

[35] Powlison, *Competent to Counsel?*, 120.

[36] Johnson, *Foundations of Soul Care*, 109.

[37] Heath Lambert, *The Biblical Counseling Movement After Adams* (Wheaton, IL: Crossway, 2012).

[38] David Powlison, "Critiquing Modern Integrationists," *Journal of Biblical Counseling* 11, no. 3 (1993): 29.

[39] Ed Welch, "Motives: Why Do I Do the Things I Do?" *Journal of Biblical Counseling* 22, no. 1 (2003): 49.

[40] David Powlison, "Idols of the Heart and 'Vanity Fair'," *Journal of Biblical Counseling* 13, no. 2 (1995): 35–50.

[41] Powlison, "Crucial Issues in Contemporary Biblical Counseling," 61.

[42] Adams, *Competent to Counsel*, 147.

[43] Johnson, *Foundations of Soul Care*, 122.

[44] David Powlison, *Competent to Counsel?*, 473.

[45] Ibid.

[46] Personal correspondence with some in Christian soul care such as Dr. Ian Jones and Dr. Phil Monroe indicate that they believe these categories are too narrow. Jones himself does not self-identify with either COMPIN or VITEX.

[47] The following is from my PhD dissertation (July, 2012). The study drew out possible changes that were potentially coming regarding the use of the term nouthetic among many within the nouthetic counseling community. My sentiments were drawn from answers given by participants certified by the organization known at the time as the National Association of Nouthetic Counselors (NANC). This organization changed its name to the Association of Certified Biblical Counselors (ACBC) in 2013. Indications that a change could be coming were present in my panelist's answers in 2012.

Contributing to the myriad of changes transpiring with the identity of biblical counselor, this study not only elicited evidence that some who are nouthetic counselors now refrain from being identified by the title biblical counselor, but there are also those who have historically identified themselves as nouthetic counselors who now prefer the identity of biblical counselor to the exclusion of the former. One participant notified the Primary Investigator (PI) that while he is certified as a nouthetic counselor, he no longer uses the term *nouthetic* but rather prefers the term *biblical* when describing his identity and work. This was further reflected in the current study in that two individuals certified as nouthetic counselors chose to self-identify as biblical counselors on the Participant Screening Survey (PSS) rather than choosing the option nouthetic counselor. Certainly the two identities have historically been interchangeable, but the preference of biblical counselor over nouthetic counselor by some who are certified by NANC is interesting and may be explained by the rationale offered by Welch and Powlison (1997):

> Given that Nouthetic Counseling has matured to become much more than the first two books by Jay Adams, given that there is increasing diversity within Nouthetic Counseling, and given the historical context behind the choice of the word *nouthetic*, many of us prefer to use the term *biblical counseling* rather than nouthetic counseling. This change communicates that we are part of a larger movement within the church and avoids the potential sectarian stereotypes often associated with the word *nouthetic*. (304)

It is not known for certain whether or not such an explanation captures the rationale of current panelists choosing biblical over nouthetic counselor in the current study; however, their choice may be indicative of a continuing and potentially growing trend in the field of nouthetic counseling.

In 2013, board members of NANC, under the leadership of Heath Lambert, chose to change the organization's name to the Association of Certified Biblical Counselors.

48 To date the BCC is now represented on an international level with council members from various countries throughout the world.

49 "The Biblical Counseling Coalition Mission, Vision, and Passion Statement," http://biblicalcounselingcoalition.org/about/mission-statement/, accessed October 4, 2014.

50 The idea that historically biblical counseling ministries have operated in isolated silos without much or any interaction or cross-pollination of ideas was first brought to me by a pioneer in the biblical counseling arena, Steve Viars.

51 Following is from email correspondence with Dr. Ian Jones summarizing his thoughts on VITEX and COMPIN. He wrote, "My concern with the terms is that they present a fallacy of bifurcation, asserting, or implying, that there are only two options, and that if you are not one (COMPIN) then you must be the other (VITEX). It is like saying that if you are not Calvinist, then you must be an Arminian. As defined, the COMPrehensive INternal resources (COMPIN) or 'everything we need to counsel others is ultimately comprehensively internal to the Scriptures' model would appear to exclude such historical theologians as Augustine (*On Christian Doctrine*, Preface, 8, 2.18.28, 2.40.60), Luther (*sola Scriptura* NOT *nuda Scriptura*), Calvin (*Institutes*, II,ii,15; *Commentary on Titus*,1:12), and Wesley. In other words,

standard, orthodox Christian theologians who affirm the primacy and authority of Scripture would not be likely to fit in the COMPIN camp. At times, research and science used in service to the Scripture can and do inform and illustrate for more effective, biblical soul care, though I might not use the term Vital (VITEX) contribution. Let me add that I do appreciate Dave Powlison's irenic spirit in attempting to avoid divisiveness in the body of Christ."

52 Heath Lambert, *A Theology of Biblical Counseling: The Doctrinal Foundations of Counseling Ministry* (Grand Rapids, MI: Zondervan, 2016), 29–30.

53 I have had the privilege of supervising many interns who graduated from Dr. Jones's counseling program (a program that prepares students for licensure), and it was clear they were effectively trained to utilize Scripture within a counseling context.

54 It is encouraging to see this trend evolving within many circles of biblical counseling and among those in the broader soul care movement.

55 This is a resource of the Biblical Counseling Coalition.

Chapter Three

1 Cornelius Van Til, *An Introduction to Systematic Theology*, 2nd ed. (Phillipsburg, NJ: P&R Publishing, 2007), 21.

2 This is my recollection of what the professor taught during the forty-hour class I attended to acquire my supervisory status.

3 Francis A. Schaeffer, *He Is There and He Is Not Silent* (Wheaton IL: Tyndale House, 1972), 37.

4 David Powlison, "Questions at the Crossroads: The Care of Souls and Modern Psychotherapies," in *Care for the Soul: Exploring the Intersection of Psychology and Theology*, eds. M. R. McMinn and T. R. Phillips (Downers Grove, IL: IVP Academic, 2001), 23–61.

5 Ron Hawkins and Tim Clinton, *The New Christian Counselor: A Fresh Biblical & Transformational Approach* (Eugene, OR: Harvest House, 2015), 15.

6 J. M. Frame, *The Doctrine of God: A Theology of Lordship* (Phillipsburg, NJ: P&R Publishing, 2002), 7.

7 Cornelius Van Til, *An Introduction to Systematic Theology*, 2nd ed. (Phillipsburg, NJ: P&R Publishing, 2007), 15.

8 To gain perspective on how our theology shapes our interaction with unbelievers, please read Appendix A.

9 Wayne Grudem, *Systematic Theology: An Introduction to Biblical Doctrine* (Grand Rapids, MI: Zondervan, 1994), 18.

10 Virginia Todd Holeman, *Theology for Better Counseling: Trinitarian Reflections for Healing and Formation* (Downers Grove, IL: IVP, 2012), 22.

11 Adams, *More Than Redemption: A Theology of Christian Counseling*, 15.

12 Ibid.

[13]   Jeremy Lelek, *The Study of the Constructs and a Proposed Definition of Biblical Counseling* (Dissertation, Regent University, 2012), 104.

[14]   David Powlison, "Affirmations and Denials," *Journal of Biblical Counseling* 19, no. 1 (2000): 18–25.

[15]   Ed Welch, "What is Biblical Counseling, Anyway?" *Journal of Biblical Counseling* 16, no. 1 (1997): 2.

[16]   Paul Tripp, "The Present Glories of Redemption," *Journal of Biblical Counseling* 17, no. 2 (1999): 32–37.

[17]   John Piper, *Toward a Definition of the Essence of Biblical Counseling*, 2001, retrieved from https://www.desiringgod.org/articles/toward-a-definition-of-the-essence-of-biblical-counseling.

[18]   John Henderson, *Equipped to Counsel* (Bedford, TX: Association of Biblical Counselors, 2008).

[19]   Lelek, *The Study of the Constructs and a Proposed Definition of Biblical Counseling*, 150.

Chapter Four

[1]   Grudem, *Systematic Theology: An Introduction to Biblical Doctrine*, 73.

[2]   It is important to note that some of the leading classical theorists in psychology were uncomfortable with the idea of value neutrality when it came to understanding people, in part because they acknowledged the influence of cultural values on an individual's perspective and development. Christian students of psychology may inadvertently assume that the current value-neutral stance has always been a universal value among the secular pioneers. This, however, is not the case. Consider two of the most prominent thinkers on the topic,

I am convinced that the value-free, value-neutral, value-avoiding model of science that we inherited from physics, chemistry, and astronomy, where it was necessary and desirable to keep the data clean and also to keep the church out of scientific affairs, is quite unsuitable for the scientific study of life. Even more dramatically is the value-free philosophy of science unsuitable for human questions, where personal values, purposes and goals, intentions and plans are absolutely crucial for the understanding of any person. –Abraham Maslow, *The Farther Reaches of Human Nature* (New York: Viking Press, 1971), 5.

The student of man is, more than any other scientist, influenced by the atmosphere of his society. This is so because not only are his ways of thinking, his interests, the questions he raises, all partly socially determined as in the natural sciences, but in his case the subject matter itself, man, is thus determined. –Erich Fromm, *The Anatomy of Human Destructiveness* (New York: Hold, Rinehart & Winston Inc., 1975), 3.

[3]   Steven Pinker, *The Blank Slate: The Modern Denial of Human Nature* (New York: Penguin Books, 2002).

[4]   Van Til, *An Introduction to Systematic Theology*, 36.

⁵   John Frame, *Selected Shorter Writings*, vol. 1 (Philipsburg, NJ: P&R Publishing, 2014), 4.

⁶   Grudem, *Systematic Theology: An Introduction to Biblical Doctrine*, 149.

⁷   Francis Schaeffer, *The Complete Works of Francis A. Schaeffer: A Christian Worldview*, vol. 1 (Wheaton, IL: Crossway, 1985), 138.

⁸   John Frame, *The Doctrine of God: A Theology of Lordship* (Phillipsburg, NJ: P&R Publishing, 2002), 316–17.

⁹   Kevin DeYoung, *Taking God at His Word: Why the Bible Is Knowable, Necessary, and Enough, and What That Means for You and Me* (Wheaton, IL: Crossway, 2014), 78, Kindle Fire.

¹⁰ Francis Schaeffer, *The God Who Is There* (Wheaton, IL: Crossway, 1972).

¹¹ Adams, *More Than Redemption: A Theology of Christian Counseling*, 17.

¹² Albert Ellis, *New Directions for Rational Emotive Behavior Therapy: Overcoming Destructive Beliefs, Feelings, and Behaviors* (New York: Prometheus Books, 2001), 104.

¹³ Ed Welch and David Powlison, "Every Common Bush Afire with God: The Scripture's Constitutive Role for Counseling," *Journal of Psychology and Christianity* 16, no. 4 (1997): 303–22.

¹⁴ Paul David Tripp, *Instruments in the Redeemer's Hands: People in Need of Change Helping People in Need of Change* (Phillipsburg, NJ: P&R Publishing, 2002), 1–16.

¹⁵ Welch and Powlison, "Every Common Bush Afire with God: The Scripture's Constitutive Role for Counseling," 303–22.

¹⁶ David Powlison, "X-ray Questions: Drawing Out the Whys and Wherefores of Human Behavior," *Journal of Biblical Counseling* 18, no. 2 (1999): 2–9.

¹⁷ David Powlison, "Human Defensiveness: The Third Way," *Journal of Pastoral Practice* 8, no. 1 (1985): 55.

¹⁸ I adapted this concept/diagram from Timothy S. Lane and Paul David Tripp, *How People Change* (Greensboro, NC: New Growth Press, 2006), 103.

Chapter Five

¹   George Carlin Quotes, BrainyQuote.com, Xplore Inc, 2017, https://www.brainyquote.com/quotes/george_carlin_379970, accessed November 24, 2017.

²   Powlison, "Questions at the Crossroads: The Care of Souls and Modern Psychotherapies," in *Care for the Soul: Exploring the Intersection of Psychology and Theology*, 33.

³   Timothy Keller, *Prayer: Experiencing Awe and Intimacy with God* (New York: Penguin Books, 2016), 54.

⁴   D. A. Carson, *Exegetical Fallacies*, 2nd ed. (Grand Rapids, MI: Baker Academic, 1996), 15.

[5] Stanton Jones and Richard Butman, *Modern Psychotherapies: A Comprehensive Christian Appraisal* (Downers Grove, IL: InterVarsity Press, 1991), 29.

[6] Bryan Maier and Philip Monroe, "Biblical Hermeneutics & Christian Psychology" in *Care for the Soul: Exploring the Intersection of Psychology and Theology*, eds. Mark McMinn and Timothy Phillips (Downers Grove, IL: InterVarsity Press, 2001), 277.

[7] Welch and Powlison, "Every Common Bush Afire with God: The Scriptures Constitutive Role for Counseling," 303–22.

[8] Powlison, "Questions at the Crossroads," in *Care for the Soul: Exploring the Intersection of Psychology and Theology*, 27.

[9] John Bettler, "Keep the Truth Alive," *Journal of Biblical Counseling*, 15:2 (1997): 2–5.

[10] See Jochem Douma, *Responsible Conduct: Principles for Christian Ethics* (Philipsburg, NJ: P&R Publishing, 2003) for further discussion on the dangers of personal presuppositions on one's interpretation of the Bible.

[11] David Powlison, *The Biblical Counseling Movement: History and Context*, 277.

[12] J. Robertson McQuilkin, "The Behavioral Sciences Under the Authority of Scripture," *Journal of the Evangelical Theological Society* 20, no. 1 (1977): 36.

[13] Frank Minirth and Paul Meier, *Happiness Is a Choice: New Ways to Enhance Joy and Meaning in Your Life* (Grand Rapids, MI: Baker Books, 1978).

[14] Walter Trobisch, *Love Yourself* (Bolivar, MO: Quiet Waters Publications, 2001), N. 236, Kindle Fire.

[15] Anthony A. Hoekema, *Created in God's Image* (Grand Rapids, MI: Wm. B. Eerdmans Publishing Co., 1986), 103.

[16] Ian F. Jones, *The Counsel of Heaven on Earth: Foundations for Biblical Christian Counseling* (Nashville, TN: B&H Academic, 2006), 67.

[17] Jochem Douma, *Responsible Conduct: Principles for Christian Ethics* (Phillipsburg, NJ: P&R Publishing, 2003), 137.

[18] Nathaniel Branden, *The Psychology of Self-Esteem* (San Francisco, CA: Jossey-Bass, 2001), 22.

[19] Eric L. Johnson, *God and Soul Care: The Therapeutic Resources of the Christian Faith* (Downers Grove, IL: IVP, 2017), 201.

[20] *Exegetical Bible Study Methods*, Francis Schaeffer Institute of Church Leadership Development, 2006, www.churchleadership.org, accessed November 19, 2012.

[21] These suggestions were provided by Darwin Jordan, pastor of Fort Worth PCA.

[22] A very important aspect of learning is a willingness to take risks and allowing yourself to be wrong. Receiving helpful correction by a trusted pastor or mentor in such instances is invaluable to counselor development.

Chapter Six

[1]   "Doxology," by Thomas Ken, *Trinity Hymnal* (Suwanee, GA: Great Commission Publication, 2004), 731.

[2]   John Calvin, *Calvin: Institutes of the Christian Religion*, ed. J. T. McNeil, trans. F. L. Battles (Louisville, KY: Westminster John Knox Press, 1960), 37.

[3]   See recommended resources at the end of this chapter.

[4]   Grudem, *Systematic Theology: An Introduction to Biblical Doctrine*, 231.

[5]   These statements are adapted from Grudem, *Systematic Theology: An Introduction to Biblical Doctrine*.

[6]   In the following section, my aim is to provide a cursory outline of the Trinity's involvement in human change. Dozens of volumes written by the most articulate scholars could never effectively capture the work of God in the lives of people, much less a single chapter. However, my hope is that a brief review here will push biblical counselors further in their study of God and his work so that they and those they serve would be struck with the awe of God's love as he personally works in their lives.

[7]   Charles Spurgeon, adapted from the *Spurgeon Commentary: Hebrews*, available digitally as part of the *Spurgeon Commentary Collection: New Testament Letters*, and coming soon to print. Retrieved from: http://www.lexhampress.com/blog/2015/6/25/spurgeon-on-jesus-as-son-of-god-and-likeness-of-god on July 8th, 2016.

[8]   Frame, *The Doctrine of God: A Theology of Lordship*, 706.

[9]   Ibid., 694.

[10]   Ibid.

[11]   It is also worth noting that obedience here is directed to Jesus Christ. This is something that would be blasphemous if he were not God. This is common New Testament language demonstrating that in the minds of these men, obedience to Jesus is obedience to God.

[12]   Michael Reeves, *Delighting in the Trinity: An Introduction to the Christian Faith* (Downers Grove, IL: IVP, 2012), 12.

[13]   The following are a few more of the many passages that reveal the unity of the Father, Son, and Holy Spirit in the work of redemption:

   1 Peter 1:10–12—These verses provide the elegant interplay of the Spirit and Christ: the Spirit predicted the sufferings of Christ, yet it was the Spirit of Christ that did this (showing their union) and then the message about Christ is preached by that same Spirit.

   2 Corinthians 3:16–18—Paul names the Lord Jesus with the same name of the Spirit, not to say they are the same person, but to indicate how united their work is, that the work of the Spirit is the work of the Lord carried out by the same Spirit.

Romans 8:9–11—Here Paul reveals the amazing unity of the work of the Trinity: the "Spirit of God dwells in you" "if anyone does not have the Spirit of Christ" "if Christ is in you" "the Spirit of Him who raised Jesus from the dead dwells in you" "his Spirit who dwells in you."

[14] The gospel is constantly set forth as the highly involved, joint work of the Father, Son, and Holy Spirit. I hope you will be further enriched by the majesty and beauty of the work of the Triune God in the following passages. Resist skipping over them, but instead read them, meditate on them, ponder them, be in awe of God through them.

Father, Son, and Holy Spirit: Romans 5:1–5; 7:4–6; 8:1–4, 14–17; 15:15–16, 30; 1 Corinthians 2:1–5; 6:11; Ephesians 1:3–14; 2:13–22; 3:14–19; 4:4–6; 5:18–21; 2 Thessalonians 2:12–13
Father and Son: Romans 2:21–26; 5:6–11; 8:31–34; notice the interplay "love of Christ" in Romans 3:35 and "him who loved us" in 37 and "the love of God in Christ Jesus our Lord" in 39; 15:5–7; 1 Corinthians 1:4–9; 4:1–5; 15:57; 2 Corinthians 4:4–6; 5:18–21; 2 Timothy 4:1; many greetings and benedictions, like Philippians 1:2; 2 Thessalonians 1:2 and 1 Timothy 1:2
Son and Spirit: 1 Corinthians 12:12–13; 2 Corinthians 3:16–18; Philippians 2:1–2; 1 Peter 1:10–12
Father and Spirit: Romans 8:5–8, 26–27; 14:17; 15:13; 1 Corinthians 2:10–14; 3:16–17; 2 Corinthians 5:5
The Spirit and the Father's involvement in Christ's work on earth:
• The Spirit: Luke 1:35; 3:21–22; 4:1, 14, 18; 10:21; Romans 1:4; 1 Timothy 3:16; Hebrews 9:14
• The Father: John 5:19–23, 26–27; 6:38–39; 7:16, 28–29, 42; 10:37–38; 14:10–11; Romans 8:11

Chapter Seven

[1] Tripp, *Instruments in the Redeemer's Hands: People in Need of Change Helping People in Need of Change,* 1–34.

[2] A. W. Tozer, *Man: The Dwelling Place of God* (City: Fig Books, 2012), 15.

[3] While the details of the "smaller story" are not the main story, they are still extremely important and significant. These details contain moments of agony and pain that must not be minimized. Biblical counselors have a duty to weep with those who weep, sit with those in need, and love the inconsolable. Yet, we cannot be swallowed up by the tragedies we will encounter. God is always up to something!

[4] Frame, *Systematic Theology,* 218.

[5] The issue of counseling the unbeliever will be covered in Appendix A.

[6] Paul Vitz, *Psychology as Religion: The Cult of Self-Worship,* 2nd ed. (Grand Rapids, MI: Wm. B. Eerdmans Publishing Co., 2001), 141.

[7] Theodore Dalrymple, *Admirable Evasions: How Psychology Undermines Morality* (New York: Encounter Books, 2015), loc. 794, Kindle.

[8] Kendra Creasy Dean, *Almost Christian: What the Faith of Our Teenagers Is Telling the American Church* (New York, NY: Oxford University Press, 2010), 30.

[9] Ibid., 36.

[10] Tozer, *Man: The Dwelling Place of God*, 19.

[11] A. W. Pink, *The Sovereignty of God* (Carlisle, PA: The Banner of Truth Trust, 1998), 48.

[12] John Piper, *Spectacular Sins and Their Global Purpose in the Glory of Christ* (Wheaton, IL: Crossway, 2008), 27.

[13] See Joni Eareckson Tada, *Joni: An Unforgettable Story* (Grand Rapids, MI: Zondervan, 2001).

[14] Philip Ryken and Michael LeFebvre, *Our Triune God: Living in the Love of the Three-In-One* (Wheaton, IL: Crossway, 2011), 72.

[15] Joe Thorn, *Experiencing the Trinity: The Grace of God for the People of God* (Wheaton, IL: Crossway, 2015), 42, Kindle.

[16] Bryan Chapell and Dane Ortlund, eds., *Gospel Transformation Bible* (Wheaton, IL: Crossway, 2014), 1587.

Chapter Eight

[1] Jonathan Edwards, *Jonathan Edwards on Knowing Christ* (Carlisle, PA: The Banner of Truth Trust, 1997), 162.

[2] John Owen, *The Holy Spirit: His Gifts and Power*, 45–46.

[3] It is not that humans are intrinsically valuable so God decided to love us, but God loved us, therefore, we become valuable as objects of his creation and love.

[4] "Arise, My Soul, Arise" by Charles Wesley, *Trinity Hymnal* (Suwanee, GA: Great Commission Publication, 2004), 305.

[5] Mike Sharrett founded Fort Worth Presbyterian Church (PCA) where I have attended for seventeen years, and he was the most influential person in my life to introduce me to the amazing theology of the Reformation.

[6] Herman Ridderbos, *Paul: An Outline of His Theology*, trans. John Richard De Witt (Grand Rapids, MI: Wm. B. Eerdmans Publishing Co., 1975), 47, Kindle.

[7] David Mathis, "The Wine Jesus Drank," Desiring God (blog), May 27, 2010, https://www.desiringgod.org/articles/the-wine-jesus-drank, accessed October 24, 2017.

[8] Kevin DeYoung, "The Holy Spirit" in *The Gospel as Center: Renewing our Faith and Reforming Our Ministry Practices*, ed. D. A. Carson and T. Keller (Wheaton, IL: Crossway, 2012), 183.

[9] Tony Reinke, *Newton on the Christian Life: To Live Is Christ* (Wheaton, IL: Crossway, 2015), N. 1383. Kindle.

Chapter Nine

[1]   Charles Darwin Quotes, Goodreads.com, Goodreads, Inc., 2017, https://www.goodreads.com/quotes/904405-in-the-distant-future-i-see-open-fields-for-far, accessed November 24, 2017.

[2]   Abraham Maslow, *Toward a Psychology of Being*, 2nd ed. (New York: Van Nostrand Reinhold Co., 1968), 189.

[3]   Stanton Jones, *Psychology: A Student's Guide* (Wheaton, IL: Crossway, 2014), 33.

[4]   Abraham Maslow, *The Farther Reaches of Human Nature* (New York: The Viking Press, Inc., 1975), 186.

[5]   B. F. Skinner, *Beyond Freedom and Dignity* (New York: Bantam Books, 1971), 123.

[6]   Rogers, *On Becoming a Person: A Therapist's View of Psychotherapy*, 35.

[7]   Joseph LeDoux, *Synaptic Self: How Our Brains Become Who We Are* (New York: Penguin Books, 2003), 302.

[8]   Steven Pinker, *The Blank Slate: The Modern Denial of Human Nature* (New York: Penguin Books, 2002), 40.

[9]   Ken Wilber, *A Brief History of Everything* (Boston, MA: Shambhala Publications, Inc. 1996), 40–41.

[10]   Wilber is an exception when it comes to embracing a materialistic view of people, however, his theory of personality is significantly influenced by Darwinian evolution.

[11]   My claims in this section assume the counselor adheres primarily to an overriding theory of personality. The popular approach embraces eclecticism—an approach wherein one draws counseling methods from various theoretical models. My opinion is that such an approach undercuts the counseling process because one does not begin with actual, defined presuppositions about human nature. In other words, counseling methods do not emerge from one's theoretical anthropology, but rather are gathered in a hodge-podge manner that facilitates a positive subjective emotional experience on the part of the client. I was first introduced to concerns regarding this approach by my professor, Dr. Phillip Captain, while pursuing my bachelor's degree in Psychology at Liberty University.

[12]   Rogers, *On Becoming a Person: The Therapist's View of Psychotherapy*, 23–24.

[13]   Ibid.

[14]   John D. Carter and Bruce Narramore, *The Integration of Psychology and Theology*; Malcom A. Jeeves, *Psychology and Christianity: The View Both Ways* (Downers Grove, IL: InterVarsity Press, 1976).

[15]   Ed Welch, "Who Are We? Needs, Longings, and the Image of God in Man," *Journal of Biblical Counseling* 13, no. 1 (1994): 25.

[16]   John Babler, David Penley, and Mike Bizzell, *Counseling by the Book* (Longwood, FL: Xulon, 2007), 93.

[17]   Eric L. Johnson and Stanton L. Jones, *Psychology & Christianity: Four Views.*

[18]   Powlison, "Crucial Issues in Contemporary Biblical Counseling," 56.

[19]   Cornelius Plantinga, Jr., *Not the Way It's Supposed to Be: A Breviary of Sin* (Grand Rapids: MI: Wm. B. Eerdmans Publishing Co., 1995), 17.

[20]   Karl Menninger, *Whatever Became of Sin* (New York: Hawthorn Books, Inc., 1974), 10–11, 13.

[21]   Scott T. Meier and Susan R. Davis, *The Elements of Counseling*, 7th ed. (Belmont, CA: Brooks/Cole, 2011), 32.

[22]   Hawkins and Clinton, *The New Christian Counselor: A Fresh Biblical & Transformational Approach*, 15.

[23]   Jeremy Lelek, *Truths That (Should) Permeate Counsel* (unpublished, 2003).

[24]   Ralph Venning, *The Sinfulness of Sin* (Carlisle, PA: The Banner of Truth Trust, 2001), 161.

[25]   Herman Ridderbos, *Paul: An Outline of His Theology*, trans. John Richard De Witt (Grand Rapids, MI: Wm. B. Eerdmans Publishing Co., 1975), 107, Kindle.

[26]   Tripp, *Instruments in the Redeemer's Hands: People in Need of Change Helping People in Need of Change.*

[27]   Robert C. Roberts, "Parameters of a Christian Psychology," in *Limning the Psyche: Explorations in Christian Psychology*, series ed. M. R. Talbot (Grand Rapids, MI: William Eerdmans, 1997), 84.

[28]   Jeeves, *Psychology and Christianity: The View Both Ways*, 69.

[29]   Robert C. Roberts, "Starting From Scripture" in *Limning the Psyche: Explorations in Christian Psychology*, series ed. M. R. Talbot (Grand Rapids, MI: William Eerdmans, 1997), 121.

[30]   Ed Welch, "Why Ask Why? Four Types of Causes in Counseling," *Journal of Pastoral Practice* 10, no. 3 (1991): 44.

[31]   Bruce Narramore and John Carter, "On Straw Men, Autonomous Spheres, and the Integration of Psychology and Theology," 74.

[32]   James K. A. Smith, *Desiring the Kingdom: Worship, Worldview, and Cultural Formation* (Grand Rapids, MI: Baker, 2009), 51.

[33]   Powlison, "Critiquing Modern Integrationists," 29.

[34]   Paul D. Tripp, "Wisdom in Counseling," *Journal of Biblical Counseling* 19, no. 2 (2001): 6.

[35]   C. S. Lewis, *Surprised by Joy: The Shape of My Early Life* (Orlando, FL: Harcourt, 1955), 226, Kindle.

[36]   I once heard R. C. Sproul expounding on this point when suddenly he paused as he sensed disagreement from the crowd. He then went on to explain that a few husbands in the crowd might argue with the point that

the will always follows the strongest desire because they would have much preferred to stay home and watch the baseball game that was on television that night rather than attend a conference on theology. Smiling he replied, "Oh yes, but your desire to avoid the fury of your wife for not attending this conference with her dominated any desire to watch a baseball game. Hence you are here at the conference and not home watching television."

37   Martin Luther, *The Bondage of the Will*, trans. J. I. Packer and O. R. Johnston (Grand Rapids, MI: Fleming H. Revell), 1957.

Chapter Ten

1   Bob Marley Quotes. BrainyQuote.com, Xplore Inc, 2017. https://www.brainyquote.com/quotes/bob_marley_109298, accessed November 24, 2017.

2   Martin Luther, *The Bondage of the Will*, 103.

3   Ezekiel 36:25–27.

4   John Murray, *Redemption: Accomplished and Applied* (Grand Rapids, MI: Wm. B. Eerdmans Publishing, 5), loc. 1637, Kindle.

5   Ed Welch, "Motives: Why Do I Do the Things I Do," *Journal of Biblical Counseling* 22, no. 1 (2003): 48–56.

6   An exceptional and more detailed treatment of the dynamics of the heart may be found in Dr. Jeremy Pierre's book, *The Dynamic Heart in Daily Life: Connecting Christ to Human Experience* (Greensboro, NC: New Growth Press), 2016.

7   Powlison, "Idols of the Heart and Vanity Fair," 35–50.

8   The following is an illustration of a Christian's battle with sin I learned from my pastor, Darwin Jordan of Fort Worth PCA:

Before a person trusts in Christ, sin was alive and its invasive tentacles reached into every part of that individual's life. In Christ, however, sin's core, dominating power has been smashed, utterly broken. The broken pieces of those tentacles must be removed from every part of the person's life (i.e., desires, thoughts, perceptions, behaviors, etc.). This is a difficult, agonizing, lifelong enduring warfare. Yet, in God's redemptive design, sin does not have a chance. The believer no longer belongs to it. In its place of dominance is the almighty Holy Spirit springing up as a river of water from the believer's innermost being (John 7:37–39).

9   This example was also provided to me by my pastor, Darwin Jordan, Fort Worth (PCA).

10   Francis Schaeffer, *True Spirituality* (Wheaton, IL: Tyndale House, 1971), 7.

11   Ibid., 9.

12   Cornelius Plantiga, Jr., *Not the Way It's Supposed to Be: A Breviary of Sin*, 44.

Chapter Eleven

[1] William James Quotes. BrainyQuote.com, Xplore Inc, 2017. https://www.brainyquote.com/quotes/william_james_160986, accessed November 24, 2017.

[2] 2 Corinthians 7:1.

[3] *The Westminster Shorter Catechism* (Lawrenceville, GA: PCA Christian Education and Publications), 13.

[4] Powlison, "Affirmations and Denials," 20.

[5] This was brought to my attention in a sermon taught by my pastor, Darwin Jordan, at Fort Worth PCA: http://fortworthpca.org/audio/491.

[6] Barbara R. Duguid, *Extravagent Grace: God's Glory Displayed in Our Weakness* (Phillipsburg, NJ: P&R Publishing, 2013), 153.

[7] D. Martyn Lloyd-Jones, *Spiritual Depression: Its Causes and Its Cure* (Grand Rapids, MI: Wm. B Eerdmans Publishing, 1986), 56.

Chapter Twelve

[1] Siang-Yang Tan, "Lay Christian Counseling for General Psychological Problems," in *Evidenced-Based Practices for Christian Counseling and Psychotherapy*, eds. Everett Worthington Jr., Eric Johnson, Joshua Hook, and Jamie Aten (Downers Grove, IL: IVP, 2013), 41.

[2] *Christianity is a Crutch for the Weak*, The Village Church Resources, 2014, https://www.tvcresources.net/resource-library/articles/christianity-is-a-crutch-for-the-weak, accessed December 2, 2017.

[3] R. B. Kuiper, *The Glorious Body of Christ* (Carlisle, PA: The Banner of Truth Trust, 2006), 230.

[4] Mowrer, *The Crisis in Psychiatry and Religion.*

[5] Tripp, "Wisdom in Counseling," 6.

[6] Jeremy Lelek, *The Study of the Constructs and a Proposed Definition of Biblical Counseling.*

[7] Powlison, "Questions at the Crossroads: The Care of Souls and Modern Psychotherapies," in *Care for the Soul: Exploring the Intersection of Psychology and Theology*, 54–55.

[8] Christopher Hull, Elizabeth Suarez, James Sells, and Marianne Miller, "Addressing Spiritual Dialogue in Supervision: Comparing Supervisor and Supervisee Perceptions," *Journal of Psychology and Christianity* 32:1 (2013): 40.

[9] Purchase at: https://store.harvestbiblechapel.org/p-2940-uncommon-community-biblical-soul-care-in-small-groups-4-part-dvd-series.aspx.

[10] Purchase at: https://store.christiancounseling.com/products/your-walk-with-god-is-a-community-project-dvd.

Chapter Thirteen

¹ Jimi Hendrix Quotes. BrainyQuote.com, Xplore Inc, 2017. https://www.brainyquote.com/quotes/jimi_hendrix_103615, accessed November 24, 2017.

² An example of encouragement not corresponding with God's Word would be encouraging a person to pursue divorce when there are no biblical grounds for doing so.

³ Adams, *Competent to Counsel*, 137.

⁴ Ibid., 193.

⁵ Adams, *The Christian Counselor's Manual*, 191.

⁶ Ibid., 53.

⁷ Ibid., 15.

⁸ Adams, *The Christian Counselor's Manual*, 117.

⁹ Jesus is not teaching one to literally pluck out the eye. Rather he is encouraging radical denial of sin. In his commentary, Matthew Henry writes the following regarding this passage: "Let the idols that have been delectable things, be cast away as detestable things . . . self must be denied, that it may not be destroyed." Such is mortification of the flesh.

¹⁰ David Powlison, "How Healthy Is Your Preparation?" *The Journal of Biblical Counseling* 14, no. 3 (1996): 2–5.

¹¹ Paul Tripp, "Data Gathering Part 2: What the Counselor Brings to the Process," *Journal of Biblical Counseling* 14, no. 3 (1996): 8–14; Paul Tripp, "Opening Blind Eyes: Another Look at Data Gathering," *Journal of Biblical Counseling* 14, no. 2 (1996): 6–11.

¹² Paul Tripp, "Strategies for Opening Blind Eyes: Data Gathering Part 3," *Journal of Biblical Counseling* 15, no. 1 (1996): 42–51.

¹³ Paul Tripp, "Homework and Biblical Counseling," *Journal of Biblical Counseling* 11, no. 2 (1993): 21–25; Paul Tripp, "Homework and Biblical Counseling: Part 2," *Journal of Biblical Counseling* 11, no. 3 (1993): 5–18; Welch, "Motives: Why Do I Do the Things I Do?," 48–56.

¹⁴ Ibid.

¹⁵ David Powlison, "Let's Talk!," *Journal of Biblical Counseling* 14, no. 2 (1996): 2–5.

¹⁶ Jay Adams, *The Biblical View of Self-Esteem, Self-Love, Self-Image* (Eugene, OR: Harvest House, 1986); John Bettler, "Gaining an Accurate Self-image: Part I," *Journal of Pastoral Practice* 6 no. 4 (1983): 46–52; John Bettler, "Gaining an Accurate Self-image: Part II," *Journal of Pastoral Practice* 7 no. 1 (1984): 41–50; John Bettler, "Gaining an Accurate Self-image: Part III," *Journal of Pastoral Practice* 7, no. 2 (1984): 52–61; John Bettler, "Gaining an Accurate Self-image: Part IV," *The Journal of Pastoral Practice* 7, no. 3 (1984): 50–58; John Bettler, "Gaining an Accurate Self-image: Part

V," *The Journal of Pastoral Practice* 7, no. 4 (1985): 46–55; Johnson, *God and Soul Care: The Therapeutic Resources of the Christian Faith*, 199–209.

[17]   David Powlison, "Picturing the Heart of Conflict," *Journal of Biblical Counseling* 16, no. 1 (1997): 43–46; Tripp, "Homework and Biblical Counseling," 21–25; Tripp, "Homework and Biblical Counseling: Part 2," 5–18.

[18]   Jay Adams, *Winning the War Within: A Biblical Strategy for Spiritual Warfare* (Woodruff, SC: Timeless Texts, 1989), 47; Paul Tripp, "Take Up Your Weapons: Ephesians 6:10–20," *Journal of Biblical Counseling* 17, no. 2 (1999): 58–60; Paul Tripp, "The Present Glories of Redemption," *Journal of Biblical Counseling* 17, no. 2 (1999): 32–37.

[19]   Powlison, "How Healthy Is Your Preparation?", 2–5; David Powlison, "How Do You Help a 'Psychologized' Counselee?" *Journal of Biblical Counseling* 15, no. 1 (1996): 2–7.

[20]   Ibid.

[21]   Jeremy Lelek, *The Study of the Constructs and a Proposed Definition of Biblical Counseling*, 104.

[22]   Ibid.

[23]   Ibid.

[24]   Ibid.

[25]   Welch, "Why ask Why? Four Types of Causes in Counseling," 40–47; Ed Welch, "Christian Doctors on Depression," *Journal of Biblical Counseling* 18, no. 3 (2000): 35–43.

[26]   Ibid.

[27]   Ibid.

[28]   Paul Tripp, "Keeping Destiny in View: Counselees View Life from the Perspective of Psalm 7," *Journal of Biblical Counseling* 13, no. 1 (1994): 13–24; Paul Tripp, "Speaking Redemptively," *Journal of Biblical Counseling* 16, no. 3 (1998): 10–18.

[29]   David Powlison, "Modern Therapies and the Church's Faith," *Journal of Biblical Counseling* 15, no. 1 (1996): 32–41.

[30]   Powlison, "Crucial Issues in Contemporary Biblical Counseling," 53–78; David Powlison, "Biological Psychiatry," *Journal of Biblical Counseling* 17, no. 3 (1999): 2–8.

Chapter Fourteen

[1]   On The David Letterman Show one week after September 11, 2001.

[2]   Abraham Kuyper, *Wisdom and Wonder: Common Grace in Science and Art* (Grand Rapids, MI: Christians Library Press, 2011). 52.

[3]   Anthony Hoekema, *Created in God's Image* (Grand Rapids, MI: William B. Eerdmans Publishing, 1986), 216.

4   Joseph LeDoux, *Synaptic Self: How Our Brains Become Who We Are*, 21.

5   Andrew Newberg, and Mark Waldman, *How God Changes Your Brain: Breakthrough Findings from a Leading Neuroscientist* (New York: Ballantine Books Trade Paperbacks, 2010).

6   Ibid., 41.

7   Francis Schaeffer, *The Complete Works of Francis A. Schaeffer: A Christian Worldview*, vol. 1, 61.

8   Newberg, and Waldman, *How God Changes Your Brain*, 127.

9   Michael Emlet, "Listening to Prozac . . . and to the Scriptures. A Primer on Psychoactive Medications," *Journal of Biblical Counseling* 26, no. 1 (2010):16, Retrieved 2012 from http://www.ccef.org/store/catalog/jbc-articles/volume-26-number-1 26(1).

10   Francis Schaeffer, *Escape from Reason* (Downers Grove, IL: InterVarsity Press, 1968), 10.

11   Johnson, *God and Soul Care: The Therapeutic Resources of the Christian Faith*, 190.

12   John Bettler, "Counseling and the Problem of the Past," *Journal of Biblical Counseling* 12, no. 2 (1994): 5–23.

Chapter Fifteen

1   Desiring God, "Thoughts on the Sufficiency of Scripture: What it Does and Doesn't Mean," https://www.desiringgod.org/articles/thoughts-on-the-sufficiency-of-scripture, accessed November 24, 2017.

2   Adams, *Competent to Counsel*, xxi.

3   Lambert, *The Biblical Counseling Movement After Adams*, 16.

4   Jeremy Lelek, *The Study of the Constructs and a Proposed Definition of Biblical Counseling*, 104.

5   Ibid., 84.

6   Ibid.

7   Ibid., 85.

8   Ibid.

9   Ibid., 86.

10   Ibid.

11   Ibid.

12   Ibid.

13   Adams, *More Than Redemption: A Theology of Christian Counseling*, 8.

14   Powlison, "Critiquing Modern Integrationists," 24.

15   David Powlison, "The Sufficiency of Scripture to Diagnose and Cure Souls," *Journal of Biblical Counseling* 23, no. 2 (2005): 2.

16   David Powlison, *The Biblical Counseling Movement: History and Context*, 276.

17   Ibid., 276.

[18]   Eric Johnson, *Foundations of Soul Care.*

[19]   Louis Berkhof, *Systematic Theology* (Woodstock, Ontario, Canada: Devoted Publishing, 2017), 129.

[20]   David Powlison, "Does Biblical Counseling Really Work?" in *Totally Sufficient: The Bible and Christian Counseling*, eds. E. Hindson and H. Eyrich (Ross-Shire, Great Britain: Christian Focus Publications, 2004), 81.

[21]   David Powlison. "A Biblical Counseling Response to Christian Psychology," in *Psychology & Christianity: Five Views*, ed. E. Johnson (Downers Grove, IL: IVP, 2010), 255.

[22]   Stephen Farra, "Biblical Counseling: Concepts from the Accountability Group Become a Christian Psychology," (2003), Christiancounsel.net. Retrieved June 17, 2013 from http://www.christian-counsel.net/acp123.htm.

[23]   Eric Johnson, *Foundations of Soul Care*, 149.

[24]   Ron Hawkins, Ed Hindson, and Timothy Clinton, "Theological Roots: Synthesizing and Systematizing a Biblical Theology of Helping," in *Competent Christian Counseling: Foundations & Practice of Compassionate Soul Care*, eds. Timothy Clinton and George Ohlschlager (Colorado Springs, CO: Waterbrook Press), 94.

Chapter Sixteen

[1]   Eminem, "Lose Yourself," in *8 Mile*, Shady Records/Interscope Records, 2001, http://itunes.com.

[2]   David Powlison, *Power Encounters: Reclaiming Spiritual Warfare* (Grand Rapids, MI: Baker Books, 1995), 27.

[3]   Anton Boisen, *The Exploration of the Inner World: A Study of Mental Disorder and Religious Experience* (New York, NY: Harper and Brothers, 1936), 221.

[4]   David Powlison, *Power Encounters: Reclaiming Spiritual Warfare*, 20.

Appendix A

[1]   Much of what is written in this Appendix was gleaned from correspondence with my pastor, Darwin Jordan, at Fort Worth PCA.

[2]   This reflects what Jesus did for me in entering my broken world and sympathizing with the utter pain of humanity (Hebrews 4:14–16).

[3]   Private correspondence with my pastor, Darwin Jordan.

[4]   Such a conversation could happen in my first meeting, third meeting, or any meeting thereafter. My ideal is sooner than later, but I want to be discerning in my timing.

[5]   Ian F. Jones, *The Counsel of Heaven on Earth: Foundations for Biblical Christian Counseling* (Nashville, TN: B&H Academic, 2006), 111.

Appendix B

[1]   Abraham Maslow, *Toward a Psychology of Being*, 2nd, 23.

[2]   Following is an excerpt from the Humanist Manifesto II published in *1973, which provides insight* into Maslow's conceptual framework of human nature: "We believe, however, that traditional dogmatic or authoritarian religions that place revelation, God, ritual, or creed above human needs and experience do a disservice to the human species. . . . We find insufficient evidence for belief in the existence of a supernatural; it is either meaningless or irrelevant to the question of survival and fulfillment of the human race" (emphasis added).

[3]   Maslow, *Toward a Psychology of Being*, 25.

[4]   Ibid., 25.

[5]   Ibid., 27.

[6]   Ibid,. 48.

[7]   Steven Pinker, *How the Mind Works* (New York: W.W. Norton & Co., 1997), 54.

[8]   Ibid., 55.

[9]   Ibid., 57.

[10]   Ibid., 58.

[11]   Ibid., 58.